Praise for *Upgrade Your Brain*

'The declining mental health and  -
ment of the brain pose a grave threa   s
of our children and theirs for whic   t
act now . . . this book provides the s

Professor Michael Crawford, Director of the Institute
for Brain Chemistry & Human Nutrition

'*Upgrade Your Brain* by Patrick Holford offers a compelling wake-up call to the alarming decline in mental health and cognitive function plaguing society today. With a meticulous blend of scientific research and real-life testimonials, Holford navigates through the intricate web of factors contributing to this decline, shedding light on the pivotal role of nutrition in brain health. From unveiling the hidden truths about what makes a good brain go bad to providing practical steps for readers to reclaim their mental acuity, this book serves as a beacon of hope in an era dominated by stress, anxiety and cognitive decline. Holford's integrated approach not only empowers individuals to enhance their own cognitive well-being but also advocates for a paradigm shift towards prioritizing brain health on a global scale.'

Dr David Perlmutter, author of No.1 *New York Times*
bestseller *Grain Brain*, and *Drop Acid*

'This approach is far more effective than medication, working with the body's own chemistry to restore balance, and without side-effects. It is the future of an enlightened approach to psychiatry.'

Dr Hyla Cass, psychiatrist and retired assistant
professor of psychiatry

'I have skin in the game when it comes to Alzheimer's. Twenty years ago I discovered I had a copy of the gene that boosted my chance of developing this awful disease. My only chance of cutting my risk seemed to be regular card and board games. *Upgrade Your Brain* is the first book that offers hope with the revolutionary idea that diet and lifestyle can help to Alzheimer's-proof your brain. It clearly explains the largely unfamiliar biology that makes this possible. It's like Zoe for the brain. The book also challenges the general assumption that the cure must come from a drug. But the brain is not isolated in a

bony box. Its health is intimately connected with the health of the body. If your brain's powers are fading, this is a must-read.'
Jerome Burne, award-winning medical journalist

'What an eye-opening book! Patrick Holford has assembled a compelling compendium of steps that we can all follow to erase Alzheimer's disease from our personal future. The practical advice he provides will not only lead to a lower risk for AD but will – if followed! – markedly improve overall health. A must read for everyone with a brain.'
Professor William S. Harris, PhD, FASN

'Healthy diet and lifestyle are critical to keep brain health and prevent brain disorders. This book is worth reading for both researchers and the public who are interested in improving their cognitive reserve.'
Professor Jin-Tai Yu, Fudan University, Director of the Memory Disorders Centre at the National Centre for Neurological Disorders, China

'Every parent, and, indeed, every person should read this book and be inspired to attain a healthier lifestyle for themselves and for their families.'
Dr Rona Tutt OBE, former President of the National Association of Head Teachers.

'*Upgrade Your Brain* by Patrick Holford takes complex scientific information and distils it simply and clearly for the lay reader. This book is easy to read, full of frightening statistics, but also practical solutions and compelling case histories that should empower every one of us to take better care of our brain or risk dire consequences. This is a must-read for anyone looking for practical non-pharmaceutical solutions and easy-to-implement lifestyle, dietary and nutrient changes to enhance mental well-being.'
Professor Julia Rucklidge, Director of Te Puna Taiora, the Mental Health and Nutrition Research Lab, University of Canterbury, Christchurch, New Zealand

'It is time we woke up to the fact that Alzheimer's is a preventable disease, not an inevitable part of ageing. Just as there is nothing inevitable about heart disease, there is nothing inevitable about Alzheimer's disease. Patrick Holford's book takes up this theme with zest and is to be greatly welcomed. Each of us needs to know that Alzheimer's disease and several other diet-related brain disorders can be prevented and governments need to recognise this too. The lesson to be learnt from this book is that we can help ourselves and our loved ones by starting to modify the way we live so that our chance of developing diseases such as Alzheimer's is greatly reduced. But we need to begin now; the disease process begins early in life, and already in our thirties some of us have signs of Alzheimer's disease in the brain, just as we have atherosclerosis in our blood vessels. Get started!'

Emeritus Professor David Smith, former Chair of Pharmacology and Deputy Head of the Faculty of Medical Science at the University of Oxford

'This great book makes it abundantly clear that nutrition is a fundamental cornerstone of mental health and brain function and should be the first, not the last, port of call for those suffering as well as their treaters.'

Uma Naidoo MD, Harvard Nutritional Psychiatrist, author, chef and nutritional biologist

What people say after following Patrick Holford's principles:

'In just three months the change has been remarkable. We both feel better. Our moods are better, our energy is better. Honestly, I feel like I've got my husband back from dementia. I am so grateful to Patrick Holford and Food for the Brain.'

Dorothy Norris

'I have been given a new lease of life.'

Eddie M, former schizophrenic

'I've been trying to feel like this for 25 years – I'm over the moon!'
Gabrielle F, former depressive

'At last, I'm sleeping like a baby and spend my days without anxiety. It's a game-changer for me.'
Audrey M, former insomniac

'My mind is back. I can do the whole crossword again.'
Dr John B, diagnosed with dementia

Other books by Patrick Holford

Balance Your Hormones

Boost Your Immune System (with Jennifer Meek)

Burn Fat Fast (with Kate Staples)

Delicious, Healthy, Sugar-Free (with Fiona McDonald Joyce)

Flu Fighters

Food Is Better Medicine than Drugs (with Jerome Burne)

Good Medicine

Hidden Food Allergies (with Dr James Braly)

How to Quit Without Feeling S**t (with David Miller and Dr James Braly)

Improve Your Digestion

Natural Highs (with Dr Hyla Cass)

Optimum Nutrition Before, During and After Pregnancy (with Susannah Lawson)

Optimum Nutrition for the Mind

Optimum Nutrition for Vegans

Optimum Nutrition for Your Child (with Deborah Colson)

Optimum Nutrition Made Easy

Say No to Arthritis

Say No to Cancer (with Liz Efiong)

Say No to Diabetes

Say No to Heart Disease

Six Weeks to Superhealth

Smart Food for Smart Kids (with Fiona McDonald Joyce)

Solve Your Skin Problems (with Natalie Savona)

The 5-Day Diet

The 9-Day Liver Detox (with Fiona McDonald Joyce)

The Alzheimer's Prevention Plan (with Shane Heaton and Deborah Colson)

The Feel Good Factor

The Homocysteine Solution (with Dr James Braly)

The Little Book of Optimum Nutrition

The Low-GL Diet Bible

The Low-GL Diet Cookbook (with Fiona McDonald Joyce)

The Low-GL Diet Counter

The Optimum Nutrition Bible

The Stress Cure (with Susannah Lawson)

The Ten Secrets of 100% Healthy People

The Ten Secrets of Healthy Ageing (with Jerome Burne)

Foreign editions are listed at www.patrickholford.com/foreign-editions/.

PATRICK HOLFORD

UPGRADE YOUR BRAIN

8 steps to optimise your
brain for better mood,
memory and sleep

Thorsons

Thorsons
An imprint of HarperCollins*Publishers*
1 London Bridge Street
London SE1 9GF

www.harpercollins.co.uk

HarperCollins*Publishers*
Macken House, 39/40 Mayor Street Upper
Dublin 1, D01 C9W8, Ireland

First published by Thorsons 2024

5 7 9 10 8 6 4

A catalogue record of this book is available from the British Library

ISBN: 978-0-00-866120-5

Printed and bound in the UK using 100% renewable electricity
at CPI Group (UK) Ltd

This book is dedicated to twice Nobel Prize-winner Dr Linus Pauling and Dr Abram Hoffer, who, in 1968, defined 'orthomolecular psychiatry', the approach this book represents; Professor Michael Crawford, who put marine food and omega-3 on the map as brain essentials; and Professors David Smith and Helga Refsum, whose comprehensive research on B vitamins and homocysteine, probably the most critical factor in dementia prevention, is worthy of a Nobel Prize. Their outstanding, and tragically largely ignored, research has laid the foundation for tomorrow's medicine, which has to put nutrition at the top of the agenda. It is the only way we can prevent the cerebral tsunami that is fuelling so much unnecessary suffering.

About the Author

Patrick Holford, BSc, DipION, FBANT, NTCRP

Patrick Holford, BSc, DipION, FBANT, NTCRP, is a leading spokesman on nutrition and mental health, and founder of the Food for the Brain Foundation, VitaminC4Covid and the Institute for Optimum Nutrition, an educational charity that offers degree-accredited training in nutritional therapy.

Originally trained in psychology at the University of York, Patrick was involved in groundbreaking research showing that multivitamins can increase children's IQ scores, which was the subject of a *Horizon* television documentary in the 1980s. He was one of the first promoters of the importance of zinc, essential fats, low-GL diets and homocysteine-lowering B vitamins, and their importance in mental health and Alzheimer's prevention, working closely with David Smith, Emeritus Professor of Pharmacology at the University of Oxford. As well as being the founder of the charitable Food for the Brain Foundation, he is the director of their 'Alzheimer's Is Preventable' campaign and chair of their Scientific Advisory Board.

He is the author of several papers and 47 books, which have been translated into over 30 languages, including the bestselling *The Optimum Nutrition Bible*, *The Low-GL Diet Bible* and *Cookbook*, *Optimum Nutrition for the Mind*, *Food Is Better Medicine than Drugs*, *The Ten Secrets of Healthy Ageing* and *The Hybrid Diet* (co-authored with award-winning medical journalist Jerome Burne), as well as *The Alzheimer's Prevention Plan*, *The Feel Good Factor*, *How to Quit* *without Feeling S**t* and *The Stress Cure* (co-authored with Susannah Lawson).

With more than 40 years of research and experience in the field of nutrition and mental health, he is a retired visiting professor at the University of Teeside and is in the Orthomolecular Medicine Hall of Fame and on the editorial board for the Orthomolecular News Service.

Contents

Acknowledgements

In this book you will meet many world-leading experts, most of whom serve voluntarily on our charity's Scientific Advisory Board, to whom I am immensely grateful for their intelligence, research, commitment and generosity in giving me time. These include Professor David Smith, Professor Michael Crawford, Professor Jin-Tai Yu, Professor Julia Rucklidge, Professor Robert Lustig, Professor Stephen Cunnane, Professor Jeremy Spencer, Assistant Professor Tommy Wood, Associate Professor David Vazour, Dr Simon Dyall, Dr William Grant and Dr Gill Hart, from whom I have learned so much.

I am also deeply grateful to the hundreds of scientists whose research I've quoted and learned from who largely go unacknowledged in the public domain and often do not see the fruits of their research put into health policy and strategy. I hope they will derive some satisfaction from seeing their research shared in the public domain. Among these are Professor Helga Refsum, Professor John Read, Professor Alessio Fasano, Drs Chris Palmer, David Perlmutter, Alex Richardson and Paul Shattock.

Susannah Lawson, my co-author of *The Stress Cure*, thank you and the team at the HeartMath Institute for your help and support. Also, Jerome Burne – our discussions and your editorial advice is always enlightening. My original teachers, Dr Linus Pauling, Dr Abram Hoffer and Dr Carl Pfeiffer, are the giants whose shoulders I stand on.

Behind the scenes, the team at Food for the Brain – Kim, Steffan, Kezia, Cath and Joyce – help us reach thousands through the Cognitive Function Test and COGNITION. Also, Ros and the team at patrickholford.com who help get the word out there to as many as possible.

I am also immensely grateful to the whole team at HarperCollins – George for the words, Sim, together with Alex at Purple Dinosaur for the images and cover, and Claire and Katie on PR, all led by the visionary Katya. Thank you all for sharing the vision and making it a reality.

Most of all, my thanks goes to my wonderful wife, Gaby, who supports me 100 per cent through the early hours and long days it takes to write a book, followed by days on the road during lecture tours.

Finally, thanks to you for your interest and I hope you'll pass this book on to many others to help them discover how our health, both mental and physical, is under our control.

Wishing you the best of health and happiness,
Patrick Holford

Guide to Abbreviations and Measures

1 gram (g) = 1,000 milligrams (mg) = 1,000,000 micrograms (mcg or μg). Most vitamins are measured in milligrams or micrograms. Vitamins A, D and E are also measured in International Units (iu) – a measurement designed to standardize the different forms of these vitamins that have different potencies.

1mcg of retinol (mcg RE) = 3.3iu of vitamin A (RE = retinol equivalents)
1mcg RE of beta-carotene = 6mcg
100iu of vitamin D = 2.5mcg
100iu of vitamin E = 67mg
1 pound (lb) = 16 ounces (oz)
2.2lb = 1 kilogram (kg)

References and Further Sources of Information

Numerous references from respected scientific literature have been used in writing this book. These sources are acknowledged with a number at the relevant position in the text. In order to save paper (there are over 400 cited sources), I have placed the corresponding details of – and links to – those studies on the webpage www.foodforthebrain.org/upgrade-your-brain so that you can delve deeper if you wish.

Important note
This book is not intended as a substitute for medical advice or treatment. Any person with a condition requiring medical attention should consult a qualified medical practitioner or suitable therapist. The recommendations given in this book are solely intended as education and information and should not be taken as medical advice. Neither the author nor the publisher accepts liability for readers who choose to self-prescribe. Do not change your medication without consulting your doctor.

Introduction

Do you often feel gelatinously exhausted? Enthusiastically negative? Do you spend your days feeling tired and wired? Your evenings with a drink in hand? Your nights restlessly searching for sleep? Do you wake up anxious and stressed and in need of a coffee to get going? Do you forget what you were doing, forget people's names, forget where you put things?

In 2010, I did a survey[1] of over 55,000 people who had completed my online '100% Health Check' at patrickholford.com. These are the results:

82 per cent become impatient quickly
81 per cent have low energy level
76 per cent have less energy than they used to
67 per cent feel they have too much to do
66 per cent become anxious or tense easily
63 per cent need more than eight hours' sleep
63 per cent have PMS/PMT (women only)
55 per cent easily become angry
48 per cent suffer from depression
47 per cent have difficulty concentrating or easily become confused
39 per cent have poor memory or difficulty learning
39 per cent feel generally nervous or hyperactive

Does this sound like anyone you know? Something depressing is happening to humanity, and possibly you. The very thing that makes us human, that is our brain and intelligence, is in rapid decline. We are fundamentally different from chimpanzees, with a brain size of under 0.4kg, despite sharing 98.5 per cent of the same genes, precisely because of our intelligence, directly reflected in our larger brain size. This gradual increase in brain size, driven by a brain-friendly diet, not genes, over 6 million years, is the unique hallmark of *Homo sapiens*. But both brain size and intelligence are decreasing – in the case of IQ, by an estimated 7 per cent a generation! Our average brain size, which peaked at 1.6 to 1.7kg 30,000 years ago, is now averaging less than 1.35kg. That means we've literally lost 20 per cent of our brain in the last 30,000 years and the signs are this brain degeneration is speeding up.

This parallels a worrying increase in mental illness across the world. Diagnoses of anxiety, depression, dementia, ADHD and autism are all increasing at an alarming rate. One in six children is classified as 'neurodivergent', with autism rates alone seeing a four-fold increase in 20 years, while one in four over 80 has mild cognitive impairment (MCI), sometimes called pre-dementia. Even more worrying is the evidence of brain shrinkage in adolescents and memory decline in those in their thirties. It is the greatest health threat we face, according to the World Health Organization.

Indeed, this is a global phenomenon that is accelerating at an alarming scale. Depression is the leading cause of disability, and in the UK alone, one in six adults was prescribed anti-depressants last year. Yesterday, again in the UK, more than nine double-decker buses' worth of people – about 800 – were diagnosed with dementia. What on earth is going wrong and what can we do about it?

'We are heading for an idiocracy,' says Professor Michael Crawford, director of the Institute of Brain Chemistry, whose research at the Chelsea and Westminster Hospital can predict which pregnant women are going to have pre-term babies with a higher risk of developmental problems. If nothing changes, by 2080 half of all children are likely to have a degree of neurodevelopmental impairment.

It is scary stuff, because our humanity is in decline, which can be seen manifesting in hate speech, extremism, mass shootings and suicides, which have become, globally, a greater killer than all wars and murders combined. Clearly, modern man, *Homo sapiens*, is neither wise nor happy. We are literally losing our higher brain intelligence – emotional control, sense of connection, sharp cognition, purpose and innate happiness. Yet intelligence is something we need more of, not less, as we face the challenges of over-population, climate change and pollution. We need to work together in an intelligent fashion, not stagger from war to war, depleting finite resources.

This is not just my opinion, but the opinion of a worldwide group of scientists, most of them eminent professors and experts in their field, whose interviews in this book are key to unravelling why our mental health is in decline, and what we can do to reverse this trend.

Fortunately, there are things we can do, individually and collectively, to reclaim our brains – to upgrade them.

Your brain upgrade may be experienced as a rapid improvement in your mood, as Gabrielle, a former depressive, found. 'I've been trying to feel like this for 25 years – I'm over the moon!' she said. Or a reduction in stress, as retail manager Andrew reported: 'My energy is through the roof, I don't feel stressed and I have no problem sleeping.' Or regaining the ability to think straight, as Stephanie, a lawyer, related: 'After a week, the brain fog and tiredness were significantly better.' Or even the reversal of serious mental illness, as Liz, a former schizophrenic, found: 'I've been fine.' You'll hear their stories, and what made the difference, in Parts 2 and 3. They are all ordinary people, like you or me, whose lives were made unbearable by changes in brain function, and put back together again by taking steps to regain brain health.

My interest in this field started back in the 1970s, when I became fascinated by the human condition. As a teenager, I read Jung and Freud and thought psychotherapy might be my career path. I went to university to study it and became fascinated by the brain, how it works and what goes wrong with it. I have been studying intelligence and mental illness ever since.

In the 1980s, I founded the Institute for Optimum Nutrition (ION) with Professor Derek Bryce-Smith, the UK chemist who campaigned to get lead out of petrol because it was lowering children's IQ, and twice Nobel Prize-winner Dr Linus Pauling as patrons. This has since trained several thousand nutritional therapists in what is now a degree-accredited profession.

In 1968, Dr Linus Pauling, together with Dr Abram Hoffer, wrote, in a seminal paper in *Science* journal, that 'The provision for the individual person of the optimum concentrations of important normal constituents (nutrients) of the brain may be the preferred treatment for many mentally ill patients.' He coined the phrase 'orthomolecular psychiatry'. I call this approach 'optimum nutrition' and others call it 'functional medicine'. Dr Pauling spent the last 38 years of his life researching vitamin C and its effects on mental health, addiction, viral infection, cancer and heart disease, and putting nutrition centre-stage in healthcare. If only he and others had been taken seriously, then we might not be facing this terrible cerebral tsunami. 'Brain health conditions have become a global health emergency,' said the Federation of European Neuroscience Societies last year.[2]

Back in 1985, when I was supervising one of my first students, Gwillym Roberts, the headmaster of a secondary school, we wondered if giving an optimal intake of vitamins and minerals might improve IQ. We designed a study and enrolled a sceptic, Professor David Benton from the University of Swansea, to run the trial and also invited the BBC documentary series *Horizon* to film it. Thirty children in Gwillym Roberts's school were given a multivitamin and mineral, thirty a dummy placebo pill and thirty nothing at all. The study found that non-verbal IQ increased by 7 per cent (roughly the average decline per generation, according to Scandinavian researchers; more on this in Chapter 3) in the children taking the multivitamin and mineral. As well as being the subject of a *Horizon* documentary, this study was published in the *Lancet*, and hit the headlines of national newspapers, firing up interest in nutrition and mental health. If we had known then what we know now, I am sure even these positive improvements could have been enhanced.

In the 1990s, I set up the Brain Bio Centre in London, at the Institute for Optimum Nutrition, to treat people suffering from a wide variety of mental health concerns.

Across these past 40 years, I've had the chance to study under the leading lights in mental health, from the late Dr Abram Hoffer, the Director of Psychiatric Research in Canada who successfully treated over 6,000 schizophrenic patients, to David Smith, Emeritus Professor of Pharmacology at the University of Oxford, and Helga Refsum,

Professor of Nutrition at the University of Oslo, whose impeccable studies of nutritional treatment have shown up to 73 per cent reduction in shrinkage of the Alzheimer's areas of the brain in a year, compared to placebo, and effectively no further memory loss in people with pre-Alzheimer's, which is leagues ahead of any anti-amyloid drug treatments.

You'll meet many other world-class experts in other fields that impact the brain health, such as Dr Robert Lustig, Professor Emeritus of Pediatrics in the Division of Endocrinology and a member of the Institute for Health Policy Studies at the University of California, San Francisco, who has unravelled how junk and ultra-processed food, clever marketing and tech have got us hooked on their products by manipulating the brain's antiquated 'reward system', with the insidious downside of a spiral into depression and anxiety and hopelessness; also, Assistant Professor Tommy Wood at the University of Washington, who's an expert on how to 'exercise' your brain for more power. I've interviewed many more, such as Associate Professor David Vazour, expert on the gut-microbiome–brain superhighway; Dr Simon Dyall and Professor Michael Crawford, experts on omega-3 and the importance of the right brain fats; Professor Jeremy Spencer, who knows the foods, high in polyphenols, that help the brain to work; also, Professor Stephen Cunnane, an expert on 'ketotherapeutics' – how ketones, made from fat, can be used for a brain energy boost. These, and other leading lights, are part of our Scientific Advisory Board at the charitable Food for the Brain Foundation, which I founded in 2006.

Each of these highly intelligent, focused, pioneering professors has a piece of why our brain function and mental health are in sharp decline, and a piece of the solution. This book is about putting those pieces together until it becomes obvious what you need to do to upgrade your brain and become part of the solution, not part of the problem.

Psychologists, often unaware of the driving force of nutrition in brain health, may tell you mental health issues are all down to psychological factors, and psychiatrists may extol the virtues of the latest anti-depressant drug or sleeping pill, while sociologists may say it's all to do with the pressures that ensue from the digital and industrial age we live in, but clearly this global decline in mental health is not happening because of a breakdown in social connection or a lack of drugs, and although you will see how the combination of junk food, junk media and tech addiction are contributing to a general dumbing down, that's not the whole story either.

In this book you will discover what has created the perfect storm that is hitting the brain right now:

- In Part 1 you'll discover why this brain drain is happening – and why you're not being told the whole truth.
- In Part 2 you'll learn the eight steps you need to take to upgrade your brain and restore full brain function.
- In Part 3 there are specific 'action' chapters that will help you improve your mood, end anxiety and insomnia, build stress resilience, break free from addiction, sharpen your mind and memory, and ultimately reconnect to your sense of meaning and purpose. There's also a chapter on how to maximize your child's attention, focus, creativity, intelligence and potential. If you want to jump to these chapters and get started, please do, but do take the time to read the eight steps, as these apply to all, and because that will also motivate you to make the necessary changes to your diet and lifestyle.
- Finally, in Part 4, I show you how to go from victim to change agent – to not only change yourself, but also help support the paradigm shift that has to happen, putting nutrition for the brain at the top of the health agenda and finding a healthy way to live in this fast-changing digital age.

With all we know now, it is not only possible to prevent cognitive decline, but to enhance brain function, intelligence, memory, concentration and mood. Take heart.

Wishing you the best of health and happiness,
Patrick Holford

PART 1

Brain Storm

Brain size is shrinking, IQ is falling, mental health problems are rising. One in six children fits a 'neurodivergent' diagnosis, perhaps of autism or ADHD, while one in four over 80 has pre-dementia, and cognitive decline is happening for many from their thirties. One in six adults is on anti-depressants. Our brains are what make us human. It is literally our humanity that is on the line. What is going wrong and how do we recover?

1. The Space between Your Ears – The Final Frontier
2. How We Became *Sapiens*
3. Why Our Brains Are Shrinking
4. Warning: Your Brain Is Being Hijacked . . . by Junk, Tech and Stimulants
5. Mind Myths, from Genes to Drugs
6. What's Really Driving the Brain Drain?

The Space between Your Ears - the Final Frontier

Outer space has been called the final frontier, but it is the space between your ears that matters most. Understanding how your brain works is the key to enhancing intelligence, concentration, mood and stress resilience, protecting yourself from age-related memory decline and minimizing the risk of mental illness. Your brain is the most important part of your body.

If you get your diet and lifestyle right for your brain, they'll also be right for your body. If your brain is working well, you'll think more clearly and be more likely to be in a good mood. While your state of mind is also determined by other things going on in your life – work and money stresses, relationships, having a life purpose or acting aimlessly, for example – if your brain isn't working properly, all these 'psychological' matters get worse. If you don't have enough brain energy, you don't have the power to resolve issues and adjust your life in ways to make you feel happy, motivated and in charge, with your needs fulfilled.

You may have read books about detoxing your liver, protecting your heart, boosting your immune system, balancing your hormones, keeping your joints healthy. Perhaps even one of mine! But even your ability to strengthen or heal a body part requires the engagement of your brain.

We humans have very big brains. Excepting elephants, only marine mammals, eating a pescetarian diet, have as big or larger brains than us. In terms of size, the sperm whale is the winner, with a brain size six times ours. Dolphins have roughly the same brain size as us. Both dolphins and sperm whales have complex language and signs of considerable intelligence. Physically, size matters, and psychologically, IQ is a reasonable indicator of intelligence. It is vital to understand why we have evolved to have such large brains, because it gives you the means to know how to upgrade your brain.

But first, let's get an overview of what's between your ears. Once you've learned how the parts work you'll see, in later chapters, how all the pieces fit together for your brain upgrade. Potentially new words for you are shown in *italics*, but soon they'll become part of your brain vocabulary.

Your brain is mainly fat

The first thing to know is that the dry weight of your brain (excluding water content) is about 60 per cent fat. That's way more than any other organ. The kind of fats you eat, which then become part of your brain, changes how you think and feel. To give you an example, if a pregnant woman lacks essential omega-3 fats, their baby's brain gets built using substitute fat, oleic acid, which is primarily what's in olive oil, which doesn't work nearly so well.[3] Measuring oleic acid in pregnant women's blood is being used to predict the risk of problems in newborn infants.

Where are these fats in your brain? They are largely in the membrane or outer layers of brain cells, called *neurons*, making the membrane water-resistant and therefore keeping the right amount of water in and outside cells. This is especially important in the brain, because each brain cell sends out thousands of tentacle-like connections called *dendrites*, which have the equivalent of an electrical wire in the middle called an *axon*, to reach and talk to other cells, and these have to be surrounded with a fatty sheath to keep them insulated and stop short-circuits.

Also, where one neuron meets another, they 'talk' to each other across a gap called a *synapse* via chemical messengers called *neurotransmitters*. So, the fatty membranes are like the 'ears' of brain cells.

Each of us has something like 86 billion neurons and about the same number of 'support' cells, called *glial cells*,[4] which help supply the neurons with fuel – either glucose or ketones, which is a brain

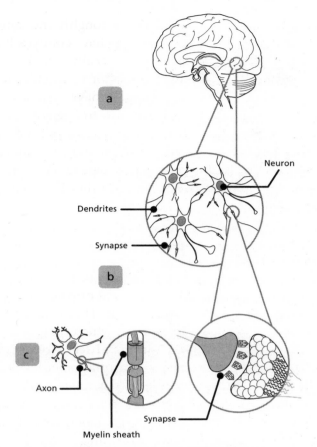

Fig 1. (a) the brain; (b) network of interconnected neurons; (c) synapse where two cells meet

fuel made from fat. So, about 170 billion cells with spindly dendrites, like tentacles – that is largely what your brain consists of, and they, in turn, contain mainly fat.

Not everything is black or white - grey matters

You've probably heard of 'grey matter' and 'white matter'. That's because when a brain is scanned, you can see grey and white matter.

The white matter is principally a very fatty protein called myelin, which is insulating those dendritic tentacles.

The grey matter is the neurons, which have other stuff in them, including more protein in the central nucleus, where all the genetic DNA instructions are banked.

So, in basic terms, a reduction in grey matter means your brain is shrinking, and a reduction in white matter means fewer functioning connections – the network is breaking down. So, for example, studies of people with dementia show grey-matter atrophy (smaller brain size) and loss of white-matter integrity, indicating 'wiring' problems. In multiple sclerosis there is a breakdown in the fatty myelin sheath, so signals don't get through and an MS sufferer starts to lose muscle control.

The two hallmarks of Alzheimer's dementia, which accounts for two-thirds of dementia, are 'neurofibrillary tangles' – think wires in a mess – which is linked to the accumulation of an abnormal protein called *p-tau*; and the accumulation of abnormal *amyloid protein*, resulting in amyloid deposits or plaque, which are found mainly in the synapses or junction points where two brain cells meet.

These two – p-tau and amyloid – are the two main targets for the new generation of dementia drugs. The trouble is, the anti-amyloid drugs don't work that well, despite lowering amyloid (*see page 57*), and have terrible side-effects – one third of patients get brain bleeding and swelling, which can be fatal. But is the cause of dementia the amyloid plaque or the p-tau-induced tangles? Consider your teeth. Is the cause of tooth decay plaque? Sure, flossing your teeth and getting the plaque scraped off by the dental hygienist helps, but what causes the plaque? The answer is a bad diet – in this case, one high in sugar and low in fibre. The same concept applies to Alzheimer's, which is as preventable as tooth decay with the right diet and nutrition.

Later on, I'll show you how to dementia-proof your brain by stopping amyloid protein and p-tau accumulating and other ways to make sure you don't suffer from this preventable but not really reversible disease.

Targeting amyloid and p-tau with the new generation of 'antibody' drugs is tackling the consequence, not the cause, of brain degeneration. The same is true for virtually every drug for mental illness. Benzodiazepines (Valium, Librium, etc.) cut the adrenalin switch, so you calm down. But what causes the adrenalin switch to be turned on in the first place? We are going to get to the root causes of these problems.

It's all about connection

A newborn baby already has at least 100 billion brain cells and, by 18 months, isn't going to generate many more. These brain cells can, however, die off if we don't do the right things, and they aren't easily replaced. Regenerating neurons is a very slow process. We can, however, improve their function and their ability to make energy, both by giving their powerhouse energy factories, called *mitochondria*, an overhaul and by improving their fuel supply. (*How to do this is explained in chapters 11 and 12.*) But what we can do at any age is to increase the number of *connections* between brain cells. This is, in effect, learning. Right now, as you read this book, you'll be making new connections.

The process of hard-wiring the human brain also involves pruning redundant connections. It's a case of 'use it or lose it', which is why it is important to have an active lifestyle physically, socially and intellectually.

As we've seen, neurons communicate by sending and receiving neurotransmitters, which are made from amino acids, except for one called *acetylcholine*, which is critical for memory and made from a special kind of fat called a *phospholipid*. Phospholipids are a vital part of the brain cell membrane, making up more than half of it. They have to bind to omega-3 DHA to make the membrane, a process that is dependent on B vitamins. More on this in Chapter 9, but you can see how this works in this one-minute film *How to Keep Building Brain Cells at Any Age* – foodforthebrain.org/building-brain-cells/.

Neurotransmitters, the chemicals of communication

So far, I've shown you how messages are sent through the brain and how they are received at the synapse, the space between brain cells, crossing through the membrane. That, if you like, is the 'listening' part of the process. But what's the 'talking'? That's where neurotransmitters come in. These are the chemicals of communication.

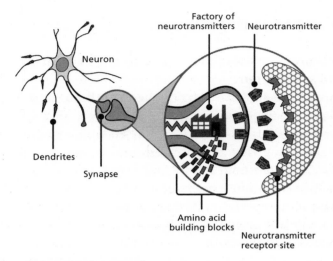

Fig 2. How neurotransmitters work

Most neurotransmitters are made from amino acids, which are the building blocks of protein. There are eight essential amino acids we have to eat in our diet, shown in the white boxes in the figure below, from which we can make the main neurotransmitters, shown in the black boxes.

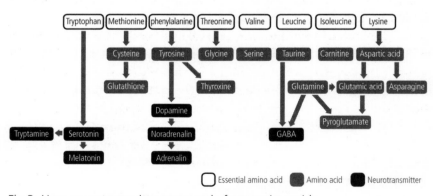

Fig 3. How neurotransmitters are made from amino acids

There are a few others that are not shown here, such as *endorphins* and *enkephalins*, which are part of the 'reward' signalling in the brain. These are released, for example, after exercise, hence the 'runner's high'.

As already mentioned, there's also one key player not made from amino acids, acetylcholine, which is made from a very important phospholipid called phosphatidyl choline, which is abundant in eggs and fish.

Neurotransmitters affect how we think and feel. For example, a low *serotonin* level correlates with depression, a high *adrenalin* level correlates with feeling stressed and anxious, and a lack of *melatonin* will make it very hard to sleep well.

All neurotransmitters are either 'excitatory' or 'inhibitory'. If they are excitatory, they switch something on. This means that when the neurotransmitter is released, crosses the gap and hits the receptor in the adjoining brain cell, it tells that cell to 'fire' and pass the message on. An example of this is adrenalin. It wakes up adjoining neurons much like switching a light on.

If neurotransmitters are inhibitory, it's like switching a light off. Serotonin and gamma-aminobutyric acid (GABA), for example, are inhibitory. Serotonin makes us feel happy. It tells the next neuron to go to rest. GABA switches off adrenalin, leading to relaxation. Alcohol, temporarily, promotes GABA, which is why we relax after a drink.

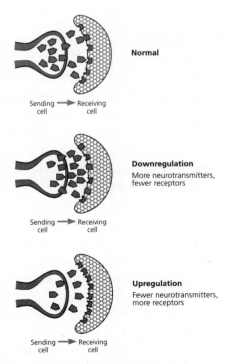

Fig 4. How overstimulation leads to downregulation

Triggering the release of excitatory neurotransmitters such as dopamine or adrenalin too much leads to the brain starting to 'downregulate' or shut down receptors, much like blocking our ears if the music is too loud. Then we crave more of whatever we are using to feel good – more sugar, more carbs, more coffee, more shopping, more cocaine, more amphetamines. Eventually the stimulant doesn't work so well. This is called tolerance. Eventually the receptors shut down. This is called addiction.

An addictive substance or behaviour, such as gambling, is basically mimicking what a natural neurotransmitter does until we no longer make it and have to have the addictive substance or behaviour. So we can become addicted to pleasure-seeking, and the marketeers know it. (*More on this in Chapter 4.*)

In serious addiction, the receptors for neurotransmitters can literally be destroyed, but otherwise they can come back to life, or upregulate, if we avoid the addictive substance. This does, however, take a few days, or weeks in more serious addiction, during which it takes will-power to resist the substance cravings.

You have three brains

Where is all this talking and listening happening? Of course, the answer is throughout your brain, but different areas are responsible for different functions. The brain is divided into lobes with different core functions, much like an industrial complex with different areas of speciality.

But let's step back a bit in time and consider the brain's evolution. The early brains of reptiles (think dinosaurs) were very small and covered core instinctual survival functions such as breathing, eating and self-preservation, but not complex thought or emotions. That is why having a snake as a pet isn't a very rewarding experience – they don't 'love' you as such. (Please excuse me if I've offended any snake lovers.) This *reptilian brain* is the core of our modern brain.

Evolutionarily speaking, the next layer is called the *mammalian brain*. Take a dog's brain as an example. Dogs do feel and do love you. But they aren't great philosophers. They've got much of what we've got in the *medial central lobes*, which include the *hippocampus*. Both are important in relation to addiction and Alzheimer's.

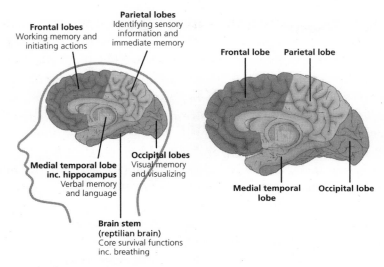

Fig 5. The brain's anatomy

Then there is the outer layer, the *neocortex*, the newest layer, which generally gets bigger as you move up the evolutionary scale. So ours is bigger than that of a monkey, which is bigger than that of a dog.

An example of how we integrate these 'layers' of the brain can be shown in a simple breathing exercise. Breathing is controlled by the oldest brain, the reptilian brain; awareness of the breath is actually in the *newest* brain, the neocortex. We integrate the experience by focusing the awareness in the big new human brain on the activities of the old small reptile brain, and at that point, we've got fully integrated brain functioning. Focusing on the breath is a way into meditation. More on this later, too.

Some would say the gut is also a brain, or at least connected to it. We'll explore this in Chapter 14. After all, thinking doesn't only happen in the brain – neurons are nerve cells, and these are found throughout the body, and there's one great big nerve, the vagus nerve, that links the gut, heart and brain together. Also, as we are learning from studying the gut microbiome, the network of around 130 different strains of bacteria in our digestive system, the whole body–mind experience that we call 'life' is orchestrated not only by us, but also by the vast intelligence that exists within us – in cells, mitochondria and the gut microbiome.

Integrated brain functioning

Integrated brain functioning changes the pattern of electrical activity across the brain, much like changing music from energizing rock 'n' roll to chill-out music or the blues. The energized state, chemically, means more excitatory neurotransmitters – adrenalin, noradrenalin (called norepinephrine in the USA) and dopamine – are flowing around the brain, and this pattern is called *beta waves*.

When we are asleep and dreaming, on the other hand, our brain produces *theta waves*. Theta waves relate to the subconscious mind and imagination. They are associated with intuitive thought and also occur during periods of strong internal focus, for example in the creation of art or music, in meditation and in prayer. They are common in children up to 13 years old and also found in advanced meditators.

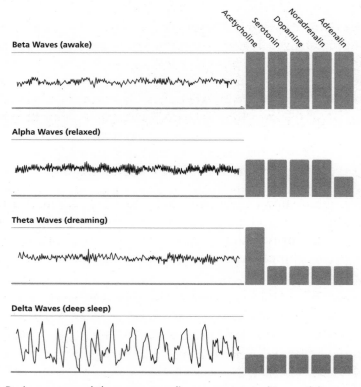

Fig 6. Brain waves and the corresponding neurotransmitter activity

An interesting finding comes from the rapidly unfolding research into hallucinogenic compounds such as LSD, psilocybin (magic mushrooms) and the Amazonian plant potion ayahuasca. These are all associated with promoting a potent neurotransmitter called di-methyl tryptamine (DMT), a cousin of serotonin and melatonin. During these trips, the brain produces more theta waves, according to research carried out at Imperial College's Centre for Psychedelic Research.[5] Also, there is much more communication across the brain between regions that don't normally talk to each other.

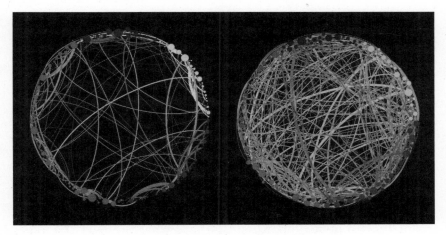

Fig 7. Brain connectivity on placebo versus psilocybin

This figure shows the connections between different areas of the brain on a placebo (left) versus on psilocybin (right). People with treatment-resistant depression report amazing break-throughs in clinical trials of hallucinogens,[6] perhaps by freeing up painful memories and making more fruitful connections. In other words, a brain upgrade. I'll be showing you how to promote more connections without psychedelics! However, the research into them is really teaching us a lot about how the brain works and how different areas communicate and stop listening to each other, filtering our experience for better, or sometimes for worse.

In summary, we have learned that:

- Our brain is made of fats, principally omega-3 and phospholipids.
- Brain cells, neurons, make energy from either glucose or ketones, which are derived from fat.
- Neurons talk to each other using neurotransmitters, which are made from amino acids.
- The basis of addiction involves a substance mimicking a neurotransmitter and leading to its receptors downregulating and ultimately becoming depleted.
- Imbalances in neurotransmitters are behind many aspects of mental health problems.
- Our brain has evolved and is still evolving (and devolving). What we eat and how we live make a difference.
- Areas of the brain have specific functions, and states of mind are reflected in waves of electrical activity across the brain.

Since the brain is a result of millions of years of evolution, understanding how we became *Homo sapiens* can give us vital clues about how to upgrade our brains. That's what the next chapter is all about.

How We Became *Sapiens*

What makes us humans so different from other apes is our larger brain, especially the outer layer, the neocortex. How did this happen? What can we learn from this?

Life began in the ocean. Millions of years ago, something like the rudimentary eye cell, probably a dinoflagellate, which is a type of marine phytoplankton, used a specific fat, the omega-3 fat docosahexaenoic acid (DHA), to convert solar photon energy into the first electrical nerve impulse, or twitch – a twitch towards food. In the same way that an electric shock makes you twitch, this organism started to twitch, and learned to move towards food. That is the origin of the nervous systems and brains of all creatures.

Back in the 1980s, when zoologist Professor Michael Crawford analysed the types of fat in different animals' organs and muscles, he found they all varied according to their dietary environment except the brain and eye. He also discovered that the brain is always rich in the omega-3 fat DHA.

Recently, it has been discovered that DHA has a unique structure involving six double bonds arranged in a horseshoe shape (*see figure on page 16*), which actually makes it a semi-conductor, meaning it is not just insulating, but can also conduct, that is, send and receive messages.

But DHA is not only involved in signalling, but also in stimulating gene expression in the brain, so the rich aquatic food sources available constantly, every day, would have powered the increase in brain size and function. Sea mammals, such as whales, seals, sealions and dolphins, also have exceptionally large brains.

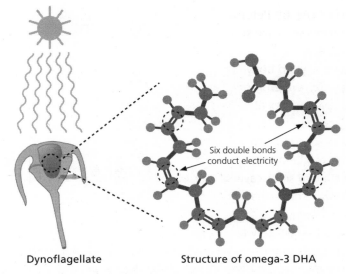

Dynoflagellate Structure of omega-3 DHA

Fig 8. The structure of omega-3 docosahexaenoic acid (DHA)

DHA's close cousins, alpha linolenic acid (ALA), found in chia and flax, and eicosapentaenoic acid (EPA), which is the other main fat in fish oils, don't have this unique property. While some EPA converts into DHA, less than 1 per cent of ALA in plant-based sources of omega-3, such as chia seeds, does. The richest source of DHA is marine-based food from rivers and the sea. What does this say about our early development?

Homo aquaticus

Over 6 million years ago, our hominid ancestors split from other apes (chimpanzees, gorillas and bonobos), culminating in *Homo sapiens* around 100,000 years ago. During this time, brain size steadily increased up to an average of 1.66kg 30,000 years ago,[7] more than four times the size of that of a chimpanzee, at 384g. It clearly wasn't genes that made us different – we share 98.5 per cent of our genome. It had to be the environment our ancestors exploited.

But before looking closely at the circumstances and diet that almost certainly drove our gain in brain size and intelligence, let's take a look at the fundamental differences between us and other apes. These have been clearly delineated in an excellent book, *The*

Waterside Ape, by Peter Rhys-Evans, an ear, nose and throat surgeon. He explores why we stand upright and have:

- (virtually) no body hair and a layer of sub-cutaneous fat
- a waxy, waterproof layer, the vernix, at birth
- a diving reflex at birth, meaning we are able to swim before we can walk, and hold our breath underwater
- a descended larynx, a precursor of being able to have complex spoken language
- enlarged sinus cavities
- a nose shape that is good for keeping the water out while swimming
- ears that actually form a protective bony protrusion called an exostosis in those who spend a lot of time diving
- kidneys that are different in how they filter salt and water
- manual dexterity
- fingers that have crinkly skin when in water for a few minutes – good for catching fish

Of course, the story we've all been told is that we came out of the trees onto the savannah and stood upright for better hunting. But anyone who has been on safari will know that a) you don't stand a chance catching anything by standing upright – you crawl; and b) all the good hunters can sprint much faster than man (lions sprint at 80 kilometres per hour, leopards 60kph, cheetahs 100kph and man under 30kph), precisely because four legs are better than two. That apart, can any of the other changes, let alone our increase in intelligence, be explained by a move from the trees to the savannah? Also, why do certain 'sea nomad' tribes exist, such as the Moken and Bajau of Southeast Asia, who can hold their breath for up to 10 minutes underwater and even give birth in the sea? Their spleen, like that of dolphins, has adapted to oxygenate tissue to enable long dives. Where did that evolutionary adaptation come from?

The only logical hypothesis that I have encountered which eloquently fits all these adaptations is that our hominid ancestors exploited the waterside – wetlands, swamplands, rivers, estuaries and coasts. In the process, they became upright and started to eat a diet high in marine foods, which provided the essential nutrients for brain development, that is omega-3 DHA, phospholipids, plus vitamin B12, iodine and all those other essential elements from magnesium to selenium. After all, the water's edge and coastlines would have been packed with easy pickings – mussels, oysters, lobsters and small fish caught in tidal pools. There is clear evidence, going back almost 200,000 years at Pinnacle Point on South Africa's Southern Cape Coast, that our ancestors were eating and cooking marine food. From this perspective, let's briefly examine all the differences between us and other apes listed above:

- standing upright – better for wading in water, so gradually our anatomy adapts, but, even so, we are prone to the problems of uprightness, e.g. with the hips and knees, because it is anatomically inferior to walking on all fours, which has a better weight distribution
- having (virtually) no body hair and a layer of sub-cutaneous fat – consistent with semi-aquatic mammals, better for floating and insulation
- having a waxy, waterproof layer, the vernix, at birth – found in no land mammals, only semi-aquatic mammals such as seals, and chemically identical[8]
- having a diving reflex at birth, meaning we are able to swim before we can walk, and hold our breath underwater
- having a descended larynx, a prerequisite of being able to have complex spoken language – being upright and diving could have led to this vital adaptation
- having enlarged sinus cavities, which help to keep the head above water, but still have drainage holes in the 'wrong' place, i.e. good if on all fours, but bad if upright, which is why we are prone to sinus problems
- having a nose shape that is good for keeping the water out while swimming
- having ears that actually form a protective bony protrusion – exostosis – in those who spend a lot of time diving, hence underwater
- having manual dexterity – if we were wading, and swimming, not walking on all fours, we'd have 'free' hands. Opening shells would develop manual dexterity
- having crinkly fingers when in water for a few minutes – perfect for catching fish

Part of the 'savannah' theory is that food became scarce with climate changes, so we switched to hunting. But the water's edge was, until recently, abundant with easily accessible food. Even 300 years ago, in 1706, Daniel Defoe wrote, regarding the Firth of Forth, 'Off the Pentland Firth the sea was one third water and two thirds fish; the operation of taking them could hardly be call'd fishing, for they did little more than dip for them into the water and take them up.' (Today, pollution has rendered mussels along this estuary toxic – unfit for either human consumption. There is a sign telling dog-walkers to keep their dogs on a lead due to their toxicity.) The metro area of New York in the 1600s was home to 350 square miles of oyster reefs and considered the oyster capital of the world. Our estuaries were packed with mussels, oysters and crabs. In the early 1900s, the barmen in the East End would fill their buckets with oysters from the Thames in the early morning and put them on the bar free for people who bought beer (*see placards in the Museum of London*).

Historically, wherever early man is found, so too is evidence of seafood consumption, with remains of shells, fish bones, etc., such as from Pinnacle Point in South Africa to Wales. When a 40,000-year-old *Homo sapiens* was found in the Gower peninsula, DNA evidence suggests that almost a quarter of its diet was seafood. In Scandinavia 10,000 years ago, people were relying on the marine food web and food in the rivers and of course any mammals on land. A fishing net, found in a bog in Finland, was 35 metres long, with sinkers and floaters dating back to 10,000 years ago.

Not everyone agrees with the aquatic ape theory championed by biologist and natural historian Sir David Attenborough. After his series about it on BBC Radio 4 in 2016[9] there was a backlash,[10] led by Alice Roberts, a professor of anatomy, claiming the fossil record wasn't consistent with this theory. But none of the opponents could explain two of the compelling facts – that only humans and marine mammals have the waxy, waterproof vernix at birth, and why our ears produce exostoses in those who dive a lot, thus spend time underwater. Nor am I aware of a better theory as to how we became *Homo sapiens*. It had to be the consequence of exposure to a diet rich in brain-building nutrients.

Professor Michael Crawford says, 'Interestingly, those supporting the savannah view of human evolution do not consider nutritional input in any qualitative way that is relevant to the brain. The idea that competition and the need to hunt led to adroitness, etc., is baseless. There is no biological mechanism, no science here!

'The brain needs nutrients to build it in the same way as a house needs bricks. Make no mistake, it is the brain that makes us different from other animals. So, to become *Homo sapiens*, our ape ancestors had to eat food which contained the building blocks for the brain: it is basic and elementary.

'The brain evolved in the sea and its building blocks came from the sea. So *ipso facto*, we had to be eating aquatic foods. But anyway, by the time we were able to hunt animals with arrows and spears, we were already quite smart.'

As Sir David Attenborough says, 'Gathering molluscs is far easier than chasing elephants and wildebeests across the savannah.'

A marine-food diet is a brain-building diet

Leaving prehistory aside, given our close genetics to apes, and assuming it must have been our environment that drove our evolution in a brain-friendly way, a marine-food diet is high in critical brain-building nutrients, especially DHA, phospholipids and vitamin B12.

'The crucial point is that without a high DHA diet from seafood we could not have developed our big brains. We got smart from eating fish and living in water,' says Professor Michael Crawford.

The dry weight of the brain is 60 per cent fat and DHA makes up the majority of the structural fat of neurons. The intelligent membrane that makes up all neurons is largely composed of phosphorylated DHA – that is, DHA attached to phospholipids. The most abundant phospholipid is phosphatidyl choline, found predominantly in fish, eggs and organ meats. These are bound together by a process called methylation, itself dependent on vitamins B12, folate and B6. While folate and B6 are found in both plant foods and seafood, B12 is only found in foods of animal origin, and is especially high in all marine foods.

So, the evidence that exists suggests we were eating a diet rich in marine food, as well as plant foods along the water's edge, enjoying the *fruits de mer*. We would have eaten much more than we do today – at least double the calories. Today's world of convenience has dramatically reduced the calories we need to expend hunting and gathering food, travelling and staying warm.

The idea that we were eating twice as much and possibly a quarter of our diet as marine foods makes sense of what we know about the optimal intake of both omega-3 fats rich in DHA, phospholipids and vitamin B12, lack of which are the main drivers of today's endemic dementia. This would be equivalent to at least half our diet today being from marine foods rich in fats, because we eat half as many calories.

The optimal amount of omega-3 from seafood is estimated at 2 grams (2,000mg) a day by Joseph Hibbeln, a leading expert in neuroscience at the US National Institutes of Health (NIH). Dr Simon Dyall, one of the directors of the International Society for the Study of Fatty Acids and Lipids, estimates an optimal intake of DHA is closer to 1,000mg.

These two highly regarded scientists base their calculations on hundreds of studies consistently showing brain-friendly benefits from higher intakes of the omega-3 fats found in fish. An example is a study of 48 studies in the *American Journal of Clinical Nutrition* in 2023,[11] concluding that 'a moderate-to-high level of evidence suggested that dietary intake of omega-3 fatty acids could lower risk of all-cause dementia or cognitive decline by about 20 per cent, especially for docosahexaenoic acid (DHA) intake'. Each 100mg increment of DHA was associated with an 8 to 10 per cent lower risk of dementia. This confirmed the results of a US study[12] that found a 49 per cent reduced risk for dementia in those with the highest DHA level (top fifth) in their red blood cells versus the lowest (bottom fifth),[12] and a study from the UK Biobank which reported a 30 per cent lower risk of dementia in those with a higher omega-3 status in their blood.[13]

There can no longer be any doubt that increasing one's omega-3 intake, by eating oily fish or supplementing, reduces dementia risk. Just eating one serving of fish a week has been shown to reduce risk of Alzheimer's disease by 60 per cent.[14] More is even better.

An optimal intake of B12 is probably 10mcg. (There are 1,000 micrograms (mcg) in 1 milligram (mg), so this is a tiny quantity.) The optimal intake of choline, the critical ingredient in phosphatidyl choline, is estimated at 400mg to 800mg. (Choline is rich in all fish, but DHA is only rich in oily fish, fish roe and liver.) To achieve these kinds of intakes, our ancestors would have needed to eat at least one serving of fish or seafood a day, if not more, which is consistent with a period in our evolution which was based on marine food. These kinds of intakes can only be achieved today by both eating fish and supplementing with fish oils. Phosphatidyl choline is rich in lecithin capsules and granules, which are also easy to supplement.

Please note that this doesn't mean there weren't periods *after Homo sapiens* arrived in full force 100,000 years ago when we survived on a different diet. But the issue here is what made our brain size triple from that of our ape ancestors. There is no evidence that eating a carnivorous only or plant-based only diet could have provided the environment for such a jump in brain size.

Brain size remained reasonably constant from 100,000 to 10,000 years ago, then started to shrink. Today, the average brain size is less than 1.35kg. That's about 20 per cent smaller than early Cro-Magnon humans.

The evolution of intelligence and self-awareness

Apart from brain size and, more pertinently, brain to body size or ratio, what sets us apart from other animals is being able to witness our own thoughts and feelings, that is, having self-awareness. This is not an easy thing to measure, but some other mammals, notably dolphins, gorillas and chimpanzees, have a degree of self-awareness. Other contenders for higher cognition include octopuses and elephants, all large-brained creatures. However, it isn't just size that matters. While elephants have larger brains than we do, they have smaller neo-cortexes. It's the neo-cortex that starts to grow in our hominid ancestors and adds that uniquely human layer of intelligence.

An indication of an advancing intelligence could be ancient rock art, as well as the use of complex tools and adornments. The most ancient rock art – which has been dated to around 80,000 BCE – is in sub-Saharan Africa, which had a vast network of lakes, rivers and wetlands at the time. One particularly significant cave painting from this period shows a group of early humans swimming. Then weather patterns changed, the monsoon moved further south and the whole area dried up. Whether the drying up of the Sahara was linked to the Younger Dryas (*see below*), a change in the Earth's tilt or overgrazing is a subject of debate.[15]

By 10,000 years ago, the Nile was the only large river left in Africa, and the longest. Further north, the Tigris and Euphrates, in modern-day Iraq, were similarly isolated water sources. It was along the banks of these rivers that human civilization started to flourish. Even today, the vast majority of the world's major cities are on the water's edge.

Campfires on the beach

However, it wasn't just the fats in seafood that shaped our development. Another significant milestone was the discovery of fire about 1.8 million years ago. Thereafter, especially after around 500,000 BCE, cooking had a huge impact on our ancestors' diet and evolution. It made previously hard to digest root vegetables and beans more edible, and therefore valuable new sources of energy because of the carbohydrates they contained.

This coincided with the ongoing steady increase in brain size, along with a parallel increase in aerobic capacity, a shortening of the gut and a reduction in tooth size. A plausible explanation for all of these physiological changes is that cooking meant our ancestors needed to spend less time chewing food in the mouth as well as digesting and absorbing nutrients in the gut. Uncooked vegetables, meat and fish all demand a lot of chewing.

Our genes support this theory. About 1 million years ago, multiple variations in carbohydrate-digesting amylase enzymes, which turn cooked starch into glucose, started to appear. This meant that more fuel was available for both the body and the brain.

'Consumption of increased amounts of starch may have provided a substantial evolutionary advantage to Mid-to-Late Pleistocene omnivorous hominins,' according to Karen Hardy and Jenny Brand-Miller from the University of Sydney.[16]

Cooked starch – a rich source of preformed glucose – greatly increased energy availability to human tissues with high glucose demands, including the brain, red blood cells and developing foetuses.

By 20,000 BCE, the hunter-gatherer *Homo sapiens'* diet consisted chiefly of lean meat, fish and shellfish, eggs, vegetables and fruit. Some wild lentils, grasses, grains and peas may have been eaten too, but these foodstuffs didn't take off in a major way until the Agricultural Revolution, more than 10,000 years later, when land-based agriculture kicked in. There was no consumption of dairy products, and of course no processed food.

Meanwhile, groups of our early ancestors who had left Africa and were living as far west as Ireland, north as Scandinavia and east as China and Australia, were also struck by cataclysmic weather changes. There is another evolutionary hotspot in Asia and China.[17]

In Europe, the Magdalenian culture, with advanced stonework, existed from 17,000 years ago, coinciding with the end of the last Ice Age, until 12,000 years ago, coinciding with the Younger Dryas, a period of extreme cooling which lasted for around 1,000 years, its start possibly triggered by a meteor shower.[18] Glaciers started to recede around 20,000 years ago, which allowed 'plant species previously confined to sheltered habitats ... to spread well beyond their regions of origin', according to Ivan Crow in his book *The Quest for Food*.[19] These were favourable conditions for the wild grains that our ancestors were already eating. Wheat, barley and lentils all grew well along the shores of the Sea of Galilee, where archaeologists have found evidence of early pestles and mortars, used for grinding.

Prime examples of these grains are wheat, rye and barley, which became mainstays of the Mesopotamian diet by about 9,000 BCE. Meanwhile, less robust, relatively low-gluten cereals were discarded. Gluten is a source of protein.

The widespread cultivation of grain, especially wheat, facilitated the formation of villages and then towns, as tribes abandoned their traditional nomadic lifestyles and settled down. The invention of ploughing led to higher yields. Grain stores provided more security during winters and droughts.

Domesticated animals began to appear around 6,000 BCE, starting with goats. As a result, consumption of meat and especially dairy products increased enormously. Rapid population growth ensued. Peasant farmers survived better than hunter-gatherers and claimed ever more of the most fertile land for themselves. The pace of civilization accelerated as the food supply became increasingly stable. But there was a price to pay. Our brains started shrinking.

In summary, we know that:

- We split from chimpanzees and gorillas 6 to 7 million years ago, and our brain size steadily increased from the 0.4 to 0.5kg brain size of a chimp or gorilla.
- We became human by eating a mixture of marine foods and plant foods along the water's edge, and became upright wading in water.
- Only a largely marine-food diet could have provided the essential building blocks for the human brain, which grew to a maximum size of 1.6 to 1.7kg 30,000 years ago. Today it has shrunk to less than 1.35kg.
- About 1 million years ago, with the discovery of fire, our diet changed as we learned how to cook previously inedible foods, allowing more nutrition to feed brain growth.
- Around 10,000 years ago, vast sections of humanity started to exploit land-based agriculture, with a consequent increase in the consumption of grains, meat and milk. This parallels evidence of the reverse of brain growth – brain shrinkage.

Why Our Brains Are Shrinking

We have a rather human-centric point of view, putting humanity at the top of the heap and assuming we are always evolving. But the evidence is now clear that we are devolving – and perhaps, like the dinosaurs, towards our own extinction, largely as a consequence of our diet. The simplest illustration of this is that our brain size, which is worked out from the space inside the skull, has actually decreased by a staggering 20 per cent over the last 30,000 years, with mental health now in increasingly rapid decline in the last 50 years.

The rise and fall of brain size

The migration of hominids to the coast occurred about 2 million years ago, according to the fossil record. Thereafter, there was a steady growth in brain space from 450cc.

After a few hundred thousand years of rapid mental and physical development on the East African coast, *Homo erectus* started to explore further afield, reaching the southern Mediterranean, the Middle East, India and East Asia. By then, the human brain had already doubled in size to 940cc.

Later, those who remained in – or possibly returned to – Africa ultimately evolved into *Homo sapiens*. Then, like their ancestors before them, they started to spread around the world. Recent archaeological discoveries in China, Israel and Morocco suggest that our species reached these places around 180,000 years ago.[20]

Around 32,000 years ago, Cro Magnon had a brain size of 1,550cc (that's 1.55kg). At Dolni Vestonice in the Czech Republic, the discovery of skulls dates back to 29,000 years ago, with a capacity of 1,660cc, which is more than four times the size of a chimpanzee's brain, at 384g. Around 10,000 years ago, average brain size was estimated at 1,550cc.[21]

Today, our average brain size is less than 1,350cc – 1,328cc according to a recent calculation.[22] That's more than a 20 per cent decrease over 30,000 years, and more than a 10 per cent decrease over the last 10,000 years, coinciding with a move to land-based agriculture, with more meat and plants and less fish, and away from hunting and gathering along coasts and rivers. Could our change in diet be the primary cause given that the fundamental for brain development is having the right brain-building materials, namely omega-3 fats and phospholipids? I am not aware of any other plausible explanations.

Nutrition drives evolution

The story of Darwin's evolutionary theories is not what you think. If you ask the average person what Darwin proposed, they will say 'survival of the fittest' – that 'natural selection' drives evolution. This misrepresentation has fuelled a mistaken notion that those genetically 'superior' took over through a process of natural selection. What he actually said was:

> The fact of variations ... occurring much more frequently under domestication than under nature ... led to the conclusion that variability is generally related to the conditions of life to which each species has been exposed in successive generations... Of the two forces [that is, natural selection and conditions of existence], conditions were the more important.[23]

Let me explain this a bit more, using dinosaurs, cats and rhinos as examples, because knowing this not only defines the nutrition you need for mental health, but also why nutrition is the driving force for our health and evolution and needs to be centre-stage in all healthcare, as well as education and policy. Natural selection, that is the survival of the fittest, only kicks in *after* a change in the environment.

The importance of food resources

Why did dinosaurs die out 65 million years ago? Were they 'dead on impact'? This is the prevailing theory that a meteor struck the Earth and changed conditions dramatically. Another possibility is a massive volcano erupting.

Professor Michael Crawford and David Marsh, in their seminal book *The Shrinking Brain*, provide a much simpler or potentially parallel and contributing explanation:

> A collapse in environmental systems brought about by giant herbivores outstripping their food resources could have finished off the dinosaurs without the need for extra-terrestrial projectiles or super-volcanoes. Indeed, both forces could have done the trick. Dinosaurs may have been responsible for their own extinction, just as we have been responsible for the present mass extinction of our fellow inhabitants of this planet – and indeed threatening our own survival.[24]

They are referring to the 500 species that have gone extinct in the last 100 years in a way linked to human activity, such as overhunting, destruction of ecosystems/habitats and pollution.

Back in the dinosaur era, it was the time of giants – giant ferns, giant vegetation, and giant dinosaurs with tiny brains eating around 46 million kilos of plant food each year. The plants grew more slowly than the animals, which trampled them with their giant feet. 'This period was the hottest,' Crawford and Marsh say, 'and it may be that dinosaurs created their own hothouse effect.'

Why omega-6 in seeds was a brain-evolution essential

What happened next? Post the dinosaurs, smaller flowering plants with protected seeds high in omega-6 fats, appeared. I should point out here that the leaves of plants provide omega-3, but only the seeds provide omega-6, which is called linoleic acid. Linoleic acid can quite easily be turned into arachidonic acid (AA), which is the second brain essential, along with omega-3 DHA. The brains of all mammals contain both large amounts of omega-3 DHA and omega-6 AA. Without this, as you will see, you cannot have a big brain.

Fish are an example of this. Obviously, they've got a ready supply of DHA in the ocean. Of the essential fats in the flesh of cod, 47% is DHA. Their flesh, however, is very low in fat, hence they are not an oily fish, so cod isn't a good source of omega-3, while cod liver oil is.

Oily fish contain even more omega-3. But there are no flowering plants in the oceans, just a little omega-6 in algae in warmer waters. This not only limits the ability of fish to develop large brains, but the arrival of abundant omega-6 on the scene is the likely change that led to the switch from egg-laying to incubation in the womb, which was the game-changer.

The reason, proposes Crawford, is simply that large brains need large hearts and circulation.

Unlike egg-layers, from chickens to reptiles, where all the nutrients ever needed for foetal development have to be packed into the egg at the beginning, mammals rely on a rich network of placental blood vessels constantly feeding a supply of brain-friendly nutrients. A cod can lay 1 million eggs. That's the mother's nutrition divided by 1 million, and all the developing cod will ever get before birth. A human foetus, on the other hand, is bathed in a rich supply of nutrients for nine months.

Omega-6 also stimulates the growth of blood vessels, hence the supply lines of the growing embryo. Why do the brains of all mammals have both omega-6 (largely AA) and omega-3 (largely DHA) in large supply?

Omega-6 fats and the prostaglandins they produce not only encourage blood vessel formation, but are also 'sticky'. It is likely that this change in diet supply led to eggs starting to 'stick' to the womb and the switch to mammalian reproduction. This is another example of Darwin's 'conditions of existence'.

Arachidonic acid is the difference between reptiles and mammals because it is essential for building the complex blood vessels that supply the brain. Twenty-six days after conception, the human foetus has a heart. The brain's butlers, the glial cells that supply neurons with fuel, are exceptionally high in arachidonic acid. Having a food source, namely the seeds of plants, is a big brain essential.

But there is a problem, which rhinos are stuck with and cats have solved. As you will see (*Figure 16, page 104*), omega-6, in seeds, starts off as linoleic acid. A couple of steps later, it turns into arachidonic acid.

There's next to no omega-6 in grass, only in the seeds. Grass contains omega-3 alpha linolenic acid (ALA). Very slowly, and several biochemical steps later, a little bit of it turns into DHA. 'So the faster an animal grows eating the green stuff, the less DHA it can make,' says Crawford. Instead it channels all its energy into extracting the protein and making muscle. As a consequence, a rhino, who effectively eats grass, just doesn't have the supply of either arachidonic acid but especially DHA to build a large brain. For the rhino, it's all about brawn – its body is 321 times larger than its brain. The rhino illustrates one of the biggest myths in nutrition, that protein is important for growth. Of the calories in grasses, which is the rhino's diet, only 7 per cent is protein. Our brain size, however, is not a result of protein intake, but fat intake. It is essential fats more than anything else, both omega-3 DHA and omega-6 AA, that have made us human.

But they are not the only critical nutrients for the brain. Minerals such as zinc, magnesium and the B vitamins, especially B6, are needed to make the 'desaturase' enzymes that respectively convert the linoleic and linolenic acid into AA and DHA. These nutrients are also rich in marine food. Zinc is the most important and the most abundant in oysters, mussels and other rich pickings from the water's edge. A lack of zinc means less ability to make these brain-essential fats.[25] A lack of B12, also abundant in marine food, means you can't bind the essential fats into cell membranes by attaching them to phospholipids.

So, why are cats not only very smart but also have brilliant eyesight? They cannot convert that omega-3 linoleic acid into AA, or linolenic acid into DHA. They've outsourced this slow and energy-expensive process to others, such as rats and rabbits. They jump up the food chain, eating a direct source of DHA and AA in the form of these animals. Lions devour the DHA- and AA-rich organs and leave the rest. All that DHA, which is concentrated in the eye, means cats see very well in the dark and have the edge over mice, rats and rabbits. The problem for the cats is that they didn't go back from the land into a marine environment, either occasionally, as we did, or permanently, as the dolphins did, so they have smaller brains. They are the fisherman's friend, as they love eating fish. But even a smart carnivore like a lion only has a 320cc brain, one quarter of ours or any marine mammal.

We, however, can make the conversion, synthesizing both AA and DHA from seeds and leaves. We can get enough AA this way, though we really struggle to get anything like enough DHA just by eating leaves, because, in us, it's also a very slow process. That's why just eating chia or flax seeds, high in omega-3 alpha linolenic acid, is no substitute for a direct source of DHA from marine food.

Another problem is that the brain needs an omega-6 to omega-3 ratio of less than 2:1, but today many people's diets are dangerously high in processed omega-6 from commercial rape, sunflower, soya and peanut oil and low in omega-3, with a ratio of something like 20:1 omega-6 to 3. This overload of poor-quality omega-6 not only fills up fat stores in cells until there's no more room for the good stuff, but also maxes out the desaturase enzymes and uses up the co-factor nutrients such as zinc, magnesium and B6, all of which are poorly supplied in most people's diets, especially those eating the processed foods high in omega-6.

As well as learning that we need both a direct supply of DHA (marine food) and AA (seeds and nuts), the story of the rhino and the cat illustrates how it is our nutritional environment that drives our evolution and why we have to take nutrition seriously in the pursuit of optimal health. That means optimal IQ too.

IQ is falling

IQ scores have been steadily falling for the past few decades, and environmental factors are to blame. Norwegian researchers headed by Ole Rogeberg, a senior research fellow at the Ragnar Frisch Center for Economic Research, analysed the IQ scores of Norwegian men born between 1962 and 1991 and found that scores increased by almost 3 percentage points each decade for those born between

1962 to 1975, but then declined steadily among those born after 1975.[26] This coincides with the demonization of fat by mistaken researcher Ancel Keys, who managed to persuade the US authorities that fat was causing heart disease and that we should all eat a low-fat, hence high-carb diet. Since then our IQ scores have been dropping by about 7 per cent per generation. This is about the same as the increase we saw in our study giving children a high-potency multivitamin versus a placebo back in 1987 (*see page 257*).

Rogeberg says, 'Similar studies in Denmark, Britain, France, the Netherlands, Finland and Estonia have demonstrated a similar downward trend in IQ scores.' He believes the change is not due to genetics: 'It's not that dumb people are having more kids than smart people, to put it crudely, it's something to do with the environment, because we're seeing the same differences within families.'

He proposes that the environmental factors could include changes in the education system and media environment, reading less and being online more – and nutrition.

Writing in *The Times* in 1972, agricultural correspondent Graham Rose predicted that we would be 'a race of morons' unless we prioritized nutrition for the brain.

Severe neurodevelopmental impairment is defined as an IQ between 90 and 70. If the current fall in IQ continues, by 2080 between a third and a half of the world's population will be severely neurodevelopmentally impaired.

Mental illness is rising

Not only this, but globally, there is an increase in mental illness, which is fast becoming the biggest health threat, according to the World Health Organization. Global rates of depression and dementia, suicide and the stress-related disorders of anxiety and insomnia are escalating. Suicide, globally, has become the most common cause of violent death, ahead of all wars and murders.

The importance of diet can be seen in the fact that a country's suicide,[27] homicide[28] and depression[29] rates correlate with seafood intake. Land-locked countries have the highest rates of pre-term babies and, at the other end of life, dementia. Globally, every three seconds someone is diagnosed with dementia.

Is it any wonder that mental health is in sharp decline, given the fact that we are simply not achieving anything like the same intake of brain-essential fats, phospholipids and micro-nutrients? And, with a growing population and declining available seafood, coupled with contamination with heavy metals, PCBs and micro-plastics, matters are likely to get much worse.

Sugar leads to shrinkage

High sugar intake, in both animals and teenagers, has been shown to lead to the shrinking of the brain's hippocampal region that is a hallmark of Alzheimer's. (*More on this in Chapter 11.*) To date, the youngest person given an Alzheimer's diagnosis was 19. This Chinese teenager had no genetically associated risk.[30] The hippo-campal region is where the *nucleus accumbens*, the seat of the brain's dopamine-based reward system, stimulated by sugar, caffeine and tech addiction, especially that based on variable rewards such as the 'like' button, resides. Alzheimer's could even be a maladaptation to what could be called the genetic programming of the 'survival of the fattest'. This hypothesis, proposed by Professor Richard Johnson from the University of Colorado, neurologist Dr David Perlmutter and Dr Dale Bredesen (see page 246 for his astonishing results on reversing dementia), suggests that in times of scarcity the consumption of fructose (fruit sugar), now so abundant in processed foods, makes you eat more, slows your metabolism, makes you store fat, raises uric acid and induces insulin resistance, having the net effect of preserving glucose supply for the brain as an evolutionary essential.[31] Now that's good if you are starving, but having all this high fructose corn syrup added to processed foods when you're not short of food could be a royal road to Alzheimer's. Neurologist Dr David Perlmutter's book *Drop Acid* explains why increased uric acid is a function of too much fructose and a driver of so many diseases of both brain and body. Marketeers, however, have learned how to use sugar, and especially fructose, to create addiction to their products by selling short-term pleasure, the dopamine-based feeling, in the guise of happiness, as we'll explore in the next chapter. The happy hour, the happy meal, happiness in a bottle – sounds great, but over-stimulation of the reward system ultimately leads to dopamine depletion and brain-cell death, coupled with a decline in serotonin, the tryptamine associated with happiness, connection, love, empathy and other essential qualities of a harmonious society – and the very qualities that make us human.

We are therefore witnessing the devolution of the brain and the decline and fall of mental health and harmonious society, a situation that is likely to get worse as population expands, unless we rapidly find a way to optimally nourish the brain.

Building healthy brains

The emphasis in human nutrition has, for too long, been on the body rather than the mind. With more protein, meat and dairy products, we have grown taller, but not smarter. As mentioned earlier, Professor Michael Crawford has been able to accurately predict which pregnant women are most likely to have pre-term babies, and the supply of DHA in the mother-to-be predicts the cognitive development of the child. In its absence, the level of a surrogate fat, oleic acid, rises to fulfil the requirement of the neonatal brain.[32] It is, however, an inadequate substitute, and thus cognitive development is impaired. Babies born of women with low blood DHA levels, compared to those supplementing DHA, have smaller brains.[33] (*Chapter 22 shows how to build healthy young brains.*)

According to Crawford, with a growing population and a shrinking fish supply, we must develop marine agriculture on a massive scale to survive and protect the brain. As he says, 'Without plentiful DHA, we face a future of increased mental illness and intellectual deterioration. We need to face up to that urgently.'

In the same way that our ancestors moved from being hunter-gatherers on the land to peasant farmers, we must move from being hunter-gatherers in the oceans to marine farmers. In Japan, Crawford has been instrumental in the creation of artificial reefs in the estuaries to attract back the marine food web, from mussels to crustaceans and fish, as well as farming seaweed on a massive scale. By processing seaweed, it is possible to create DHA, the critical brain fat that is crucially lacking in a plant-based diet. But first we have to clean up our oceans and intelligently repopulate the marine-food web with marine agriculture, regenerating the ocean floor devasted by trawling by planting sea grasses and kelp forests, as they are doing in Japan, creating artificial reefs that attract back marine life.

According to Crawford, 'Marine agriculture would also provide brain food for us and offal for fish aquaculture, instead of chicken feathers and vegetable oils, with the kelp forests providing food, and fertilizer for land-based farming, and fixing CO_2 similar to the Amazon forests, so helping with global warming – a multiple whammy. Then there would be jobs, so economic benefits, and the need for new infrastructure, education, fish, shellfish, and marine flora breeding and research, creating a new agro-industrial revolution whilst making us self-sufficient in food and combating the shrinking brain, the escalation of mental ill-health and climate change.'

It is not rocket science. It is simply recreating the 'conditions of existence' favourable for a return of marine-food life.

Crawford's brilliant book lays out the solutions in more detail, politically and agriculturally, which is beyond the scope of this book. In Japan, he has been awarded the Order of the Rising Sun. In the UK, nothing is being done. Yet unless we address the fundamental issue, which is that we evolved to thrive on a wild and marine-food diet which bears no resemblance to what we eat today, we will not solve our mental health crisis.

Without fully functioning brains, we will neither have the insight nor the cooperation to face and resolve the challenges of a growing population, reducing food supply and increasing pollution, climate change and energy demands. At the age of 93, using quantum physics, Professor Michael Crawford has solved the mystery of vision – how photons entering the eye turn rapidly into the precise image we see. It's all about DHA. Without enough we have no clear vision, which is exactly what we need right now.[34]

What the human mind can achieve when we put our mind to it is extraordinary. After 18 years and over 100 million man-hours, NASA scientists and engineers, at a cost of £8 billion, are now getting images from deep space from the James Webb Satellite, orbiting 1 million miles from Earth. What a bold vision that is, looking back into the beginning of the universe, just after the Big Bang, when stars were born.

Yet here we are, looking into the abyss of declining physical and mental health, lower life expectancy and rising incidence of cancer, diabetes, obesity, dementia and mental illness – and we know the solutions. What is lacking is the vision of our politicians. Furthermore, our brains are being hijacked, as I'll show you in the next chapter.

In summary, we have learned that:

- The brain needs omega-3 DHA, and our supply from food has been falling, first as a consequence of moving to land-based agriculture and more recently due to processed food, high in omega-6 but lacking in omega-3, that bears no resemblance to the wild food diet that allowed our evolution to occur.
- Carnivorous animals, although inferior to marine mammals in brain size and intelligence, have outsourced the conversion of plant-based omega-3 and 6 into DHA and AA, which they cannot do, so get one step ahead of herbivores by eating them.
- The switch from egg-laying to mammalian womb development needed a rich supply of omega-6, which builds the rich blood supply to the womb. Brains are high in both omega-3 DHA and omega-6 AA.
- Not only is brain size shrinking, but IQ has been steadily falling since the 1970s, coinciding with the demonization of fat, which led to be a big increase in sugar-laden and carbohydrate-rich foods. Mental health problems are rising in parallel.
- Too much sugar shrinks the brain, producing the kind of shrinkage and cognitive deficits seen in the early stages of Alzheimer's. The youngest age of a non-genetic Alzheimer's diagnosis is 19!
- Having sufficient DHA during pregnancy is a brain essential for the baby.
- We have to clean up our oceans and get serious about marine agriculture, recreating the conditions of existence to attract back marine life and the marine-food web.

Warning: Your Brain Is Being Hijacked ... by Junk, Tech and Stimulants

So far, we've explored the kind of diet and environment that would have allowed our *Homo sapiens* brains to develop and why today's diet, lacking in brain-friendly fats and other nutrients and high in sugar and ultra-processed food, is likely to be shrinking our brains, dumbing us down and triggering a big increase in mental health problems. But it isn't just nutrition that is creating the perfect storm for our mental demise.

'Got to have it'

The digital culture we exist in is pushing us towards a whole new paradigm of background stress, partly because the marketeers have learned how to get us addicted to their products by applying a level of stress and variable reward to trick the brain's reward system so we've 'got to have it'.

Variable reward was discovered by psychologist B.F. Skinner in the 1930s. I was studying his research as a psychology undergraduate in the 1970s. Mice, he found, responded most frequently to reward-associated stimuli when the reward was administered after a varying number of responses, so the animal didn't know when it would get the prize. We are no different; if we perceive a reward to be delivered at random, and if checking for the reward comes at little cost, we end up checking habitually. This is the 'like' button on Facebook and the pings of messages. It is also the basis of gambling addiction, as with slot machines. You keep putting a little money in, hoping for a jackpot. Pull the lever and you get a stress response, activating the feel-good dopamine circuitry. The variable reward cranks this up.

The brain's reward system is based on dopamine and adrenalin, and clever marketing executives have learned how to exploit this and get us addicted to a variety of things, including our smartphones and the ads they expose us to.

The stress/reward response – one of oldest mechanisms of the brain – is both core for our survival, but also makes us more impulsive, open to manipulation and, effectively, stupid. Most of all, it makes us good consumers.

We are living in Space Age times with Stone Age minds, and multinational companies have learned how to get us literally neurochemically addicted to consuming their products. We are being sold pleasure in the guise of happiness. We even buy 'goods'.

The problem is, as Professor Robert Lustig, author of the excellent book *Hacking the American Mind*, says, 'The more pleasure you seek, the more unhappy you get.' Why? 'Dopamine release suppresses serotonin, the happy neurotransmitter,' he says, 'which then promotes feeling unhappy and depressed.'

This brain hijack is also why depression, suicide and psychiatric drug prescriptions have rocketed to the point where, in the UK and USA and probably elsewhere, there are almost twice as many prescriptions for psychiatric drugs per year than there are people.

'We are the most in debt, the most obese, the most medicated and the most drugged-up adult population in human history,' says Lustig.

We have literally learned how to fool our brains and in doing so, have fooled ourselves by creating addictive behaviours and addictive foods.

Sugar addiction

An example of this is what happens in our brains if we eat sugar. Sugar, just like cocaine and heroin, stimulates dopamine and endorphins, triggers the reward system and, with overuse, leads to reward deficiency.

In 1999, Dr Candace Pert, Research Professor in the Department of Physiology and Biophysics at Georgetown University Medical Center in Washington, DC, and author of the seminal book *Molecules of Emotion*, was the first to point this out in no uncertain terms: 'I consider sugar to be a drug, a highly purified plant product that can become addictive. Relying on an artificial form of glucose – sugar – to give us a quick pick-me-up is analogous to, if not as dangerous as, shooting heroin.'[35] At the time, this was heresy, but today most people are well aware of this. Guitarist Eric Clapton said his addiction started with sugar, before heroin and alcohol.[36]

Sugar and fats

Neuropharmacologist Professor Paul Kenny, originally a Dubliner, working in his Manhattan lab at Mount Sinai Hospital, discovered the importance of this combination when he started feeding rats different diets. When he fed one group of rats lots of sugary foods and another lots of fatty foods, neither group would gain much weight. They'd control their intake and it would take over a month to see a small weight gain. However, when he fed them a combination of 50 per cent sugar and 50 per cent fat, such as in a cheesecake, he said a rat would 'dive head first into a slice and gorge so vigorously that it covers its fur in blobs. It's not pleasant.' After a binge on cheesecake, the rats continued to graze on the food, constantly eating it, Kenny says, as if the off-switch telling them they were full had malfunctioned. 'It completely changed them.' They stopped exercising and gained significant weight after only seven days. They also became addicted.[37] When he took away the junk food and replaced it with healthy food, they went on a hunger strike.

Kenny even tried to stop them eating the junk food by giving them an electric shock to their feet: 'We then warned the rats as they were eating – by flashing a light – that they would receive a nasty foot shock. Rats eating the bland chow would quickly stop and scramble away, but time and again the obese rats continued to devour the rich food, ignoring the warning they had been trained to fear. Their hedonic desire overruled their basic sense of self-preservation.'

Overeating, he had found, juiced up the reward systems in the brain – so much so in some that it had overpowered the brain's ability to tell them to stop eating when they had had enough. As with alcoholics and drug addicts, the more such people had, the more they wanted.

It's all to do with dopamine, the brain's key neurotransmitter of reward and desire. Overeaters, like cocaine and heroin addicts, become more and more dopamine resistant – that is, their brain's receptors for dopamine shut down. Obese people, and drug addicts, have been shown to have fewer dopamine D2 receptors (D2R).[38] People who are born with reduced levels of D2R are at greater genetic risk of developing obesity and drug addiction, so you can be genetically predisposed to addiction.

Researchers at Brookhaven National Laboratory and the Oregon Research Institute have shown that the reward system in obese people responds weakly to food, even to junk food.[39] How does an individual overcome this absence of pleasure? By eating more pleasure foods to gain a temporary boost, thereby perpetuating the cycle. What the researchers found was that obese people may overeat just to experience the same degree of pleasure that lean individuals enjoy from less food.

Nicole Avena of the University of Florida and others have found that particular fats or sugars, sugars together with fats, and possibly salt, are the most addictive.[40] A study by Professor David Ludwig of Boston Children's Hospital suggests that highly processed, quickly digested fast carbs could trigger cravings.[41] But research overall indicates that no one ingredient stokes food addiction better than the combo of fats and sugars, high in calories. Nature just doesn't make these kinds of foods. Only the food industry does.

Similarly, cola drinks combine the stimulant caffeine with sugar and salt to make us drink more. When it was learned that we'd drink more if fructose, rather than glucose, was used, out went glucose, derived from cane sugar, and in came high-fructose corn syrup, derived from corn. This is a key ingredient in today's ultra-processed food.

But it's not only food that can be addictive.

Are you addicted to your smartphone?

Of all the changes that have taken place in the 21st century, it is the 'digital revolution' that has changed our world beyond recognition. Yes, our diet and environment have changed a lot, but what's really changed, especially in cities, which now house half of humanity and will house an estimated 60 per cent by 2030, is the pace of life. People all over the world are sleeping less, having less downtime, feeling more anxious and stressed, and burning out at a far higher rate. This is reflected in increasing rate of work absenteeism, depression and suicide, especially in cities.

The speeding up of communication – via e-mails, smartphones and digital media – means that we are supposed to react to demands, and are bombarded with them, at an ever-increasing speed. So, we have literally become addicted to our phones.[42] The average person picks up their phone 352 times a day – more than once every three minutes – and swipes it 2,617 times a day.[43] A UK survey reports 62 per cent cannot make it through dinner without checking their phone. Almost half of us (42 per cent) report anxiety if we don't have our phone, or a signal, suffering 'nomophobia'.[44] We are going to sleep with our phones and checking them first thing on waking up. One survey found that one in ten university students in the USA admitted to having checked their smartphones during sex!

Whether it's Facebook, Instagram, Twitter, Snapchat, LinkedIn or any other platform, the core design is to get your attention, then show you ads tailored to your attributes and behaviours which the technology learns about you. Facebook, for example, has learned how to do this with prompts, swipe downs, red icons that you press and don't know what you receive. Why? Basically, to sell stuff. But, of course, we have all our contacts and social life organized on our phones, which is partly what makes them irresistible.

Facebook even knows when you're feeling 'insecure', 'worthless' and 'need a confidence boost' or are bored, and can make sure you receive notification of a 'like' just when you 'need' it to keep you hooked in. If you find yourself checking your phone at the slightest feeling of boredom, purely out of habit, know that programmers work very hard behind the screens to keep you doing exactly that.

'I feel tremendous guilt,' admitted Chamath Palihapitiya, former Vice President of User Growth at Facebook, to an audience of Stanford students. 'The short-term, dopamine-driven feedback loops that we have created are destroying how society works.'

Not only this, but our overuse and reliance are leading to a decline in mental health. A study of 143 undergraduates at the University of Pennsylvania, limiting use to 30 minutes a day versus a control group found significant reductions in loneliness and depression.[45] The researchers concluded: 'Our findings strongly suggest that limiting social media use to approximately 30 minutes per day may lead to significant improvement in well-being.'

Problems start young. A study in Japan reported that the more screen time one-year-old children have, the more their communication and problem-solving development is delayed at the ages of two and four.[46] The increase in developmental delay occurred with more than an hour of daily screen time. Those children having four or more hours of screen time versus under an hour were approximately four times more likely at the age of two and twice as likely at the age of four to have developmental delay in communication and problem-solving.

The key is to first understand how our reward system works and how to prevent its demise, then take action to free your brain from addiction, which is what Chapter 20 shows you.

The brain's reward system

Whether it's a text, a notification or a like, it triggers a reward signal in your brain. The programming times and withholds likes to get that extra-addictive quality of a variable reward. As we learned earlier, it's to do with a tiny organ in the central 'hippocampal' area of the brain called the *nucleus accumbens*. This is the headquarters of our dopamine-based 'reward' system.

The more dopamine we release, the more receptors shut down, so we seek more pleasurable behaviours and foods. Gambling, gaming, overeating, sex, drugs, food, social media and other digital addictions are all part of it. Insidiously and unknowingly, our brain has been hijacked and the symptoms we feel are the direct consequences of an intended addiction. We end up needing constant stimulation and, to fuel that, need instant-energy foods and drinks – sugar and coffee. Ironically, that leads to mental exhaustion and little energy to make sensible choices to redesign our lifestyle away from this insidious path that leads to getting sucked into, and stuck in, addictive behaviours.

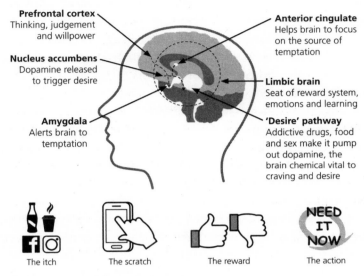

Prefrontal cortex
Thinking, judgement and willpower

Nucleus accumbens
Dopamine released to trigger desire

Amygdala
Alerts brain to temptation

Anterior cingulate
Helps brain to focus on the source of temptation

Limbic brain
Seat of reward system, emotions and learning

'Desire' pathway
Addictive drugs, food and sex make it pump out dopamine, the brain chemical vital to craving and desire

The itch   The scratch   The reward   The action

Fig 9. The brain's variable reward system

Alcohol – the opiate of the masses

Whether you've become addicted to sugar, food, caffeinated drinks, social media, gambling, gaming or non-stop stimulation, or are simply caught in the stress trap, perhaps due to work and life demands and debts, you may be unable to quell the background feeling of anxiety and stress without alcohol. Alcohol, a well-established neurotoxin,[47] surely is the opiate of the masses.

It can easily become another addiction, too. If you start with, say, a glass of wine a night, you may find, in time, that your need for alcohol increases – to two glasses, three, half a bottle or even more. Consumption keeps going up. After all, alcohol is the currency of a good time, normalized as a response to stress, glorified in movies and at the core of our modern culture, with a $1.5 trillion industry, which is expected to rise to $2 trillion by 2027,[48] promoting its use. Much more than religion, it has surely become the opiate of the masses. While smoking has become frowned upon, anything other than heavy drinking is considered socially acceptable. Yet alcohol, in the UK, is in the top five causes of death and disability, has become the most common cause of death in men under 50 (and soon will be for women), accounting for one fifth of all deaths under 50 and almost 30,000 deaths a year overall. This is roughly a third that of smoking and 10 times more than opioids (including heroin and painkillers), and is ranked more harmful than any other drug, including opioids.[49] This addictive drug is so socially acceptable that governments avoid calls by scientists and health campaigners to curtail its use, for fear of voter reprisals.

A commonly unknown fact is that death or disability from alcohol doesn't only occur in heavy drinkers. The risk goes up exponentially with the quantity you drink, whether the source of alcohol be beer, wine or spirits. The good news is that small reductions have big positive effects on your health. To make this real, for those drinking 50g of alcohol a day (two-thirds of a bottle of wine or equivalent), the risk of premature death is 16 per cent. An average of 20g, two regular glasses of wine, brings that risk below 1 per cent. In terms of mitigating serious health risk, including death, the advice of the UK government's former advisor, Professor David Nutt, is for women to consume no more than 15g, men no more than 20g, per day, and to have at least two alcohol-free days a week. Professor Nutt was sacked for saying that alcohol was a 'time bomb' and more dangerous that the drug ecstasy (MDMA), which is patently true.

The trouble is, when you get snookered in the cycle of seeking rewards, you become more tired, more anxious and may even be more depressed. You may 'need' a stimulant.

Are you addicted to stimulants?

The other major acceptable and glorified drug is caffeine, mainly in the form of coffee, although strong tea has as much caffeine as a regular cup of coffee. Like nicotine, sugar and chocolate, which also contains caffeine, coffee stimulates that dopamine release and the feeling of pleasure or reward. Imagine a day with *no* coffee, tea, sugar, chocolate, cigarettes. If you shout, 'No way!', there is a very real possibility that you have some level of addiction to these stimulants. This can range from a mild addiction that you can live with quite happily to a major problem that is controlling your life.

However, whatever the level of addiction, the net consequence is always less energy, not more. The caffeine in both coffee and tea increases the release of adrenalin, cortisol and dopamine in your body and brain, while inhibiting the action of adenosine, a brain-calming chemical. The release of adrenalin into your system gives you a temporary boost, but frequently makes you fatigued and depressed later.

One of my clients, Bobbie, serves as a case in point:

Bobbie was already eating a healthy diet and taking a sensible daily programme of vitamin and mineral supplements. She had only two problems: a lack of energy in the morning and occasional headaches. She also had one vice: three cups of coffee a day. After some persuasion, she agreed to stop the coffee for a month. To her surprise, her energy levels rose and the headaches stopped.

To make an accurate assessment of your current relationship to stimulants, you need to be honest with yourself about how you use them. So, fill in the stimulant inventory below for three days (or photocopy it and fill that in). Note down how much coffee you consume and when, and do the same for tea, chocolate, sugar (or another sweet treat) and cigarettes. Alcohol is included because it's part of the addictive cycle.

Stimulant Inventory

	A unit equals	Day 1	Day 2	Day 3
Tea	1 cup	☐	☐	☐
Coffee (espresso)	½ shot	☐	☐	☐
Coffee (filter or instant)	1 cup	☐	☐	☐
Green tea	2 cups	☐	☐	☐
Cola or caffeinated drinks	1 cup	☐	☐	☐
Caffeine pills (eg No-Doz, Pro Plus, Excedrin, Dexatrim)	1 pill	☐	☐	☐
Chocolate (milk)	200g	☐	☐	☐
Chocolate (dark)	70g	☐	☐	☐
Added sugar	1 teaspoon	☐	☐	☐

(continued)

Stimulant Inventory (Continued)

	A unit equals	Day 1	Day 2	Day 3
Hidden sugar (i.e. sugar listed in ingredients)	1 teaspoon/5g	☐	☐	☐
Alcohol				
Half-pint of beer, lager or cider (4 per cent) = 1 unit				
One 25ml spirit measure = 1 unit				
Small (125ml) glass of wine (12.5 per cent) = 1.5 units				
Large (250ml) glass of wine (12.5 per cent) = 3 units				
Beer, lager or cider		☐	☐	☐
Spirits		☐	☐	☐
Wine		☐	☐	☐
Cigarettes	1 cigarette	☐	☐	☐

Also, consider what your relationship is to these substances. Do you, for example, ever buy sweets and hide the wrappers so other people don't know you've eaten them? Do you swoon at the dessert menu in restaurants and always grab a mint or two on the way out? Do you always add ketchup? How much do you think about and look forward to that morning cup of coffee or a mid-morning second cup? How important is that drink after work? Does everyone really know how much you smoke? Have you cranked up your caffeine intake to 'double expresso' equivalent drinks using more coffee at home than you used to? Do you need more to get a 'kick', if you even get one, or does coffee now just relieve the fuzzy tiredness you feel without it?

This kind of relationship to stimulants, often cloaked in an attitude that they are just some of the innocent pleasures of life, is indicative of an underlying chemical imbalance that depletes your energy and peace of mind and, at its worst, feeds into mental health issues.

Coffee, caffeine withdrawal and sleep

If you wake up feeling good and can function without a coffee, and have no major mental health issues, sleeping well, for example, but enjoy one coffee a day which will give you a dopamine kick, that's not a problem. If you overuse coffee, this is a good target to aim for. But bear in mind that non-caffeine consumers report as much alertness on waking as coffee drinkers do after one cup of coffee. So, being caffeine-free is perhaps the ideal.

The best measure of your relationship with coffee or caffeine, and whether your brain has 'downregulated' dopamine and adrenalin receptors, is what happens when you quit. If the answer is nothing, then there's no issue. If, on the other hand, you get a variety of withdrawal symptoms,[50] including headaches, tiredness and irritability, that means your neurotransmitter receptors have downregulated and it will take a few days for them to upregulate and bring you back to normal. For many, just one cup of coffee a day can result in withdrawal effects if stopped.[51] It's also worth knowing that coffee, or caffeine, consumed six hours before sleep, which is about as long as caffeine stays in the system (although some metabolize caffeine much faster than others), is associated with disturbed sleep[52] – either difficulty falling asleep or waking in the night – so, it is wise to consume no caffeine after midday, especially if you have issues with sleeping.

Tea or coffee?

Tea also contains caffeine, but also theanine, which is a more calming amino acid that has been shown to enhance cognitive abilities.[53] It also protects GABA receptors, which are the brain's adrenalin off-switch. Overall, tea with its theanine content as well as caffeine, is better for you than coffee. Green tea may also have some benefits over black tea, which is the same plant, but processed in a different way such that green tea contains more antioxidants and polyphenols.

Benefits or excuses?

A whole chapter could be written on the apparent benefits of tea, coffee and even some forms of alcohol. We read about the beneficial effects of resveratrol in red wine, polyphenols in coffee and cacao and other antioxidants in tea, and even the possible benefits of coffee in relation to prostate cancer and Parkinson's. But please bear in mind that the nature of *any* dependence creates a psychological set of excuses that we use to justify having the addictive compound. This could be anything from 'That's a lovely sauce' (sugar) to 'A bit of what you fancy does you good' to 'I've got to focus, so I need a coffee' to 'I'm so stressed, I have to have a drink' and so on. Of course, all these substances work, otherwise we wouldn't be attracted to them, and the conscious use of them in certain circumstances makes sense. For example, if something tragic happens and you feel completely gutted, having a mind-numbing drink is both a valid and attractive way to cope. (In Chapter 18 you'll learn different ways of coping, though.) If you have an unusual deadline and need to burn the candle at both ends, caffeine is going to help. But if you are already drinking a lot of coffee every day, it won't help that much.

In summary, the issue here is to understand how the combination of sugar, caffeinated stimulants, alcohol, tech and social media addiction, shopping, gambling, gaming and so on can hijack your brain's natural feel-good reward system and result in the opposite - feeling more tired, anxious, unfulfilled and depressed than ever. If that has happened to you, then here are some simple suggestions that, step by step, will help you reclaim your brain's full potential for feeling good, energized, clear, focused and purposeful:

- *Limit your time spent on social media.* Thirty minutes a day max. is a good target. Depending on your use, you may need to build down to this. Turn your phone off or to 'airplane' mode at least an hour before bed and keep it that way for at least an hour in the morning. Or, if you have to have it on, don't check social media for a couple of hours after you wake up. Instead, do something productive or health promoting.
- *Limit your intake of caffeine to under 100mg a day.* That's a strong cup of coffee or two weaker cups of tea. If you have a second cup, use the same tea bag, or have a filter coffee 'run through'.
- *Avoid all caffeine after noon.*

- *Avoid buying food that contains added sugar, dates or raisins.* (Dates and raisins, containing primarily glucose, are akin to sugar, with a very high glycaemic load. That's why they are used as a sugar substitute in so-called 'sugar-free' foods.) Read the label. Remember, 4.5g of sugar is a teaspoon of sugar. This is about the most added sugar to aim for. Ideally, only have sugar in whole fruits. Fruit juice is also high in sugar, so best avoided or limited. (*Chapter 11 will give you the sugar lowdown.*)
- *Limit your daily intake of alcohol to 20 grams,* or a maximum of two regular glasses of wine. One small glass of red wine (125mls or 12.5g) reduces the risk of Alzheimer's, but more increases it.
- *Have at least two days a week alcohol-free.*
- *If you have other addictions – gaming, gambling, drugs, etc. – read Chapter 20.*

In the chapters that follow, I will go into more detail about how you can naturally enhance your feel-good factor, favouring serotonin over dopamine, happiness over pleasure.

Professor Lustig explains the difference in this way:

- Pleasure is short-lived. Happiness is long-lived.
- Pleasure is visceral. Happiness is ethereal.
- Pleasure is taking. Happiness is giving.
- Pleasure can be achieved with substances. Happiness cannot be achieved with substances.
- Pleasure is experienced alone. Happiness is experienced in social groups.
- The extremes of pleasure all lead to substance or behavioural addiction. There is no such thing as being addicted to too much happiness.

Mind Myths, from Genes to Drugs

In ancient Greece diseases were blamed on offending the gods and penances were prescribed to appease them. That is, until Hippocrates came along and changed the medical approach to looking for true causes, of which he thought diet was key. Since the discovery of DNA and our genetic code, there's been a tendency to blame diseases, especially those we don't know how to cure, on genes. But again, is diet key instead?

Genes are far less relevant to our health, both mental and physical, than most people believe. Our health is driven much more by what we eat and how we live – that is, 'the conditions of existence' that Darwin proposed as the critical driver of our evolution.

This broad statement is based on studies of identical twins, who inherit exactly the same genes, looking at whether or not they get the same diseases. Overall, it has been found that the inherited component accounts for about 20 per cent of the risk, leaving 80 per cent to a person's 'environment'.[54] But even that 20 per cent of 'heritability' isn't all accounted for by genes, since the twins also share many environmental factors in their upbringing. That doesn't mean that inheriting certain genes isn't important, however, and knowing what genes and gene variations you have can also help you personalize your perfect nutrition for both mental and physical health.

But first, what are genes and how do they exert their effect?

Genes

Much of our body is built up by proteins, which are made out of amino acids that are delivered in the food we eat. We digest the proteins down to the amino acids. They are the building blocks and our genes are the builders or, more exactly, the blueprint. Each gene is a bit of 'code' that instructs our body to assemble amino acids in a particular configuration to make, for example, insulin or adrenalin or skin or bone.

All genes exert their influence across our biology. What this means is that changing our biology, for example by changing what we eat, changes the effect of the genes. The effect of outside factors on our genes is called *epigenetics*.

Genetic variations

Most genetic variations – also called polymorphisms, because there are many forms and you might not inherit the best one – might predict a greater risk of something, but don't cause it. For example, we've already learned that some people have inherited a less functional D2 receptor gene, which means they are not so good at making the receptors for the feel-good neurotransmitter dopamine and have a greater risk of addiction.

In some people genes are missing, or there's an extra gene. This is what happens in Down's syndrome – there's a whole extra set of genes, strung on a spirally chromosome. In Turner's disease, there's a missing chromosome. These diseases *are* caused by genes.

In some people, the presence of a particular gene causes a disease such that everyone, or nearly everyone, who has that gene gets the disease. For example, if a person has the genes APP or PSEN (short for presenilin), they are, unfortunately, highly likely to get Alzheimer's. Fortunately, they account for less than 1 per cent of cases of Alzheimer's. If either your mother or father has such a 'causative' gene, then your risk is 50 per cent.

Someone with Down's syndrome or a rare causative Alzheimer's gene is likely to have some part of their biology askew. For example, certain enzymes may not work so well, which largely leads to more oxidation, a sign of which is premature ageing. But even these people can be supported by the right nutrition. I'm reminded of the work of Dr Henry Turkell, who achieved amazing results through optimizing a person's nutrition.

An example is Wendy:

> *Wendy was four years old but her mental age was 21 months. She had an IQ of 44 and was classified as retarded. When she began megavitamin therapy, her attention span went from 10 seconds to 15 seconds to 10 minutes. Within three months she began speaking in complete sentences. After six months of treatment, her IQ score had jumped to 72. By the age of eight, her IQ score was 85, classifying her as no longer retarded – a 40-point shift in four years.*[55]

One genetic risk you are able to do something about is caused by the ApoE gene or, specifically, a variation of it called ApoE4.

The ApoE and other exaggerations

ApoE helps the production of cholesterol and transports it, and fats, around your body. If you inherit the Apoe4 variation, you are more likely to have higher cholesterol and, statistically, you've got a 4 to 6 per cent greater chance of developing Alzheimer's. One in five people has the ApoE4 gene variant. This is the gene that the actor Chris Hemsworth has that got him all worked up about his future risk of Alzheimer's. However, if you do the right things, for example eat a healthy diet, drawing this short straw may be irrelevant.

An example of this is a hugely significant study in the *British Medical Journal* into age-related cognitive decline and dementia, which found that making improvements in your diet and lifestyle cuts your future risk of developing dementia by a massive nine times.[56] The study also showed that inheriting the ApoE4 variation made no difference to the positive reduction in risk achievable by simple diet and lifestyle changes.

According to Professor David Smith from the University of Oxford, 'Genes can only exert effects via non-genetic mechanisms, and these mechanisms are often susceptible to modification by, for example, improving one's diet. This study shows that diet and lifestyle are much more important than inheriting a gene variant such as ApoE4. Less than 1 per cent of Alzheimer's is directly caused by genes.

'This study shows that switching from an average to a healthy lifestyle, with positive diet changes being key, can dramatically reduce a person's future risk of developing cognitive decline and dementia.'

Lots of the recommendations I'll make for your overall mental health exert effects on these 'risk' genes. The negative effect of ApoE4 is mitigated by eating a low-glycaemic load (GL, a measure of the sugar and carb load) diet or a more ketogenic diet (*see page 138*), with specific Mediterranean-style food choices, including fatty fish, cruciferous vegetables and olive oil and having low alcohol consumption. There is reasonably good evidence of certain supplemental nutrients dampening down the negative effects of ApoE4. These are omega-3 DHA, B vitamins (B2, B6, B12 and folate), vitamins D3 and K2, quercetin and resveratrol.[57] These kind of nutrition improvements help us all, but they are particularly important for those with the ApoE4 gene variation.

Another example of a gene variant that about one in three have relates to a gene called MTHFR and its variant MTHFR677TT. This gene affects a process called methylation. (*More on this in Chapter 8.*) Inheriting this variant increases the risk of many mental health issues, including autism, Alzheimer's, depression, Parkinson's and schizophrenia,[58] because methylation is a cornerstone of mental health.

Poor methylation also raises the level of homocysteine, a toxic amino acid that damages the brain and blood vessels. This increases the risk of heart disease, stroke and messed-up circulation in the brain, called cerebrovascular dysfunction, by 17-fold.[59]

However, in studies where people were given homocysteine-lowering, methylation-friendly B-vitamin supplements, whether a person did or didn't have this faulty methylation gene made no difference to the beneficial effect of the B vitamins on preserving memory or preventing brain shrinkage. So, whether or not you have the gene variation, measuring your homocysteine level, and keeping it below 10mcmol/l, is the important action. If it turns out you have this gene variation, you may just have to work a bit harder to keep your homocysteine level below 10.

So many of these so-called predictive genes are like having a model of a car that has a tendency to a particular fault. However, if the car is properly serviced, it's not an issue.

Having a gene test (*see Resources*), which shows you, for example, whether you have the ApoE4 or the MTHFR677TT variation, shows you where in your diet and lifestyle you have to be careful. But it shouldn't be a cause for high anxiety that you'll get the related disease. Your health is largely under your control.

Drugs

Worldwide, the whole medical system is geared to prescribe drugs as the solutions to health problems. To even question this is often considered medical heresy.

Why drugs don't tackle the cause and are rarely the answer

To take psychiatric drugs as just one example, each year prescriptions go up and the incidence of psychiatric disorders also goes up, so whatever is driving our psychological demise is certainly not being solved by medication. Far more factors need to be taken into consideration. As we've seen, a country's rate of depression and suicide tracks their omega-3 intake. Similarly, as intake of sugar and carbs cranked up from the 1970s onwards, so did depression, while a person's B12 and folate intake predicts their risk of dementia later in life. The Covid lockdown also escalated mental health problems. Anti-depressant prescriptions escalated. But they don't solve loneliness.

Even if you aren't concerned about these diseases as such, they are the 'thick edge of the wedge', the thin edge being the near universal breakdown in mental energy, clarity, mood and emotional stability. Understanding what these drugs are doing, or attempting to do, and which nutritional and lifestyle approaches work and how, helps us to understand how to upgrade our brains and gain more mental health resilience.

Time and time again we find that a drug is a) not tackling the true cause of the disease and b) is far less effective than it is assumed to be and c) has adverse effects that are sometimes as serious as the condition it is treating. However, very often a nutritional and life-style approach tackles the true cause(s) far more or at least as effectively and has the advantage of no adverse effects, or often positive side-effects.

Even drugs for schizophrenia or Parkinson's, which we assume are essential, only become so because the underlying causes have been ignored for too long.

Schizophrenia drugs are chemical strait-jackets

Before there were schizophrenia drugs, sufferers got locked away in asylums. Schizophrenia drugs are basically tranquillizers or sedatives, acting much like chemical strait-jackets and having the advantage of keeping sufferers at home and reducing their risk of harming themselves and others. Despite this, about one in 20 end up committing suicide.[60] The reality is that the drugs don't actually 'treat' the disease, they just dampen everything down. Here's the conclusion of one review:

> Although anti-psychotic medication has persisted as the optimal treatment and is effective in managing the positive symptoms, it is limited in terms of treating negative symptoms. In addition to this drawback of drug treatment, this type of therapy is based solely on symptomatology and dosage is often determined by a process of trial and error. In those who respond to anti-psychotic medication, side-effects can be distressing and often intolerable ... Often the side-effects themselves require further pharmacological treatment and/or result in treatment discontinuation leading to subsequent relapse. Furthermore, approximately one-third of individuals with schizophrenia do not respond to anti-psychotic medication, either alone or in conjunction with psychodynamic counselling and other pharmacotherapy.[61]

The review, part of a master's degree which we funded at the Food for the Brain Foundation, goes on to show that methylation problems (indicated by high homocysteine levels) and food intolerances make a difference, and supplementation with B vitamins, antioxidants and essential fats can make an improvement. Placebo-controlled trials with B vitamins going back 60 years have been remarkably effective in stopping hallucinations.[62] These were the first ever 'double-blind controlled trials' in the history of psychiatry and were carried out by my mentor Dr Abram Hoffer, the director of psychiatric research in Saskatchewan, Canada. He ended up treating thousands of schizophrenics successfully, rehabilitating them into a normal, drug-free life. More recent studies are showing great promise for low-carb, ketogenic diets (*covered in Chapter 12*).

Later, I'll share case histories with you of formerly diagnosed schizophrenics who now have no need of medication.

B-vitamin deficiency is part of the cause of Parkinson's

In Parkinson's, an extremely unpleasant neurodegenerative disease, the brain becomes unable to make or transport dopamine and the drug levodopa must be supplied, as it readily crosses from the blood into the brain, where it can be used to make dopamine. But what causes this problem in the first place?

Dopamine is made from tyrosine, an amino acid. For this to happen, various enzymes, which are dependent on various nutrients, must be working. The vitamins B6, B12 and folate are very important in this process, as they are for dementia. If you're not getting enough your homocysteine level goes up. According to one recent study:

> Homocysteine may be associated with the development and progression of Parkinson's disease. Plasma homocysteine levels in patients with Parkinson's disease are elevated compared to those of healthy individuals. High homocysteine drives Parkinson's disease development and progression.[63]

Both raised homocysteine and lack of vitamin B12 or folic acid potentially predict the onset and development of Parkinson's, concludes another.[64]

According to another: 'Levodopa treatment of Parkinson's disease tends to further elevate circulating homocysteine levels. This begs the question of whether Parkinson's disease patients on levodopa should be concurrently treated with ongoing B-vitamin therapy.'[65]

This doesn't conclusively prove that raised homocysteine or lack of B12 or folic acid is part of the cause of Parkinson's, but it is highly suggestive that it might be. Only 3 to 5 per cent is 'in the genes', according to a recent review in the *Lancet* medical journal.[66]

Alzheimer's illusions and delusions

The amyloid illusion

There are deposits of amyloid plaque in the brains of those with Alzheimer's. There are calculus deposits on degenerating teeth. There is damaged cholesterol in atheroma blockages in arteries. There are bone spurs on arthritis joints. Are these the 'cause' of the disease or the consequence? What should treatment be targeting?

Quoting an editorial in the *Journal of the American Medical Association*, 'Although many researchers believe that amyloid is involved in the pathology of Alzheimer disease, as of June 2023, the protein has never been proven to be the cause. In clinical trials, drugs that targeted (and successfully reduced) amyloid failed to show any benefit.'[67]

Another editorial, this time in the *British Medical Journal*, reviewing the latest anti-amyloid drug, donanemab, asks, 'Are these new treatments for Alzheimer's disease blazing trails or the road to nowhere?'[68] It concludes that the clinical benefit is unclear against a backdrop of terrible adverse effects, even deaths:

> These modest absolute differences are smaller than conventionally defined minimum clinically important differences... Oedema [swelling] was seen in 24 per cent of participants treated with donanemab and haemorrhage [bleeding] in 19.7 per cent, necessitating monitoring with serial MRI and leading to three deaths.

The rate of whole brain shrinkage also went up by over 20 per cent.

Danish researchers reviewing another anti-amyloid drug in the *Journal of Alzheimer's Disease*, write:

> Benefits of lecanemab treatment are uncertain and may yield net harm for some patients, and that the data do not support the

amyloid hypothesis. We note potential biases from inclusion, unblinding, dropouts, and other issues. Given substantial adverse effects and subgroup heterogeneity, we conclude that lecanemab's efficacy is not clinically meaningful, consistent with numerous analyses suggesting that amyloid and its derivatives are not the main causative agents of Alzheimer's disease dementia.[69]

Yet newspaper headlines claim anti-amyloid drugs are a 'breakthrough', a 'turning-point' and the 'beginning of the end of Alzheimer's'. Despite the hype, the new 'anti-amyloid' antibody injections have produced very small, if any, meaningful clinical improvements, with about a third of test subjects getting brain bleeding or swelling. Five people died in two recent trials, thought to be as a consequence of the treatment.

Meanwhile, the combination of sufficient B vitamins and omega-3 has not only surpassed the clinical benefit of these medications, but also markedly slowed the rate of brain shrinkage, by two-thirds, and with no side-effects.

The p-tau delusion

Tau is a structural protein that helps build the skeleton, much like pipes, through which nutrients and nerve signals are delivered to different parts of the brain. Our brains contain a balance of tau protein and phosphorylated-tau, abbreviated to p-tau. An abnormal accumulation of p-tau makes these tubular channels tangled and dysfunctional and triggers brain-cell death.[70]

Too much p-tau also messes up the mitochondria, the cells' energy factories, potentially leading to brain fatigue. The more p-tau accumulates, the greater the risk of cognitive problems and Alzheimer's dementia. Also, those with memory decline have been shown to have relatively more p-tau to tau protein.

The next target for dementia drugs is reducing p-tau. Consequently, drugs are being developed and tested that block the kinase enzyme and activate the phosphatase enzyme,[71] which is exactly what the homocysteine-lowering B vitamins do. But so far, there are no human clinical trials reporting significant benefit.

The critical prevention question is what stops too much of the tau protein from turning into the potentially harmful p-tau in the first place and what helps restore p-tau to normal tau protein.

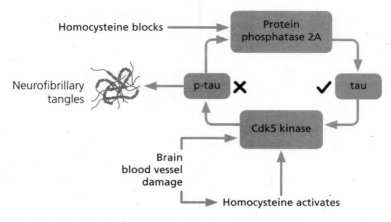

Fig 10. How lowering homocysteine stops p-tau formation

The answer is remarkably simple – a lack of B vitamins raises the blood levels of homocysteine, which activates an enzyme, Cdk5 kinase, which adds the bad 'p' to tau and blocks another enzyme, protein phosphatase A2, which removes the dangerous 'p'.[72,73] High homocysteine levels also damage the tiny blood vessels in the brain, leading to 'mini strokes' or transient ischemic attacks (TIAs), which further raise the levels of p-tau. Homocysteine not only raises the levels of the dangerous p-tau,[74] but can also bind to tau,[75] further generating the neurofibrillary tangles that then trigger brain-cell death.

So, the simplest way to stop the formation of p-tau, and neurofibrillary tangles, and keep your brain healthy, is to keep your plasma homocysteine level below 10mcmol/l. (*Details follow in Chapter 8.*) Half of those above 65 have a homocysteine level higher than this.

By now you're surely wondering why, if these natural approaches are at least as good, if not better, than drug treatments, and without adverse effects, why this isn't common knowledge and common practice, especially if the cost is a fraction of the drug treatments. For example, supplementing B vitamins and omega-3 fish oils might cost you £100 a year, while anti-amyloid drugs are pitched at around £20,000 a year.

I'm convinced that it is exactly this last point that explains the anomaly. Naturally occurring nutrients cannot be patented; only a man-made invention, such as a drug, can be. Holding a patent means only the company making that product can sell it, and they can determine the price. The price of a drug will include a hefty margin for marketing the drug and creating all the hype to get you, the media and the medical profession to buy into it. Once the patent expires, the price plummets. The price of a leading branded statin dropped by 93 per cent, from close to £30 down to just over £2 a month.[76] That's a lot of margin for marketing. By then, the manufacturers are on to the next 'new' patented drug. Up to 2022, $45 billion[77] has been spent developing the latest ineffective dementia drugs, but the real cost, including the most recent trials and marketing, could be double this. That's a lot of money to recoup.

The depressing anti-depressant problem

You might be equally surprised to hear that anti-depressants, for the most part, don't work better than placebos. According to NHS statistics, one in eight adults in the UK takes anti-depressants[78] – surely they have been proven to work? But the very basis upon which they are sold doesn't stack up. Many people who visit their doctor with depression are told that low levels of serotonin can cause depression and consequently they are prescribed SSRI (selective serotonin reuptake inhibitor) anti-depressants. The idea is that the drug will raise their serotonin levels and they'll feel much better. But the evidence for this just isn't there. A major review in 2022, headed by Professor Joanna Moncrief from University College London, concludes:

> The main areas of serotonin research provide no consistent evidence of there being an association between serotonin and depression, and no support for the hypothesis that depression is caused by lowered serotonin activity or concentrations.[79]

This doesn't mean that some depressed people may not have low serotonin, but the majority do not have it.

An analysis of six large studies found that: 'The magnitude of benefit of medication compared with placebo ... may be minimal or non-existent, on average, in patients with mild or moderate symptoms.'[80]

Another report in the *British Medical Journal* states, 'New generation antidepressants achieve almost no benefit compared with placebo in mild to moderate depression, with slightly more benefit in severe depression but only because of less response to placebo, a meta-analysis of clinical trial data has shown.'[81] The researchers analysed all available data from clinical trials submitted to the US Food and Drug Administration (FDA) for the licensing of four selective serotonin (SSRI) or serotonin-noradrenaline reuptake inhibitors (SNRI): fluoxetine (Prozac), venlafaxine (Efexor), nefazodone (Serzone) and paroxetine (Seroxat, Paxil). These were the drug company's own trials. Yet, over 100 million prescriptions were written in 2023 in the UK, for an adult population half this number.

That is not to say these drugs don't work at all, just not much better than placebos in most cases. If a doctor prescribes you something in good faith and you take it with great hope, it is likely to have some beneficial effect. This is called an *enhanced placebo effect*.[82] But adverse effects have also been reported from taking anti-depressants, two of which are suicidal thoughts and actual suicide. Another *British Medical Journal* review, of 702 studies on SSRI anti-depressants, showed that people taking them were more than twice as likely to attempt suicide as those taking a dummy pill.[83] The researchers also noted that the actual number of suicide attempts is likely to be much higher, because many of the studies did not gather information on suicide.

But it gets worse. When a person tries to stop taking anti-depressants, the withdrawal effects can be horrendous.

The conservative estimate, based on research by Professor John Reid and colleagues from the University of East London, is that 46 per cent of people who try to come off anti-depressants experience withdrawal symptoms, and a third of these experience severe and debilitating withdrawal symptoms.[84]

If you've been on anti-depressants for several years, the chances are you will experience withdrawal symptoms. In one study, 61 per cent reported some degree of withdrawal effects, and 44 per cent of these described the effects as 'severe'. The most common of six listed withdrawal effects were anxiety/panic (66 per cent) and irritability (62 per cent). The most common spontaneously reported 'other' withdrawal effect was suicidality (2 per cent). Forty per cent reported that they felt addicted, with 39 per cent of these describing their addiction as 'severe'. Over half (55 per cent) reported some degree of difficulty coming off, with 27 per cent ticking 'very difficult', and 11 per cent 'very easy'. Only six people out of 867 (0.7 per cent) recalled being told anything about withdrawal, dependence or addiction by the prescriber.[85]

As a consequence, there are an estimated 4 million long-term anti-depressant users in the UK who can't get off them and are given no help to do so. Is this addiction? The World Health Organization rates SSRI anti-depressants as among the highest-ranking drug dependencies.

If you want to come off anti-depressants, you should talk to your doctor, but in reality they probably don't know how to help you because no one has ever taught them. In Chapter 17 I'll show you some ways to minimize withdrawal effects and to support your mood. (*See also Resources for some avenues for help with withdrawal.*)

Addicted to tranquillizers

The most common anti-anxiety drugs are the benzodiazepine family of tranquillizers, such as Valium (diazepam), Librium and Ativan. These are highly effective at reducing anxiety in the short term, but highly addictive in as little as four weeks. For this reason, doctors are strongly advised not to prescribe them for more than four weeks. Despite this, a poll carried out by current-affairs programme *Panorama* in 2001 found that 3 per cent of people questioned, equivalent to one and a half million people in the UK, had been on tranquillizers for more than four months. Of these, 28 per cent had been on them for more than 10 years.[86] A report by the National Addiction Centre, King's College, London, on prescriptions up to 2009, also found that a third were for more than eight weeks.

These highly addictive drugs are now less likely to be prescribed, having been replaced by newer and more profitable non-benzodiazepines such as zolpidem, eszopiclone and zaleplon on the apparent basis that they are safer.

However, even leaving the addictive nature of these drugs aside, a study in the *British Medical Journal* found that patients prescribed zolpidem, temazepam and other hypnotics for reducing anxiety and aiding sleep suffered four times the mortality compared to matched patients not prescribed hypnotics.[87] 'Even patients prescribed fewer than 18 hypnotic doses per year experienced increased mortality, with greater mortality associated with greater dosage prescribed,' reports the author, Dr Scripps, an expert on insomnia from California. There was also a 35 per cent overall increase in incidence of cancer among those prescribed high doses.

The sad truth is that tranquillizers, much like alcohol, increase anxiety and depression in the long run, as well as being addictive. With tranquillizers, however, the reason is slightly different. Tranquillizers open up the brain's receptor sites for GABA, making you more sensitive to its effects. So you feel more relaxed, less anxious. The next day, however, you can feel hung-over. The more often you take the tranquillizers, the more you need to get the same effect, and without them, you can get rebound anxiety and insomnia. (*As well as the advice given in Chapter 20, do also see Resources for some avenues for help with withdrawal.*)

Of course, one of the biggest and most insidious of all addictions is to opioid drugs, akin to heroin, one of which is oxycodone hydrochloride (OxyContin) which has been the subject of numerous films such as *Painkiller, Dopesick, This Might Hurt, The Crime of the Century, Recovery Boys, Do No Harm: The Opioid Epidemic, 7 Days: The Opioid Crisis in Arkansas, Heroine, The Pharmacist* and more. Yet, despite this massive media exposé and exposure, codeine-related prescriptions and addictions continue to rise. Somehow, the lesson from the OxyContin scandal of corruption between the manufacturer, the government agencies that are meant to protect us, the medical system and doctors, the prescribers, just isn't being learned in relation to psychiatric drugs.

Whether you are suffering from low mood, anxiety, insomnia, failing memory or lack of mental energy and alertness, none of these are a consequence of a lack of medication. While medication may provide temporary relief, sometimes at a high cost, it isn't tackling the true underlying causes of brain dysfunction and mental malaise.

In the next part you'll discover the eight essential ways to upgrade your brain and in Part 3, I'll give you natural alternatives to these issues.

In summary, we have learned that:

- Genes rarely cause mental diseases.
- Even the apparent risk of 'predictive' genes such as ApoE4 and methylation genes can be mitigated by following the advice in this book.
- There are no real-life clinically effective Alzheimer's drugs at present, and none that tackle the true causes of cognitive decline. Also, those that exist carry significant risk of serious adverse effects, including death.
- Anti-depressants are not only remarkably ineffective for most people with depression, and less so than other approaches explained in this book, but also carry the real risk of major withdrawal effects leading to dependency.
- Both antipsychotics and tranquillizers should be prescribed with extreme caution, after having explored other effective and less toxic approaches, as both are remarkably difficult to come off and are not really addressing the potential underlying causes of disperceptions, anxiety or insomnia.

We live in a 'drug first' medical culture. This book argues the case for a 'nutrition first' paradigm shift for all mental health disorders, but also recognizes that a major cause of depression, anxiety and craziness is often depressive, stressful and crazy things happening in life, and these difficult circumstances are hard to recover from if your brain's chemistry is already all messed up. Just taking medication, in these situations, is unlikely to help in the long term and, in some cases, may make matters worse. So, before you go on medication, do ask your doctor how long they intend you to be on the drug for and how easy it is to come off it.

What's Really Driving the Brain Drain?

We are witnessing a 'perfect storm' that is driving our brains to devolve. Each factor on its own may not seem such a big deal, be it diet, lifestyle changes or the consequences of the digital age in which we live. We are so close to all these changes that in any case it is virtually impossible to step back and connect the dots. It is hard to conceive that all these apparent advances and conveniences are feeding a decline in mental health, brain size, even IQ, to such an extent that we are already in a terrible mess and fast heading towards a future where it is normal to be on anti-depressants, take sleeping pills and eventually lose our minds to dementia with possibly a quarter of our children mentally deficient by 2050.

Consider the situation in China. They have 264 million people over the age of 60, a fifth of their population. Already, 14 million have dementia, a quarter of the global number of cases. By 2050 the global prediction is that more than 150 million people will have Alzheimer's,[88] and if this ratio continues, China will have 37.5 million cases and predicts that the cost of treatment will be $1.8 trillion.

Remember, this is a *preventable* disease, just like diabetes. In fact, the latest research, carried out by members of our Scientific Advisory Board, based on UK Biobank data and published in *Nature* journal, estimates that up to 73 per cent of dementia could be prevented by putting into action the kind of recommendations you'll read in Part 2.[89] (This estimate excluded the homocysteine and omega-3 factor explained in chapters 7, 8 and 9, so it is likely that even more, perhaps up to 90 per cent of cases, and your risk, can be eliminated.)

The three drivers of brain degradation

As Marcel Proust said, 'The real act of discovery is not finding new lands [think drugs], but seeing through new eyes.' In a medical context, those new eyes see that all the risks for brain degradation either affect:

- the structure of the brain and neural network, or
- the function of the brain, including its fuel supply and ability to deal with the oxidant exhaust, or
- the utilization of the neural network, and its recovery, which is blocked by stress and lack of sleep.

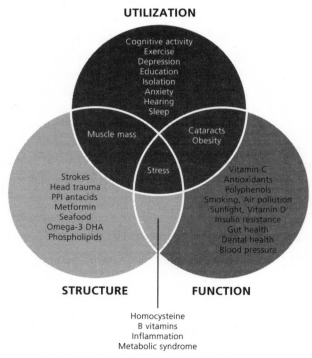

Fig 11. Structure, function and utilization – risk factors

All these seemingly disparate risk factors for mental illness and cognitive decline fit into one or more of these three fundamentals, as the figure on the previous page shows you.

In Part 2, I'll show you how these jigsaw pieces fit together to optimize the structure, function and utilization of your brain and neural network, and how you can, and will, experience a brain upgrade simply by addressing what is driving these risk factors in your diet and lifestyle. The great news is that these risks are literally under our control.

This systems-based approach is the only way out. There will never be a 'cure' for depression, dementia or any other mental illness, because there is no one place, no one thing, no one answer for mental health. No amount of money, or love, buys brain function. Even 'enlightenment', whatever that might be, requires a functioning neural network to be fully experienced and enjoyed. Psychologists, gurus and philosophers may claim the secret to happiness is all in the mind. Neuroscientists and nutritionists may claim it's all in the brain and the diet. The truth is, one cannot be separated from the other. I believe we need all the mental energy we can muster and insightful intelligence to resolve the psychological issues that drive negative patterns of behaviour and to break free from cultural 'norms' which are too often driven by commercial forces that would rather have us addicted to their products.

After all, we don't just eat out of ignorance, we eat and drink for effect. This could be for reward, driven by the dopamine release we get, for example, from eating sweets, programmed into so many during childhood by their use as reward for doing something good, or bribery to get us to do something, like 'Eat your vegetables, then you can have your dessert', or consolation to make us feel better. We use alcohol to cut the adrenalin switch and induce a level of mind numbing so our problems and cares melt away, at least temporarily. We use excess of all kinds until we numb out and gain temporary relief from the world. And, as a consequence, we get addicted. (*If this is you, Chapter 20 will show you the way out.*)

The great news is that you can take back control of your mental health and, in the process, gain energy, build resilience against disease and slow down the ageing process, since what's good for your brain is good for your body.

Your personalized brain upgrade is called COGNITION

At this stage, as you are about to discover the eight brain-upgrade essentials in Part 2, then how they are applied to specific mental health issues in Part 3, you'll be wondering which apply to you, how do you start to make changes, step by step, and what keeps you motivated, so you don't just drift back to your current habits. After all, it takes discipline to change. Psychologists tell us it takes three weeks to break a habit, six weeks to make a new habit and 36 weeks to hard-wire a habit.

That's why I strongly suggest you accompany your journey through this book with your own free online assessment of not only where you are starting from, cognitively, but also which of these eight brain essentials explained in Part 2 are most pertinent for you to address. How?

Step 1 – Measure your cognition

At foodforthebrain.org, the educational charity, there is a free online, validated Cognitive Function Test. Almost half a million people have taken the test and become 'citizen scientists', which helps us all learn what really upgrades the brain. It takes about 15 minutes to complete. It is not a questionnaire, but an interactive test that measures your cognitive resilience, based on the three critical functions that show decline on the path to cognitive decline and, ultimately, dementia. These are called executive function, episodic memory and attention. Subtle decline can be picked up 40 years before a diagnosis of dementia. That is why the test is most essential for anyone from the age of 40. You'll get a score on a scale from red to orange to green. If you're young and healthy, you'll be in the green zone, but there is always room for improvement. By doing the test now, and again in six months, you'll be able to track your progress as you initiate and progress through your brain upgrade.

This test has to be done without interruption. So, find some uninterrupted time, turn your phone off if you're doing the test on your computer or iPad, and take the test.

Step 2 – Complete the 'brain-upgrade' questionnaire

The Cognitive Function Test is immediately followed by a question-naire, with questions about your diet, lifestyle, medical history and any supplements you take. (It is good to have your supplements on hand so you can check the doses.) This takes about 10 minutes to complete.

This works out your risk for future cognitive decline. It's technic-ally called your Dementia Risk Index (DRI), but don't be put off by the term, as it's just as relevant for building resilience at any age against any mental health issue including against depression and anxiety. (Foodforthebrain will soon launch COGNITION for Smart Kids and Teens; *see Resources*.)

If you are doing everything wrong in your diet and lifestyle, your risk will be in the red, 100 per cent being the highest. If you are doing everything right, your risk will be low, in the green, perhaps below 20 per cent, with 0 per cent being the best possible. (This assessment is based only on things that you can change, so every-one has the ability to drive their DRI score towards zero.)

Your results are then broken down into a score for each of the eight brain-upgrade essentials explained in Part 2. There's an example on the next page.

Yours will be in colour, so the darkest grey will be red and the white domains will be green. In this particular example, the person is on the edge of cognitive decline, with plenty of room for improvement. Their future Dementia Risk Index is 83 per cent and they want to drive this down to closer to 0 per cent. Their weakest domain is 'Low Carb and GL', which is about diet and sugar (*see Chapter 11*). 'GL' stands for 'glycaemic load' and is the best measure of your brain's total sugar load from all foods. Their next weakest is 'Antioxidants', which is about fruit, vegetables, anti-oxidant vitamins and foods rich in polyphenols (*see Chapter 13*). Their strongest domains are 'Active Mind' (*Chapter 15*) and 'Sleep and Calm' (*Chapter 16*). By tackling your weakest domains, you'll achieve the most improvement in your cognition and mental health.

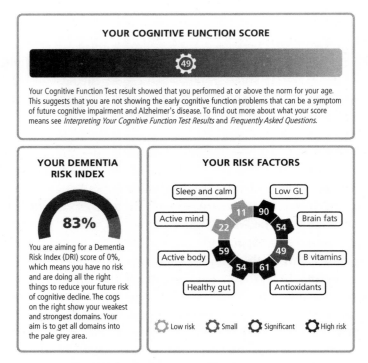

YOUR COGNITIVE FUNCTION SCORE

49

Your Cognitive Function Test result showed that you performed at or above the norm for your age. This suggests that you are not showing the early cognitive function problems that can be a symptom of future cognitive impairment and Alzheimer's disease. To find out more about what your score means see *Interpreting Your Cognitive Function Test Results* and *Frequently Asked Questions*.

YOUR DEMENTIA RISK INDEX

83%

You are aiming for a Dementia Risk Index (DRI) score of 0%, which means you have no risk and are doing all the right things to reduce your future risk of cognitive decline. The cogs on the right show your weakest and strongest domains. Your aim is to get all domains into the pale grey area.

YOUR RISK FACTORS

Sleep and calm · Low GL

Active mind · 11 · 90 · Brain fats

· 22 · 54 ·

Active body · 59 · 49 · B vitamins

· 54 · 61 ·

Healthy gut · Antioxidants

⚙ Low risk ⚙ Small ⚙ Significant ⚙ High risk

Fig 12. Example of Cognitive Function Test results

Step 3 – Start COGNITION, your brain-upgrade personalized programme

You then have the option to start COGNITION and will be offered your two weakest domains and asked to choose one. Let's say, for sake of an example, yours was also 'Low Carb and GL' and you picked that one to transform. You'll then receive e-mails every three days giving you something to read, watch, listen to or put into action. You'll also get reminders by e-mail, or WhatsApp if you prefer, to keep you on track. There are Zoom groups you can join, and a Facebook group, so you can ask questions and share results and learn from others what works best. So, step by step, with support along the way, you'll be encouraged and motivated to make changes to drive your 'Low carb and GL' score down into the green zone, shown as white in the example above.

This guidance is reinforced by reading this book in full, especially the chapter in Part 2 that relates to the domain you're working on.

The recommended actions will mirror those in Part 4, which is your brain-upgrade action plan.

After a month, you'll be invited to recomplete only those questions in the questionnaire that count towards the domain you've been focusing on, for example those that score you for 'Low Carb and GL'. You'll then see, hopefully, that you've moved from red to green. Then you'll be shown your new two weakest domains and can select the one you want to work on.

In this way, step by step, you'll effect your own brain upgrade. Most people have two greens, so the process usually takes six months. After six months, you'll be invited to redo the Cognitive Function Test, and track the progress that you've made and how it has improved your cognition. All this is shown in your online COGNITION Dashboard.

You'll also be invited to take a home pinprick blood test measuring homocysteine (B vitamin status), omega-3, vitamin D and HbA1c (blood sugar status). Why it is so important to know these will become clear in Part 2. Collectively, that allows the calculation of your DRIfT score (Dementia Risk Index functional Test), which is a biological measure of your brain resilience. Again, you want to bring this into the green zone. All this is tracked and shown in your online COGNITION Dashboard.

Becoming a Food for the Brain citizen scientist

All you need do to get started is take the free test at foodforthebrain.org. Almost half a million people have taken the test so far. Your results, and theirs, are immediately 'anonymized' to protect your privacy. Collectively, behind the scenes, the charity's research team are continually exploring which changes, and combination of changes, most protect and improve cognition over time. Everything they learn then gets shared back to you, both to inform and motivate you to keep moving in the right direction and to build resilience into the future.

All this testing, and support, and the research that is going on behind the scenes is supported by people like you becoming a Friend of Food for the Brain, which is not-for-profit, and not funded by vested interests but by individuals like you. Through this, you can become a citizen scientist, supporting and contributing to what might become the biggest brain health and dementia prevention project in the world. With your help this project will teach us all what really works in the real world for optimizing brain health.

By taking the test alongside reading this book, it will become impossible for you not to make changes towards your brain upgrade. It's like learning to ride a bicycle. Do you remember the moment you 'got' balance? Even if you haven't ridden a bike for a decade, you still have that internal distinction of balance. By taking the online test at foodforthebrain.org and reading the book, it will be impossible for you not to make changes, because those things you unconsciously do that are not brain-friendly will become obvious to you.

You don't have to change everything at once. Step by step, month by month, you'll make changes to your diet, your frame of mind and your lifestyle that will form into your new 'brain-friendly' habits. Then you can let go of any future fears about cognitive decline, because it won't be happening to you.

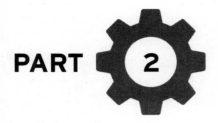

PART 2

Eight Brain-Upgrade Essentials

Learn the essentials for building new brain cells at any age, fuel your brain for better memory and connectivity, and keep your brain young and functionally fit at any age. Each chapter gives you a 'brain upgrade essential'. Some may be new to you. Others you'll have under control already. Collectively, they form the basis for building resilience against mental health problems, keeping your mind sharp and mood good, and building stress resilience.

7

Eight Ways to Upgrade Your Brain - Assess Your Need

While there are a myriad of *bona fide* reasons why our mood might dip, anxiety increase, concentration flag and so on, ranging from purely psychological, such as something depressing happening in our life or being overwhelmed by insoluble problems, to purely biochemical, such as a lack of a nutrient or excess of an anti-nutrient such as alcohol, these two realms – psychological and biological – are not separate. Each affects the other.

Almost every known mental health risk factor falls into one of eight domains. These eight domains represent the key steps you need to take to optimize your brain function, and hence your ability to optimize your experience of life and traverse the tough times to find your way forward.

These eight domains and key steps are:

- *Low Carb and GL* – eat a low-carb and low-glycaemic load (GL) diet
- *Brain Fats* – up your brain fats – omega-3, phospholipids and vitamin D
- *B vitamins* – keep your homocysteine low with B vitamins
- *Antioxidants* – eat and drink anti-ageing antioxidants and polyphenols
- *Healthy Gut* – a healthy gut is a healthy brain

- *Active Body* – exercise and keep physically active
- *Active Mind* – keep yourself socially and intellectually active
- *Sleep and Calm* – sleep well, stay calm and live purposefully

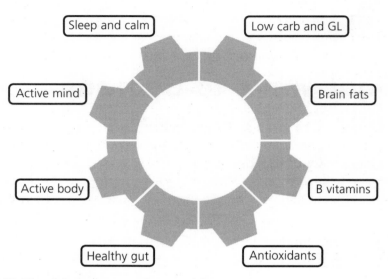

Fig 13. The eight brain-upgrade essentials

At the not-for-profit Food for the Brain Foundation, which I founded in 2006, we invited world experts in different aspects of mental health to help us define what it really meant to upgrade your brain and minimize the risk of mental health problems from ADHD in children to Alzheimer's later in life, and everything in between. You'll meet these world-leading professors, from America to China, New Zealand to the UK, as I interview them and share their research in the chapters that follow. As is inevitably the case in academia and research, each digs deeply into their area of speciality. My job, as chair of the Scientific Advisory Board, is to bring all that specialist knowledge together in a way that you can use.

To that end, Food for the Brain now offers a free Cognitive Function Test, followed by a questionnaire, which works out exactly what your future risk of problems is likely to be, and shows you exactly what is driving that risk and what to do about it. By completing this online at foodforthebrain.org, you'll know which of the factors, and chapters that follow, deserve your special attention. By the time you've worked through this book, and made the recommended step-by-step changes, you can rescore yourself on the online test, which also tracks your improvement over time.

Your results are shown in a traffic-light system, from red, orange, yellow to green (*an example of which is shown on page 70 in shades from black to white*), so you can see exactly which domains are your weakest link. You then have the option to join COGNITION, a personalized interactive programme, which enables you to pick the domain you wish to transform. You then receive e-mails, text reminders and the option to join Zoom groups, all designed to motivate and encourage you to take simple steps to transform your risk.

In the chapters that follow, you'll learn how and why these domains are the keystones for your brain upgrade, not just to sharpen and preserve your mind and memory, but also to support a good mood, reduce anxiety and insomnia, and help you build stress resilience.

'I've got my husband back from dementia, thanks to COGNITION'

But to make this real, even very late in the process of cognitive decline, consider the case of Alan, nicknamed Nodge, from Worthing in southeast England, as told by his wife, Dorothy.

Last December my husband, Nodge, was diagnosed with mixed dementia (vascular and Alzheimer's). He constantly lost his keys, wallet and glasses. He asked the same question and told the same stories repeatedly. He couldn't remember where he lived. He'd even get lost on the way to the toilet in the night. He couldn't join conversations, because he couldn't follow them. He was unable to drive, because he couldn't think about more than one thing at once. There were lots of signs of dementia.

At the memory clinic, we wanted to discuss a prevention programme, but instead were given a virtual pat on the head and a pile of depressing leaflets about where to go for support. There was no hint of hope.

We went to the Alzheimer's prevention charity foodforthebrain. org and watched a four-hour 'masterclass' by some of the world's leading prevention professors. It was mind-blowing. Nodge did their free online Cognitive Function Test and questionnaire, which work out your Dementia Risk Index and tell you what actions to take to reduce your risk. His score was 56 per cent – it should be zero.

The test not only measures your actual cognitive function, but shows you what is driving your risk across eight domains.

We were both horrified at the yellow and amber results and decided to act immediately to rectify each area as recommended by the COGNITION 'brain-upgrade' programme that sends you emails to read, things to watch and actions to take. Now there are Zoom groups and text reminders.

In just three months, the change has been remarkable. We both feel better. Our moods are better, our energy is better. Honestly, I feel like I've got my husband back. I am so grateful to Food for the Brain.

Nodge repeated the online test at foodforthebrain.org. In just three months his cognitive function has improved dramatically, more than doubling his score, and his Dementia Risk Index has fallen from 56 per cent to 43 per cent. While before he had four out of eight domains showing red flags, he's now only got two just below green – 'Active Mind' and 'Active Body' – and he's working on them.

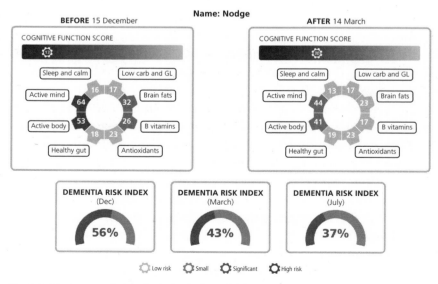

Fig 14. Nodge results, before and after COGNITION

Six months on, his Dementia Risk Index has dropped to 37 per cent. He's joining conversations, he's organizing his own diary, he uses his computer without help (still talking to and swearing at it), he's taken himself back to Morris Dancing practice and taken himself to a dementia support group so he can show them, over time, his recovery.

Nodge is also back in the garden. 'I'd completely forgotten how to garden, apart from making compost, which I'm an expert at,' he says. 'I'd had allotments for over 35 years, so it was a shock. Since I've been following the COGNITION programme, I've had the seeds out, got the pots ready for planting and planned when and where things should go.

'We couldn't discuss plans for the week or for holidays without getting muddled and cross, because I couldn't hold the idea of something in the future in my head. Now my brain is functioning better, we can, once again, plan together. It's been really exciting. We're looking forward to getting increased improvements.

'Now we know dementia is preventable, I'm sticking to the programme too. We look forward to a healthy old age together – sound of mind and fit of body!'

What is good for the brain is good for the body

Focusing on these eight domains of your life and health isn't just going to give you a brain upgrade. It is great for your body, with knock-on benefits for the prevention of diabetes, heart disease, cancer, arthritis and just about every prevalent 21st-century disease, including weight gain.

On the one hand, this might sound too good to be true, but on the other hand, if we go to the true causes of disease, we end up with exactly the same fundamental drivers, the same gradual break-down in core processes that affect both mind and body.

Seven core processes that determine your health

I first wrote about these in my book *Ten Secrets of 100% Healthy People*, based, as I mentioned earlier, on a study of over 55,000 people who had completed my online '100% Health Check' at patrickholford.com. They are:

- *Glycation* – being a master of your blood sugar control by eating a low-GL diet high in soluble fibres
- *Oxidation* – increasing your intake of antioxidants and polyphenols and reducing your intake of oxidants from smoking, frying and pollution
- *Methylation* – bringing your blood homocysteine down with 'methylating' B vitamins and other nutrients
- *Lipidation* – optimizing your intake of essential fats, phospholipids and vitamin D
- *Hydration* – optimizing your intake and quality of water
- *Digestion* – optimizing digestion and a healthy microbiome with enzymes, prebiotics (nutrients that feed bacteria) and gut-friendly foods
- *Communication* – activating 'central control' role of hormones, neurotransmitters and the immune system's communication with cytokines and inflammation control

These are the core biochemical processes that determine health, with the central control communication systems overlaying them all. Cancer, for example, is the breakdown of communication between cells such that cancer cells become disrespectful neighbours, growing uncontrollably, while the overlay of the brain in a diseased state is inflammation. The hallmarks of inflammation in the brain include increased amyloid and p-tau, the target for the next generation of dementia drugs, but that is no different from taking an anti-inflammatory drug when you are in pain. The critical question is always 'What is tipping my body and brain's biochemistry into an inflamed state?' That is what I will show in this part, and how to prevent it.

(In my *Ten Secrets of 100% Healthy People*, the other secrets were about the importance of exercise and generating vital energy; psychological health and stress; and meaning and purpose. These are reflected in the eight domains shown above, and assessed in the online questionnaire as 'Active Body', 'Active Mind' and 'Sleep and Calm'.)

Others who have thought deeply about and researched what is really driving disease have come to the same conclusion. An example of this is Professor Robert Lustig. In his book *Metabolical*,

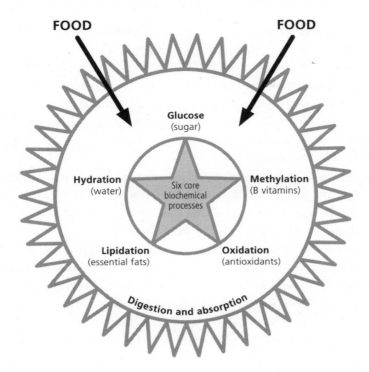

Fig 15. Six of the seven core biochemical processes necessary for health

he concludes there are eight drivers of the metabolic degeneration that results in the core diseases we now face as a consequence of how we live and what we eat.[1] These are: glycation; oxidative stress; methylation; membrane instability, which is dependent on essential omega-3 fats and phospholipids; mitochondrial dysfunction, which is a subject we'll frequently visit; insulin resistance, which then messes up brain energy; inflammation, which overlays everything from depression to dementia; and autophagy, which is the process by which the body's cells break down and recycle damaged proteins and organelles, rebuilding mitochondria.

The diseases humanity face in the 21st century are a consequence of a breakdown in one or more of these eight core processes impacting different organs – the brain for mental illness; the heart for heart disease; the joints for arthritis; the energy system and liver for diabetes and weight gain; the immune system for autoimmune diseases and cancer. Not surprisingly, each of these diseases increases the risk of the others. Not surprisingly, all are on the increase.

Another way to understand these as a whole is to start with a cell, be it a neuron or a body cell. All cells have a central nucleus, where the DNA instructions reside. This is like the yoke of an egg. Then there are various 'organelles' in the white, the cytoplasm, but for now we can focus on the mitochondria, the cigar-shaped energy factories that turn the fuel from our food (glucose, ketones, fatty acids, amino acids) into energy. The mitochondria, however, are much more than energy factories.

Then, as we learned earlier, the cell membrane, rich in intelligent fats, controls communication with the world outside, delivering messages and supplies to the cell. So, a cell needs the right fats to make these membranes. This is *lipidation* (a fat is a lipid).

A cell needs energy. This is the *glycation* shown above.

When sugar levels are out of balance, the excess damages all sorts of things, including brain cells. This energy production also generates exhaust fumes, which are neutralized by antioxidants and polyphenols – think fruit and veg. That's the *oxidation*.

Fundamental to all life processes is *methylation*, which is primarily dependent on B vitamins and other nutrients. There are over 100 diseases associated with faulty epigenetics due to messed up methylation, showing just how key this process is to health.

Then there's *hydration*. You'll know that roughly two-thirds of your body is water, but this isn't just 'plumbing'. The hydrogen and oxygen that make up H_2O are vital for so many biochemical reactions, and the change in structure of water around cell membranes is part of the communication processes that occur between cells and their surroundings.

These five processes cannot happen unless you eat, digest and absorb the right food. This is the sixth process, *digestion*, and includes the complex interaction that occurs between food and our gut microbiome.

Then there are the system-wide overlaying *communication* networks, which include the brain's main messaging neurotransmitters as well as hormones and immune messengers with strange names such as IgE and IgG (*which we'll learn about in Chapter 14*) and cytokines such as IL6, TNF alpha and others. These are all part of the body's defence systems, putting both brain and body into a state of inflammation as a kind of 'warning' system when there are too many insults. Inflammation is a core driver of so many mental health problems and strongly linked to everything from depression to dementia.

Systems-based approaches work better than reductionist medicine

This is a 'systems-based' approach to health as opposed to a reductionist approach, and better reflects how we are designed.

Reductionism, which has been the dominant approach in medical science for a century, supposes that if we study, in great detail, every individual organ and process, then put all the pieces together, we'll understand what's going on. In this way, understandably, we have a different department in the hospital for each part of the body. This reductionist approach has also been hijacked by the pharmaceutical industry with their shareholder imperative to make money. How this works is to identify, for example, one marker of disease, be it amyloid protein, or p-tau, for Alzheimer's, or cholesterol for heart disease, then one means to block or destroy it with a drug. At one level we could say this approach has fundamentally failed. Despite trillions of dollars going into medical science, fuelling a tremendous increase in understanding the details of what goes on in and between cells, giant leaps forward in genetics, big steps forward in diagnostic medicine and massively increased healthcare expenditure, we are getting sicker and sicker.

What's even more telling is that countries which spend more money on so-called healthcare, or have more doctors *per capita*, often have worse, not better, rates of disease. (I explored this in detail in my book *Food Is Better Medicine than Drugs*, co-authored with award-winning medical journalist Jerome Burne, for those who wish to dig deeper.)

A systems-based approach considers that our body and mind are a complex adaptive system, like the environment in the study of ecology or the financial markets in the study of the economy. Complex adaptive systems usually have a few key underlying processes or players that determine the health of the whole. In ecology, these are called keystone species – organisms that help define an entire ecosystem. Without its keystone species, the ecosystem would be dramatically different or cease to exist altogether.

In our bodies, if any one of our 'keystone' processes, such as glycation or methylation, breaks down, it has a dramatic effect on our entire mental and physical health.

Metabolic approaches

Metabolism is defined as 'the chemical processes that occur within a living organism in order to maintain life'. 'Metabolic syndrome' is a breakdown in these processes, the diagnosis of which depends on key 'markers' of each of the fundamental processes shown above.

A new approach in psychiatry is emerging, called 'metabolic psychiatry', which is looking at mental health in this systems-based way. It puts nutrition as a mainstream element of psychiatry. Writing in the *Lancet* medical journal in 2015, almost a decade ago, in an article headed 'Nutritional medicine as mainstream in psychiatry', a group of psychiatrists argued that 'Nutritional medicine should now be considered as a mainstream element of psychiatric practice, with research, education, policy, and health promotion supporting this new framework.'[2]

Systems-based medicine, metabolic psychiatry and nutritional medicine are more akin to organic or regenerative farming than industrial, chemical farming. In the latter, we destroy weeds and bugs with herbicides and pesticides, unwittingly weakening the soil. Then we have to use fertilizers to renourish the soil and grow plants quickly, primarily for profit, not health. Inevitably, these fast-growing plants have fewer nutrients. In regenerative farming, you study the ecosystem and learn what conditions nourish the soil. Principles like 'no-dig', where you don't plough to allow the often miles of fungal networks in the soil to interact with and nourish the plants, are the opposite of using pesticides to kill bugs, and killing the microbiome in your gut in the process.

Interference medicine and the new generation of biologics

The opposite of metabolic psychiatry is the move by the pharmaceutical industry, rebranding itself as the biotech industry, into 'biologics' and 'immunotherapy'. In effect, the industry, which has to sustain over a trillion dollars in annual sales to keep shareholders happy, is running out of profitable and patentable new chemical pathways to block. Statins, for example, block the production of cholesterol, and benzodiazepine tranquillizers block the production of adrenalin.

So, the new frontier for future profits, as the older drug patents expire, is 'biologics' – drugs and treatments that manipulate the immune system in some way. This includes the new generation of mRNA vaccines, antibody treatments such as the new Alzheimer's drugs that introduce antibodies to destroy amyloid protein or p-tau in the brain, and the new 'immunotherapy' drugs being used for autoimmune diseases, arthritis and cancer.

It's a worrying trend, because this level of interference with fundamental and complex immunological processes inevitably induces a lot of unwanted and uncontrollable adverse effects, often triggering inflammation. In a bid to protect the profitable market, these adverse effects are often vigorously downplayed, denied or resisted. This area of risk was why the makers of the first generation of mRNA covid vaccines refused to sell them into the healthcare systems without the governments accepting legal liability for potential deaths and adverse effects. More than 4,000 people in the UK have claimed vaccine damage. Some are now suing the makers, according to the *Telegraph*.[3] By July 2023, the Office for National Statistics recorded 64 vaccine-related deaths and the NHS had paid out £12.6 million in damages,[4] but this figure is likely to escalate considerably, as of July 2023. The true downside of mRNA vaccines, strongly linked to heart inflammation (carditis), and potentially a driver of increased incidences of heart failure and cardiovascular deaths, is a hot topic, with over 200 investigative scientific studies.[5]

A classic example of biologics are the monthly anti-amyloid injections being touted for dementia. No one can deny that roughly a third of people in trials to date have experienced some pretty serious adverse effects – mainly brain bleeding and swelling – for remarkably little benefit (*see page 58*). A small number of trial participants have died as a consequence. Therefore, the monthly treatment will need to be followed by costly brain scans to check for this and then act accordingly. Writing in the *British Medical Journal*, in an editorial letter entitled 'Anti-amyloid trials raise scientific and ethical questions', David Smith, Emeritus Professor of Pharmacology and former deputy head of the Faculty of Medical Science at the University of Oxford, asks, 'Is it justifiable to ask patients to undergo yet more trials of anti-amyloid treatments?'[6] Yet these drugs are forging forward, with campaigns to get them widely licensed and into the system.

Manipulating our immune system and biology in this way is proving to be, as one would expect, dangerous. It is about interfering with fundamental biological processes with a profit motive pushing hard against ethical principles.

'Hands-off' metabolic psychiatry

Much like regenerative farming, in metabolic psychiatry, nutrition is a fundamental keystone, not an afterthought. It's a more 'hands-off' approach, providing the complex adaptive system with the 'environment' it needs to be healthy. It assumes the body and brain are intelligent and will go towards health if given the right environment. We are learning more and more how intelligent our biology is. As an example, those thousands of mitochondria inside your cells don't just make energy. They are part of a complex network of communication micro-adjusting our metabolism.

Writing in his book *Brain Energy*, Chris Palmer, Assistant Professor of Psychiatry at Harvard Medical School, puts mitochondria at the centre of everything:

> Some mitochondria help with the production and release of hormones and neurotransmitters. Others serve as janitors, helping to clean up reactive oxygen species and other debris. Some communicate with the nucleus – sending signals to turn genes on and off. They work together and communicate with each other – they fuse with each other, move around cells, and communicate with other mitochondria in other cells through hormones, such as cortisol. And of course, they provide most of the power – or ATP – to make the factory work. When workers in one cell aren't doing well, they not only affect the rest of the workforce in that cell, but they can also affect the workers in other cells.[7]

He puts them at the centre of our brain health.

As the fields of neuroscience, genetics, gut microbiology, immunology and nutrition evolve, we realize more and more just how interconnected and complex our whole 'system' is. On the one hand, this can be overwhelming, creating more and more 'detail', complexity and scientific specialisms, until we become 'dependent' on the experts and resigned to whatever treatment they recommend. Although this knowledge is useful, it could be seen as an extension of reductionism.

On the other hand, when we realize our job is simply to create an environment that allows us to thrive, and then let our body and brain get on with it, life becomes so much easier. An example is the microbiome. As we learn about the fascinating connections between the gut and the brain, and the complexity of the hundreds, if not thousands of micro-organisms inside us and how they influence so much, the core message is still to eat healthy food and thus take nutrition seriously.

While what we eat is a fundamental part of that 'chemical' environment, we are not just chemical. We are physical, chemical, psychological and spiritual beings, living in an environment. Our health depends on these realms being in harmony. When this is achieved, we are naturally full of energy, free of pain, happy, alert and purposeful.

So, your brain upgrade depends not only on getting your nutrition right, but also exercising body and mind and having a healthy social, intellectual and purposeful life. The last two 'secrets' in my book *Ten Secrets of 100% Healthy People* are 'Get your past out of your present' and 'Finding meaning and purpose'. Of those scoring highest on the health questionnaire, 95 per cent consider relationships to be 'extremely' or 'moderately' important for health, 85 per cent consider their primary relationship as 'excellent' or 'good' and 83 per cent have a close circle of family and friends.

'Finding meaning and purpose' is in the spiritual domain. For those who consider themselves atheist, 'spiritual' in this context is about the context in which we place our life, the meaning and purpose we ascribe to our existence, the greatest connection we have, be it to family, nature, society, or even concepts that we fundamentally believe in and would fight for. Of those scoring most highly on the health questionnaire, 96 per cent said they had 'a clear sense of purpose or direction in life', 88 per cent said that spiritual factors were 'extremely' or 'moderately' important for health and 83 per cent considered being in natural environments important.

Against this backdrop of a systems-based approach, let's now dive deeply into the eight brain-upgrade essentials that underpin mental health and resilience.

In summary, we have learned that:

- You cannot separate your biology and your psychology. Everything you eat, drink, breathe, think and feel has an effect on both your body's chemistry and your state of mind.
- Almost all risk factors for almost all diseases, mental and physical, are driven by imbalance in one or more of seven 'keystone' biological processes, allowing disease states to develop. These are abbreviated to glycation (sugar); oxidation (antioxidants); methylation (B vitamins); lipidation (fats); hydration (water); digestion (healthy gut); communication (hormones, neurotransmitters and immunity).
- Together with our physical, mental and social activity, stress and sleep, these define our overall brain health, happiness, alertness and cognitive abilities.
- By taking the test at foodforthebrain.org you'll know which of these is driving your brain and body's health, now and in the future. The chapters that follow explain the eight domains that you can influence namely; 'Low Carb and GL' – Eat a low-carb and low-GL (glycaemic load) diet; 'Brain Fats' – Up your brain fats – omega-3, phospholipids and vitamin D; 'B Vitamins' – Keep your homocysteine low with B vitamins; 'Antioxidants' – Eat and drink anti-ageing antioxidants and polyphenols; 'Healthy Gut' – A healthy gut is a healthy brain; 'Active Body' – Exercise and keep physically active; 'Active Mind' – Keep yourself socially and intellectually active; 'Sleep and Calm' – Sleep well, stay calm and live purposefully.

- Your brain and body are intimately intelligent, and the best approach is to create the right circumstances, through your diet and lifestyle, for them to regain health.
- Very few, if any, chronic diseases are 'in the genes' or ultimately solved by pharmaceutical medicine.
- *Your health is in your hands.*

8

B Vitamins – the Brain-Makers

Have you ever wondered how your brain adjusts? The fire alarm goes off and in 0.2 seconds you're pumping adrenalin. You meet someone you love who gives you a great big hug. Now serotonin is coursing through your brain. You eat something sweet and the insulin level in your blood increases to get the glucose into your brain. Nightfall is approaching and your brain's melatonin level goes up to give you a good night's sleep. None of this can happen without B vitamins, because the production of each of these vital biochemicals depends on *methylation*, which in turn depends on B vitamins, especially vitamins B6, B12 and folate.

Not only this, but as we learned earlier, the membranes of neurons cannot be made without methylation, and the 'dimmer switches' that turn our genes up or down work through methylation too.

Folate, or folic acid (the form found in most supplements), is recommended in pregnancy because it prevents neural tube defects, also called spina bifida. That's an extreme version of neuronal damage where the spinal neuronal tube doesn't develop properly, with lifelong consequences. Some countries even fortify flour with folic acid for this very reason.

A deficiency of B12, called pernicious anaemia, results in tingling, burning, numbing and loss of sensation in the extremities, because nerves stop working. Those are the physical symptoms to watch out for. The mental symptoms include memory problems, mental fatigue, anxiety and depression. A quarter (26 per cent) of those with pernicious anaemia are undiagnosed after five years, suffering along the way, with many ending up with irreversible nerve degeneration.[8] These, and dozens of other health problems, are the knock-on effects of faulty methylation, due to a lack of B vitamins.

Homocysteine

Fortunately, there is a simple blood test measuring *homocysteine* that determines whether or not you are doing methylation properly. Homocysteine is a toxic amino acid that literally damages your brain as well as your arteries. The higher your homocysteine level, the worse you are at methylation.

Methylation is so key to the brain and body that we now know a raised homocysteine level is a biomarker for over 100 diseases and is associated with their increased risk, thanks to the tireless research of Helga Refsum, Professor of Nutrition at the University of Oslo. It is perhaps the most important biomarker of all, since not even our glucose or iron levels, and certainly not our cholesterol level, predicts so many diseases, both physical and mental. In relation to the brain and mental health, these include Alzheimer's, autism, anxiety, bipolar, children's behavioural problems, cognitive decline in both children and adults, dementia, depression, hearing loss, migraine, multiple sclerosis, motor neuron disease, neural tube defects, obsessive compulsive disorder, post-traumatic stress disorder, schizophrenia and strokes.[9]

A child's homocysteine level even predicts their school grades. A study compared the sum of school grades for 10 core subjects with homocysteine levels in a group of 692 Swedish schoolchildren aged 9 to 15. Increasing homocysteine levels were associated with reducing grades, as was folate intake.[10]

At the other end of life, if homocysteine is going up, memory is going down. If homocysteine goes down, memory goes up.[11] Your homocysteine level predicts your cognitive function better than almost anything else including your age. (Bear in mind, however, that there are many other factors playing a part, so don't think it's only about homocysteine and B vitamins.)

Test and optimize your homocysteine level

So, your first brain-upgrade essential is to make sure you're doing methylation optimally, which means keeping your homocysteine level down, which requires an optimal intake of B vitamins. The levels you need depend on your homocysteine score. Homocysteine can be measured in a skin-prick blood test, either via a home-test kit which you then send back to the lab or by going to a lab. It should be a standard test when you go to your doctor for a check-up, but it isn't. There are only, after all, over 29,000 studies on it.

Until recently, it has been really hard to get your homocysteine measured. All doctors can request it, but few do. At Food for the Brain we've succeeded in making it easy and inexpensive to test with a home-test kit. (*See foodforthebrain.org/tests.*)

One reason to test it is that a level above 11mcmol/l is strongly associated with accelerated brain shrinkage.[12] How likely is that? It does depend somewhat on your age, your sex, and your diet and lifestyle habits, but if you're over 50, it is definitely worth testing, and many younger people have raised levels too. In a study of almost 8,000 people in China in 2020, the average level in men was 12.5 and in women was 9.1. So most men were already in the 'brain-shrinking' zone. A US study found approximately 40 per cent over the age of 60 had a level above 11.[13] It's probably not much different in the UK, but all we know is that two in five adults over 61 in the UK have insufficient B12 to prevent accelerated brain shrinkage.[14] It is realistic to assume that over a third of older people have an homocysteine level over 11.

Professor David Smith recommends treatment with B vitamins for anyone with a homocysteine level above 10. But does that mean that a level of 9 is optimal? One way to explore this question is to look at pregnancy, since building a baby's brain is so dependent on good methylation. Raised homocysteine is a very good predictor of pregnancy problems.

One study looked into this by measuring pre-conceptual homocysteine levels in 81 healthy women who then became pregnant, then measured various aspects of mental health in their children at the age of six.[15] The children of the women whose homocysteine before conceiving was above 9 were significantly more withdrawn, anxious and depressed, and had more social problems, including increased aggressive behaviour.

It is reasonable to assume that if homocysteine is bad for a baby's brain, it is bad for yours too. So you certainly don't want to have a level above 9 if you're going to get pregnant. I recommend no woman attempts pregnancy until their homocysteine level is below 7.5mcmol/l. This is also the level above which chromosomal damage appears.[1] I'd recommend ensuring your 'H score' is below 7.5 (going forward, for ease of reading, I'll refer to your homocysteine level as your 'H score' and leave out the measure mcmol/l 'µmol/l').

In 'normal' pregnancies with no complications in either mother or child, homocysteine remains below 7.5, often between 5 and 7. In five out of seven studies, women who have spontaneous abortions or miscarriages have a level above 15. The risk of having a pre-term baby is four times higher in women with a homocysteine level above 12.4.[16]

Our homocysteine level is often said to go up with age, and this seems to be true from the age of 50 onwards. An interesting, and worrying, finding from this recent study in China is that the lowest levels were in those aged 40 to 50 (averaging 13.9), then increasing with each decade, with 50- to 60-year-olds up to an average of 15, then 60- to 80-year-olds averaging 16.3, and above 80-year-olds averaging 18.7. But those aged 20 to 30 had higher levels than those aged 30 to 50, averaging 15.7. So all these people, regardless of age and sex, were already in the brain-shrinking zone. The situation may not be so bad in the UK, where folate intake may tend to be higher and fewer men smoke. Smoking is one factor that also raises homocysteine. While 15 per cent of men and 11 per cent of women smoke in the UK, in this Chinese study 46 per cent of men and 3.4 per cent of women were smokers.

Smoking isn't the only thing that can raise homocysteine. Excessive drinking, high stress levels, lack of sleep,[17] being overweight, lack of exercise, any of the mental health problems listed above, also cardiovascular disease, stroke or high blood pressure, and general ill-health may all indicate a potential risk of raised homocysteine.

While the presence of these risk factors can predict that your homocysteine level may be raised, it is best to test. The questionnaire at foodforthebrain.org assesses your risk, in the 'B Vitamins' domain, based on such factors, but you'll also be asked if you've tested your homocysteine, which you can add in anytime and which will make your B-vitamin status assessment much more accurate. In truth, your optimal intake of B vitamins is whatever keeps your homocysteine low. You may well find you need more as you age.

I'm reminded of a mother and daughter who attended one of my lectures.

The mother had had a stroke and the daughter, in her twenties, encouraged her to have a homocysteine test. Homocysteine is a strong predictor of stroke risk.[18] She said, 'I will if you will.' So they both got tested. The mother's H score was below 7, so her stroke would appear to have had nothing to do with faulty methylation. The daughter's H score was over 20. She had suffered from chronic fatigue for several years following a car accident.

Within one month of taking the homocysteine-lowering supplement (see page 320), her chronic fatigue resolved itself. A few months later, she retested her homocysteine, which was now below 7.

The moral of this story is that you can't assume your homocysteine level is optimal just because you're under the age of 50. If you have any health problems or any of the risk factors for raised homocysteine, I'd recommend you get tested. I consider homocysteine to be possibly the single best predictor of overall health. If you find your H score is below 7, then you can tick that box as the first completed step towards your brain upgrade. If your H score is above 7, I'll show you how to lower it later (*see page 104*).

If none of the risk factors apply to you, your diet is good, perhaps you even supplement B vitamins, and your homocysteine is still high, there's a good chance you aren't absorbing vitamin B12 very well. This is increasingly common as you age, but some people, with pernicious anaemia, produce antibodies which attack the cells in your stomach that make stomach acid and intrinsic factor, which are needed to absorb vitamin B12. This is a type of auto-immune disease.

Leaving this aside, a UK study found that as many as two in five people over 60 had a raised homocysteine level and a low level of vitamin B12 in their blood, and accelerated brain shrinkage.[19] I'll explain how this happens, and what to do about it, in Chapter 21.

Is schizophrenia an example of what happens when methylation goes wrong?

But first, let's look at the role of methylation in schizophrenia, an extreme form of brain dysfunction. About one in 100 suffer from this debilitating mental illness and more men than women, with onset often occurring in the late teenage years. Before a diagnosis, there are often signs such as problems at school and difficulty socializing, often leading to social withdrawal. We also know that excessive cannabis use can be a trigger, as can major stresses.

'Schizophrenia' is a scary word to many people, but the reality is that most of us have experienced one or more of its symptoms, albeit at a lower level, at some point. These include confused thinking and delusions, as in losing touch with reality, possibly hearing or seeing things, or seeing things in a distorted way. These are disperceptions that can occur when the brain isn't working right. Anxiety, disturbed sleep and depression are also common symptoms of schizophrenia, perhaps as a consequence of messed-up thinking and disperceptions.

What has this got to do with methylation? Every 5-point increase in homocysteine increases the risk of being diagnosed with schizophrenia by 70 per cent![20] Many diagnosed schizophrenics have an H score above 15. There's also a genetic twist: about a third of people have a gene variation called MTHFR677TT, mentioned earlier, which means the instructions to make a key methylation enzyme called MTHFR are passed on in a less functional way. Having this variation increases the risk of schizophrenia by 36 per cent. As a consequence, such a person is more likely to have a raised level of homocysteine. As with so many mental health issues, the combination of high stress, lack of sleep, bad diet, smoking and perhaps this genetic weakness would certainly raise homocysteine and could be enough to send someone over the edge.

So, what happens to such a person if they then supplement B vitamins? Does their brain function recover? Professor Joseph Levine from the Stanley Research Center and Beersheva Mental

Health Center in the Ben Gurion University in Israel devised a study to find out.[21] He gave half of a group of 42 schizophrenic patients B vitamins (B6, B12 and folic acid) and the other half a placebo. Those taking the B-vitamin supplements had both a dramatic reduction in their homocysteine levels and a significant improvement in their symptoms of schizophrenia, except for one patient, who didn't comply with the B-vitamin treatment, didn't improve and didn't have a reduction in their homocysteine level. They were the exception that proves the rule.

Other studies giving B12 and folic acid have also proven to be effective. A review of studies back in 2014 concluded: 'Overwhelming evidence indicates that Hcy is also involved in the pathophysiology of schizophrenia and affective disorders.'[22]

Despite this 'overwhelming evidence', which has existed for over a decade, hardly anyone diagnosed with schizophrenia ever gets tested for homocysteine or given B vitamins.

Earlier, I referred to the first ever double-blind controlled trials in the history of psychiatry, in the 1950s, which gave high-dose vitamin B3 (niacin) versus a placebo and reported outstanding improvements in those with recent diagnoses of schizophrenia, so still 'drug naïve'. This remarkable breakthrough, made by my mentor Dr Abram Hoffer, the director of psychiatric research in Saskatchewan, Canada, ultimately got buried in favour of pharmaceuticals. This suppression was achieved by running B-vitamin trials on chronic schizophrenics who had been on heavy-duty medication for several years. For them, the B vitamins didn't work well enough to reach significance. (Those interested in both medical science and politics can read both the science and how niacin got culled in a paper by Abram Hoffer's son, a professor of medicine, 'Vitamin therapy in schizophrenia'.[23])

There are a few key points we can take from all this. The first, which we touched on earlier, is that most psychiatric medication, especially if taken for years, messes up the brain, making a full recovery or 'upgrade' slower. In the case of the major tranquillizers used for schizophrenia, this may make a full recovery impossible.

The second is that not everybody who has a serious mental illness like schizophrenia has faulty methylation and a raised homocysteine, although many do.

The third is that there are several critical factors that are needed for optimal brain health and they interact with each other. There isn't a single cause of Alzheimer's or depression. Anyone who

suggests that 'amyloid' is the cause of Alzheimer's, or 'low serotonin' is the cause of depression, is just perpetuating a myth
designed to sell drugs.

A lack of homocysteine-lowering B vitamins is one piece of the
puzzle, however, because – as we will explore later on – B vitamins
and omega-3 fats are synergistic. Neither can work without the other.

The last 'sad but true' point is that if a treatment involves a
non-patentable, thus relatively inexpensive, treatment, as opposed
to a patentable and profitable drug, it is highly likely to be sidelined
and ignored. There are very few exceptions to this rule, vitamin D
being one of them.

But the key takeaway message is that even if you have inherited
the apparent weakness of having the MTHFR677TT gene variant,
which you can discover with a DNA test (*see Resources*), this can be
mitigated by having enough B vitamins. Your optimal level will be
what brings your homocysteine down to 7 or less.

So, what we've learned is that, in pregnancy, in children and in both
young and older adults, raised homocysteine downgrades the brain,
with problems for learning, memory, behaviour and mental health. So,
to not only avoid these kinds of problems, but also ensure your brain is
working optimally, the first step is to do whatever is necessary to optimize your H level, which certainly means bringing it below 7.

That brings us on to the B vitamins and understanding what it is
they actually do.

B6, B12 and folate - the three musketeers

It's worth knowing why these three B vitamins are so vital for brain
health. But it's not so easy to explain.

Methylation is actually done by a vital brain nutrient called SAMe,
pronounced 'Sammy', which is short for S-adenosyl methionine.
SAMe is called a 'methyl donor'. A methyl unit is a simple molecule,
CH_3, with three hydrogen atoms attached to one carbon atom. It's a
tiny molecule that is added and taken away from other body chemicals
to change them from one thing to something else. Noradrenalin, for
example, has a methyl group added to become adrenalin.

Methylation is the process of moving these methyl groups
around. It's like a biological switch with literally billions of methylation reactions taking place every minute in your brain and body.

In order to make SAMe, which your brain is doing every second of every day, it has to turn the methionine from your food protein into it, and this process is dependent on B vitamins. Without enough B vitamins, you get a chemical log-jam, which then makes homocysteine go up. How all this works is shown in this short film: foodforthebrain.org/the-h-factor/.

B12, folate, B6, glutathione and N-acetylcysteine (NAC)

Vitamin B12: Are you absorbing it properly?

Vitamin B12, which is only found in foods of animal origin (meat, fish, eggs, dairy), is, for some, especially later in life, the most critical B vitamin for brain health. This is because its absorption from your food into your bloodstream uniquely depends on the presence of stomach secretions, including stomach acid and intrinsic factor, and these tend to go down as you age. Some people just don't make enough even early in life and therefore depend on B12 injections, which bypass this problem.

Stomach acid is called hydrochloric acid and can be raised by supplementing betaine hydrochloride. Betaine is another name for tri-methyl glycine. Hydrochloric acid is made by an enzyme dependent on zinc. So, if you have a methylation problem, perhaps due to a lack of B vitamins, and don't get enough zinc, your ability to make stomach acid is impaired.

Earlier in this chapter I referred to a study that found that two in five people had insufficient B12 in their blood to prevent accelerated brain shrinkage. You may appear to be eating enough, but if it isn't getting into your bloodstream, it won't work.

To put this into context, most servings of meat, fish, eggs or milk will provide something like 0.5 to 2.5mcg. An egg gives 0.5mcg and a serving of fish 2.5mcg. That's the Nutrient Reference Value (NRV) you'll see on the back of a vitamin supplement – 2.5mcg. Will that lower a high homocysteine level and stop your brain shrinking? Unlikely. Almost all the studies that have shown a measurable reduction in brain shrinkage and reduction in homocysteine have given 500mcg. That's 200 times more! That's because if you aren't absorbing it very well, you'll need to supplement a lot more to get a little more through into your bloodstream.

For example, Professor David Smith and his group at the Optima Project at the University of Oxford investigated the effects of giving B vitamins (B6 20mg, folic acid 800mcg and B12 500mcg) versus a placebo in a randomized controlled trial to those with mild cognitive impairment (MCI), also known as pre-dementia, measuring their homocysteine level both before and after and the rate of brain shrinkage with an MRI scan, as well as testing cognitive function.[24] Those with homocysteine above 11 who were given the B vitamins had half the rate of overall brain shrinkage and almost nine times less shrinkage in the Alzheimer's-related areas of the brain, as well as significant cognitive improvements.

The lack of B12 and consequent increase in homocysteine directly damages your brain and arteries and means you don't have enough SAMe to do methylation, and raises both p-tau, promoting those neurofibrillary tangles, and amyloid protein, which, as we have seen, are the hallmarks of Alzheimer's.[25]

Supplementing vitamin B12 lowers homocysteine and helps prevent all this degeneration. In one study in people with dementia, those given a combo of B6 (25mg), folic acid (2,000mcg) and B12 (400mcg) for two years had almost a quarter of the increase in homocysteine of those in the placebo group.[26]

There are lots of studies showing the benefits of B12, and lots of mechanisms through which it protects the brain. One of the latest reviews concludes:

Clinical studies showed homogenously that vitamin B12 in combination with further representatives of the B-vitamin family or alone have beneficial effects on cognitive function, inflammation and brain atrophy in elderly adults without cognitive decline or in mild cognitive impairment patients. Studies dealing with patients suffering from Alzheimer's disease found reduced vitamin B12 plasma levels compared to healthy controls. Moreover, supplementation of B vitamins was reported to improve cognitive functions in numerous (randomized) clinical trials.[27]

If medicine were based on the evidence, everyone with cognitive decline would be recommended to supplement B12. I've been campaigning for this for over a decade, yet still in the UK, a GP is not allowed to prescribe B12 for cognitive decline.

But it is isn't just dementia that supplementing B12 helps prevent, but also depression.[28]

My advice is to both eat foods containing vitamin B12 and supplement 10mcg a day in a multivitamin, but you'll need more like 500mcg of B12 if your homocysteine level is high (*see page 92*). The higher your homocysteine, the more B12 you need. If you are vegan, you simply must supplement B12 to protect your brain, as no plant foods contain it.

The majority of people, even those with pernicious anaemia, get better on high-dose supplemental B12. But some need B12 injections to bypass the absorption issue. If you have had a B12 injection and immediately had more energy and mental clarity, that's a good indication that you need B12. It is stored in the liver, so injections are needed every one to three months.

Vitamin B12: Beware of antacids and metformin

Stomach acid is one of the body's most vital chemicals. It is secreted when we eat protein and does four things: i) it tells the circular muscular valves at the top and bottom of the stomach to close to make a sealed 'acid bath'; ii) it then digests protein down to individual amino acids; iii) it sanitizes our food, killing bugs; and iv) it also helps B12 to be absorbed.

If we don't make enough stomach acid, we get indigestion. The bacteria in our gut then get to feed on our partially digested food. They then make gas, so we belch, and since the valves don't shut properly, some acid in the stomach can get up into the oesophagus, leading from our stomach to our throat, and we experience heartburn. Then the doctor gives us an antacid 'proton pump inhibitor' (PPI) drug, which stops us making stomach acid, so the heartburn goes away. These drugs, which usually end in '…azole', lower B12 levels and raise homocysteine. The latest review of all studies concludes: 'Our review showed significant changes in diagnostic biomarkers of vitamin B12 status in long-term PPI users, including elevated homocysteine and methylmalonic acid (MMA) concentration levels defining cellular vitamin B12 deficiency.'[29]

In terms of future dementia risk, those taking PPI antacids for more than 4.4 years have a 30 per cent increased risk.[30] Short-term use does not appear to be a problem.

When nutritional therapists suspect a client has these symptoms as a result of low stomach acid, they give them supplements of betaine hydrochloride with meals containing protein, thus raising stomach acid levels, and more often than not the symptoms of indigestion and heartburn go away.

Another drug that knocks out B12 is the diabetes drug metformin. The latest review of studies concludes: 'Metformin at ≥1500 mg/d could be a major factor related to vitamin B12 deficiency, whereas concurrent supplementation of multivitamins may potentially protect against the deficiency.'[31]

Some drugs used for lowering high blood pressure, especially diuretics, also raise homocysteine.[32]

If you are on any of these drugs, make sure your homocysteine and B12 levels are monitored.

The best test for determining your B12 status is called holo-trans-cobalamin (HTC). The next best is methylmalonic acid (MMA), then serum B12. Serum B12 is the standard test used by doctors. It's more readily available but not nearly as accurate as HTC, but gives a good starting point. The UK reference range of above 180pg/ml being sufficient is out of date and in need of revision,[33] along with the US lower level of 200pg/ml. In Europe and Japan, anything below 500pg/ml is considered deficient. Accelerated brain shrinkage due to a lack of B12 does happen with B12 levels below 500pg/ml. The amount of B12 you need is whatever both normalizes your homocysteine level and your blood B12 level. Bear in mind that if your homocysteine is raised, you're either not getting enough B12, folate or B6.

Folate: Why you need to eat your greens

Folate, which used to be called B9, is the main reason we say, 'Eat your greens.' It's actually found in greens, beans, nuts and seeds. In fact, all vegetables and most fruits contain this vital B vitamin. If you are not consciously eating at least five servings, ideally seven servings, of vegetables and fruit a day, you are probably not getting enough. Half a plate of vegetables for a main meal counts as two servings. So, if you make sure half of what you eat at two main meals is vegetables, that's four servings. Our physically active Stone Age ancestors would have been eating twice as much food, and all of it fresh, and many times more folate. These foods need to become a regular part of your diet.

The best foods for folate are:

Food	Amount per 100g serving
Wheatgerm	325mcg
Lentils, cooked	179mcg
Millet flakes	170mcg
Sunflower seeds	164mcg
Endive	142mcg
Chickpeas, dried, cooked	141mcg
Spinach	140mcg
Romaine lettuce	135mcg
Broccoli	130mcg
Kidney beans, dried, cooked	115mcg
Peanuts	110mcg
Brussels sprouts	110mcg
Orange juice, fresh or frozen	109mcg
Asparagus	98mccg
Hazelnuts	72mcg
Avocado	66mcg

These foods need to become a regular part of your diet.

Few people achieve 400mcg of folate in their diet, which is likely to be an optimal intake for most, although studies aiming to prevent cognitive decline and dementia mostly give double this – 800mcg.

The list below gives examples of daily diets that would give you 400mcg. Consider these and ask yourself if you think you achieved 400mcg yesterday…

- a salad with romaine lettuce, endive, half an avocado and a handful of sunflower seeds, accompanied by a glass of orange juice

- a dish made with a serving of lentils or millet, with a serving each of spinach, broccoli and parsnips
- a fruit salad with papaya, kiwi fruit, orange and cantaloupe melon in orange juice, plus a handful of unsalted peanuts
- an orange, a large serving of broccoli, spinach, Brussels sprouts and a bowl of miso soup

But even this might not be enough for a brain upgrade. Consider this experiment in Holland. A group of 818 people aged 50 to 70 were given a folic acid supplement of 800mcg for three years, versus a placebo. At the end, compared with those taking the placebo, those taking folic acid were functioning at the equivalent of being 5.5 years younger.[34]

My advice is to both aim to eat 400mcg of folate and supplement an additional 200 to 400mcg, the higher amount being appropriate if your homocysteine level is raised.

Vitamin B6, glutathione and N-acetylcysteine (NAC)

You won't have seen vitamin B6 in the film on page 92 because there is another way homocysteine gets lowered. This is by turning it into a non-toxic amino acid, cysteine, and then into a very important antioxidant called glutathione. This both removes the toxic homocysteine from circulation and helps protect the brain from harmful oxidants, which we'll discuss in Chapter 13 as a key part of your brain upgrade. Vitamin B6 is essential for this detoxifying pathway to work. So, without adequate vitamin B6, homocysteine accumulates. This pathway, called the sulphuration pathway, is shown in the figure on the next page.

You'll learn, in Chapter 13, that anything that raises the master antioxidant glutathione, which supplementing NAC and B6 also does, is great news for your brain health. These are key anti-ageing nutrients for both brain and body.

Vitamin B6 is also found in those folate-rich foods listed above, and also protein-rich foods such as those rich sources of vitamin B12 (meat, fish, eggs, dairy), so if you aim to eat enough B12 and folate you'll always achieve a reasonable amount of B6. The basic Nutrient Reference Value (NRV) you'll see on a supplement or food is only 1.4mg but most decent multivitamins, and those used to

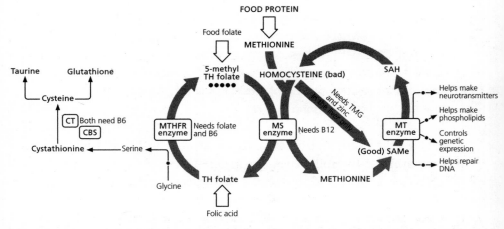

Figs 16 and 17. The methylation cycle involving homocysteine, SAMe and B vitamins. The sulphuration cycle involving vitamin B6, making glutathione

lower homocysteine, will provide 20mg. This kind of level is used in almost all studies. This is both safe and beneficial.

The older you get, the more antioxidants you need, so you want to do everything you can to promote glutathione. The best homocysteine-lowering supplements will also include a form of cysteine, N-acetylcysteine or NAC, or glutathione itself, which helps raise glutathione in the brain (*see Resources*).

Lowering homocysteine

While I've said that there is a good case for keeping your homocysteine level below 7, given that homocysteine does go up with age, if you are pursuing optimal health and aiming to minimize the risk of developing any disease, including Alzheimer's, my rule of thumb is to keep your H score below your age, divided by 10. So, if you are 80, keep your level below 8.

That being said, a study of Australians aged 18 to 34, calculating the level of both homocysteine and B vitamins that correlated with the least damage to cellular DNA, concluded that the best protection of genetic DNA occurred 'when plasma homocysteine is below 7.5

μmol/l and serum vitamin B12 is above 300 pmol/l and dietary supplement intake of 700mcg folic acid and 7mcg vitamin B12 is sufficient'.[35]

Vitamins B6, B12, folate and also tri-methyl glycine (TMG) and zinc – used to lower homocysteine in the liver – are all helpful in lowering homocysteine. (TMG is an amino acid with three 'methyl' groups which can be used to turn toxic homocysteine into helpful SAMe.) Best of all is a combination of these, together with either glutathione or NAC. These are the nutrients you'll find in the best homocysteine-lowering supplements.

Combinations work best. For example, one study found homocysteine scores were reduced by 17 per cent on high-dose folic acid alone, 19 per cent on vitamin B12 alone, 57 per cent on folic acid plus B12, and 60 per cent on folic acid, B12 and B6.[36] All this was achieved in three weeks! However, even better results could have been achieved by including TMG and zinc, and possibly NAC or glutathione. TMG is the best methyl donor, with three methyl groups, to supplement. This is because it – and only it – can immediately donate a methyl group to homocysteine, thus detoxifying it.

In one New Zealand study, the homocysteine scores of patients with chronic kidney failure and very high homocysteine levels were reduced by a further 18 per cent when 4g of TMG was added to 50mg of vitamin B6 and 5,000mcg of folate, compared with patients taking just B6 and folate.[37]

In my experience, you can halve a high homocysteine level in two to three months with the combination of these nutrients, plus a healthy diet. Some companies produce combinations of them (*see Resources*). These are the most cost-effective supplements for restoring a healthy homocysteine level.

Chris proves the point:

Chris felt very unwell, with constant tiredness, worsening memory and concentration and little zest for life. He was depressed, had no sex drive and felt brain dead. His homocysteine score was 119.

He changed his diet and took homocysteine-lowering nutrients, and within three months his homocysteine level dropped to 19. After six months it had dropped to 11.

He cannot believe how well he feels now. His memory and concentration have been completely restored. He has boundless energy from 6 a.m. until 10 p.m. He now exercises for an hour every day and has lost weight.

'You have saved my life,' he said, 'or at least made it worth living again. I'm a new man and my love life has perked up.'

Supplementation to normalize homocysteine levels

Your homocysteine level is a very good indicator of the amount of certain B vitamins, and other nutrients, you need. The chart below shows you the approximate level that is worth supplementing on a daily basis if your homocysteine level is below 7, and also what to supplement if your level is higher, until it normalizes.

Nutrient	Very low risk Below 7.5	Low risk 7.5–9.9	At risk 10–15	High risk Above 15
Folic acid or MTHF*	200mcg	400mcg	800mcg	800mcg
B12 or methyl B12	10mcg	250mcg	500mcg	750mcg
B6	10mg	20mg	25mg	40mg
B2	5mg	10mg	15mg	25mg
Zinc	5mg	10mg	15mg	20mg
TMG	500mg	750mg	1,500mg	1,500mg
NAC or glutathione	250mg	500mg	750mg	750mg

*Note: the most functional form of folate is called MTHF. This may be slightly more effective in lowering homocysteine than folic acid and is often used in homocysteine-lowering supplements. I also prefer the methylated form of B12, methylcobalamin.

- *If your level is below 7.5,* it is still advisable to take a high-potency multivitamin and mineral supplement, especially later in life, providing the levels of nutrients shown in the table above for the purposes of maintaining a healthy low level.
- *If your level is above 7.5,* you will need to take a homocysteine-lowering supplement containing larger amounts of these nutrients, as well as a high-potency multivitamin and mineral. Since most of these are water-soluble, you are best to divide the dose and take a supplement two or three times a day. For many

supplements, the 7–9.9 level equates to taking one, the 10–15 level to taking two, and above 15 to taking three of the homocysteine-lowering formula a day. But do then recheck your H score after three months, as you will probably be able to reduce supplementation to one homocysteine-lowering formula a day. The web page foodforthebrain.org/homocysteine-lowering-b-vitamins/ shows you supplements that meet these optimal levels for lowering homocysteine.

Increasing your intake of omega-3 and phospholipids (*see the next chapter*), and antioxidants (*see Chapter 13*) may also help to lower homocysteine. In Chapter 16, we'll address stress and stimulants, as both can raise homocysteine, and lowering both is part of your brain upgrade.

In summary, we have learned that:

- Homocysteine is a toxic amino acid that damages the brain. It is also a biomarker for over 100 diseases, including almost all mental and neurological diseases.
- Probably a third of people over 60 have a level above 11µmol/l, which means their brain is shrinking. Anyone over the age of 50, and anyone with a mental or neurological health concern, should get their level tested.
- It is especially important to test before getting pregnant and aim for a homocysteine level below 7.5µmol/L.
- A doctor can get your homocysteine tested, but few do. Foodforthebrain.org can send you a home-test kit.
- Anyone with an H score above 10 needs to supplement 20mg of B6, 400mcg of preferably methylfolate and 500µg of B12.
- Antacid 'PPI' drugs, the diabetes drug metformin and diuretic drugs used for high blood pressure knock out B12 and raise homocysteine. So do too much coffee, alcohol and stress.
- Eating vegetables, nuts, seeds, beans and greens, rich in folate, lowers homocysteine.

Often homocysteine is high because a person isn't absorbing vitamin B12, which is found only in foods of animal origin (eggs, milk, meat and fish). That is why, if homocysteine is high, it is important to supplement enough (500mcg) of B12. This is also essential for vegans.

9

The Fats That Build Your Brain

We now know that the omega-3 fat DHA and other marine-food nutrients would have been essential in developing our big brains. Also, that all brains, including ours, are largely made of fats. The two main types are omega-3 fatty acids and phospholipids. These bind together to form phosphorylated fats, which are found in both oily fish and the brain. Obtaining an optimal intake of all these fats is the second essential for your brain upgrade.

To explore how much you need for optimal brain function, we'll look at the benefits of fats in reducing your risk of so many diseases, from arthritis to diabetes, heart disease and cancer, to name but a few. But we'll also look at what the brain actually needs. Let's start by looking at which kinds of fats the brain needs and why.

Omega-3 and omega-6

You'll recall that 50 to 60 per cent of the brain weight is fat, rich in omega-3 DHA and omega-6 AA,[38] the rest being mainly phospholipids and cholesterol. A quarter of all the cholesterol in the body is in the brain, with low cholesterol (below 4mmol/l) being a major risk factor for dementia[39] (*see page 122 for more on this*).

Omega-3 is a family of fats, shown in the figure below, which starts with the plant-based source of omega-3, found more in cold-climate leaves, and sea plants such as algae and seaweeds, the difference between the two being that seaweed clings to things, while algae float. This is called alpha linolenic acid (ALA). A very small amount of this converts to eicosapentaenoic acid (EPA), which is a potent anti-inflammatory good for both the heart and brain, as well as joints. It also helps improve mood (*see Chapter 17*). That's because it's a slow and energy-expensive process that's also dependent on various nutrients (vitamin C, B3, B6, magnesium, zinc) to drive the enzymes that do the work. A lack of these nutrients makes the process of making EPA even harder. EPA converts quite readily to docosahexaenoic acid (DHA) when we need it. In between EPA and DHA is DPA, docosapentaenoic acid, which can swing both ways, converting to either DHA or EPA as we need it.

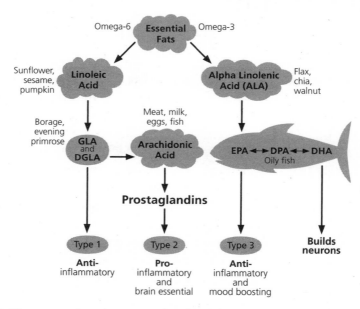

Fig 18. The omega-3 and omega-6 fats family tree

Of all the fats in the brain, the omega-3 fat DHA is the most important. It accounts for about 40 per cent of brain fats, while EPA comprises less than 1 per cent.

You'll also recall there's another important fat in the brain called arachidonic acid (AA), a type of omega-6 fat derived from linoleic acid and found in nuts and seeds and their oils. Animals accumulate it, so there's plenty in meat, fish, eggs and dairy. If you eat enough fish for omega-3 fats, you'll get enough AA.

While omega-6 fats are highest in hot-climate foods, such as sesame and sunflower seeds, omega-3 fats are highest in cold-climate foods, such as green leafy vegetables – cabbage, kale and Brussels sprouts, for example – but also colder-climate nuts or seeds such as walnut, flax and chia.

It's fish that swim in colder water, higher up the food chain, for example fish with teeth that eat other fish, that provide the most omega-3 EPA and DHA. When you eat fish, especially oily fish, you're getting a bit more DHA than EPA. The chart below shows how much. The single richest source of DHA is caviar. It is literally caviar for your brain. A 25g serving would give as much as an 85g serving of salmon. Other fish roe is also good, as is taramasalata, which is about 12 per cent fish roe when bought from the supermarket, and can of course be more if you make your own. Although not shown here, another delicacy in many parts of the world is eyes. The brain is the extension of the eye, which is phenomenally rich in DHA.

Fish and Seafood (per 85g)	EPAmg	DHAmg	EPA+ DHAmg
Caviar	2,428	3,279	5,707
Fish roe	836	1,159	1,995
Anchovy	1,366	2,310	3,576
Atlantic salmon (farmed)	587	1,238	1,825
Atlantic herring	773	939	1,712
Atlantic salmon (wild)	349	1,215	1,564
Bluefin tuna	309	970	1,279
Mackerel (canned)	369	677	1,046
Sockeye salmon (wild)	451	595	1,046
Rainbow trout (farmed)	284	697	981
Sardines (canned)	402	433	835
Albacore (or white) tuna (canned)	198	535	733
Shark (raw)	267	444	711
Swordfish	117	579	696
Sea bass	175	473	648
Pollock	77	383	460
Flat fish (flounder/sole)	207	219	426
Halibut	77	318	395
Oysters (farmed)	195	179	374

(continued)

Fish and Seafood (per 85g)	EPAmg	DHAmg	EPA+ DHAmg
Dungeness crab	239	96	335
Scallops	141	169	310
Mixed shrimp	145	122	267
Taramasalata (12 per cent fish roe)	139	100	239
Clams	117	124	241
Yellowfin tuna	40	197	237
Catfish (wild)	85	116	201
Catfish (farmed)	42	109	151
Cod	3	131	134
Mahi-mahi (dolphin fish)	22	96	118
Tilapia	4	111	115

Fish-oil supplements also provide a combination of EPA and DHA. Some provide some DPA, the 'in-betweener'. Some concentrate EPA and are taken for mood; others concentrate DHA and are taken for brain function. There are also vegan supplements of DHA, derived from algae which is highly concentrated in a laboratory. Just eating seaweed won't give you much at all.

Let's imagine, for a minute, that you are big into mackerel or sardines, especially my sardine pâté or smoked mackerel kedgeree (*page 275*), and have three servings a week. You'll be getting about 2 grams of DHA (2,031mg) and about 1 gram of EPA (1,107mg) in total.

There are lots of studies showing that either increased fish consumption or supplementation with omega-3 reduces symptoms of depression, risk of suicide, schizophrenia, bipolar, ADHD, aggression, dementia and Alzheimer's, post-natal depression and anxiety during pregnancy, and increases the cognitive function of infants and children, with a strong link between the maternal intake of omega-3 and the risk of mental and brain deficits in the offspring. An example is a recent study in the *American Journal of Clinical Nutrition* of over 100,000 people, which showed that an increased intake of omega-3, either from diet or supplements, or having a higher omega-3 blood level, cuts the risk of dementia by a fifth (20 per cent).[40] But how much omega-3, and DHA in particular, is optimal and for whom? Do older people need more? Do healthy people need less?

Let's take a look at some studies to explore this. The most comprehensive review and meta-analysis of 19 trials on patients with mild and major depression concludes that 'the use of omega-3 fats is effective both in patients with major depressive disorder and milder depression'.[41] The greater the amount of EPA (not DHA), the more effective the treatment was likely to be. The most effective studies gave 1,000mg of EPA a day.

What about memory and dementia prevention? Again, it depends on the amount of fish oils consumed. Studies, generally in older people, usually fail to find protection when 500mg or less are given a day, but in studies giving above 700mg of DHA, which usually means 2 grams of more of fish oil, are usually effective in either improving cognition or slowing the rate of decline. Also, generally, the higher the dose, the greater the benefit.[42]

Most of these studies were in people already showing cognitive decline. What about healthy people? Dr Veronica Witte and colleagues from the Department of Neurology at the Medical University in Berlin decided to find out by giving 65 healthy 50- to 75-year-olds 2.2g a day of omega-3 fish oils for 26 weeks and seeing what happened to their brains.[43] Not only did they get some significant cognitive improvements, with better memory and more flexible thinking and ability to focus, but their brains also got a physical upgrade, with an increase in grey-matter volume and more white-matter integrity, which indicate better wiring. In just six weeks you could see evidence of a brain upgrade! Also, the higher their blood levels of omega-3, the greater the improvements.

What about younger people? Philippa Jackson, Associate Professor of Biological Psychology and the Associate Director of the Brain, Performance and Nutrition Research Centre in Northumbria University in Newcastle, devised a study to find out. She gave healthy 18- to 29-year-olds either 1 or 2 grams of DHA, not only to explore the effects on cognitive tasks, but also what happened in the brain during cognitive tasks. She found both doses increased brain function by improving blood flow.[44] Her latest study actually found that an EPA-richer fish oil outperformed a DHA-rich fish oil in improving cognitive function in healthy adults,[45] which is why I prefer to add together the EPA and DHA as the measure of what I'm wanting to take in.

Her research suggests studies that administer less than 2 grams of omega-3 per day, which would give you about 1.2g of DHA plus

EPA, are unlikely to produce clinically relevant cognitive performance enhancements in healthy people.

All of this evidence concurs with the decades of research by Joe
Hibbeln MD, who worked for the US National Institutes of Health,
concluding that the majority are protected from chronic diseases,
not just brain disease, by an intake of 750mg a day of omega-3 EPA,
DHA and DPA.[46]

Taking all this into consideration, an intake of 2 grams of omega-3
from fish or fish oil, providing at least 500mg and ideally 750mg of
DHA and about the same amount of EPA, seems to be optimal. More
may be better for those suffering from omega-3-related health problems. 'My patients tell me,' says Hibbeln, 'on 4 grams of EPA and
DHA a day, they feel an emotional state of being content, accompanied by better skin, hair and nails and a better sex life.'

Less omega-3 may be sufficient if your intake of omega-6 fats,
which have rocketed in our diet from processed foods using
soybean oil, corn oil and sunflower oil, were reduced. This is for
two reasons.

First, the enzymes that turn omega-3 linolenic acid (think chia
or flax) into EPA and DHA are the same enzymes that convert
linoleic acid (think soy or corn oil) into either AA (arachidonic
acid), which is needed in the brain, and GLA, an anti-inflammatory.
The enzymes, dependent on B vitamins, magnesium, zinc and
vitamin C, get used up with too much omega-6 intake, so the
omega-3 in plants doesn't get converted so readily.

A diet high in refined food is highly likely to lack these critical
nutrients, as well as being high in omega-6.

So, stay away from processed foods using these oils and orient
your fat intake towards omega-3. That means more walnuts, pecans
and chia than sunflower or sesame, and stay away from processed
foods containing soybean oil, corn oil and sunflower oil and don't
use these oils in frying. Also, eat more seafood than meat. Ideally,
you want a 2:1 ratio of omega-6 to omega-3 in your diet. The
average modern diet is 10:1 – lots of hidden and probably damaged
omega-6 and little omega-3.

However, the best yardstick is the level of omega-3 in your blood,
or actually the red blood cell membranes, which are generally repre-
sentative of most tissues in the body. This can be easily measured
with a home-test kit using a technique called dry bloodspot analysis,
which gives you your 'omega-3 index'. This the percentage of fats

stored in red blood cell membranes that is omega-3 EPA or DHA. Above 8 per cent is optimal. Below 4 per cent is bad. We classify this as red, while 4 to 6 per cent is orange, or at risk, and 6 to 8 per cent is yellow, which is adequate but not optimal. If you're flooded with omega-6, it will be less. In Japan, where they eat a lot of seafood, many people will score 10 per cent. You will probably have to take in 2 grams of omega-3 fish oil a day and eat fish to get above 8 per cent, but we are all different. The only way to know is to measure your level (*see Resources*).

That's what psychologists at the Linda Loma University in California did for a group of older people, publishing their results in the journal *Brain Sciences*.[47] They found that the higher a person's omega-3 index was in their blood, the more white matter there was in their brain, and the better they performed in cognitive tests that predicted less risk of dementia. A study using data from 267,312 people from the UK Biobank found that compared with people with the lowest omega-3 status, those with the highest had a 31 per cent decreased risk of developing dementia.[48]

So, what do you have to eat and/or supplement to achieve the optimal level? You can approach this from two different directions. If you do it just with diet, it means a serving of seafood a day. A serving of mackerel or salmon, for example, will give you over 2 grams of omega-3. It would also provide at least 750mg of DHA.

If you didn't eat any seafood but just took supplements, that's about 2 or 3 capsules a day, providing 2,000mg of omega-3 and sufficient DHA and EPA. (*See Resources for examples of higher-dose supplements.*)

If you took one capsule a day and ate oily fish three times a week, or any seafood four times a week, with at least two servings of any of the seafood sources above the dotted line in the chart above, that would get you into the optimal zone.

Perhaps you could get away with less if you also had a handful of omega-3 rich nuts or seeds (walnut, pecan, chia, flax) a day. However, the conversion of the omega-3 linolenic acid into, for example, DHA, is very small.

I aim to have a serving of omega-3-rich nuts or seeds most days and fish four times a week, with oily fish making up three of these portions. This could be a salmon steak, smoked salmon with scrambled eggs, a mackerel dish, or in salad, perhaps in the form of mackerel pâté and some taramasalata.

Delicious recipes for a brain-friendly diet follow in Part 4.

Phospholipids

Phospholipids are not widely known, but they are undoubtedly a brain essential, as omega-3 fats or arachidonic acid must be attached to them to work. There are a number of kinds of phospholipids, all starting with 'phosphatidyl'. These are:

Phosphatidyl choline (PC)
Phosphatidyl serine (PS)
Phosphatidyl inositol (PI)
Phosphatidyl ethanolamine (PE)

They then get attached to an omega-3 fat, for example DHA, to build that brain-cell membrane. Most DHA in your brain is attached to PI, PE or PC. So that's, for example:

> *Phosphatidyl + choline + DHA = PC-DHA,*
> *sometimes called phosphorylated DHA*

The more PC-DHA you have, the lower your risk of Alzheimer's, and the less you have, the greater your risk. Those with Alzheimer's have 2.5 times less in their blood and 20 per cent less grey matter (brain volume).[49]

Phosphatidyl choline (PC) is also the raw material for the brain to make one of its most important neurotransmitters, acetylcholine. The first generation of drugs for dementia were based on helping to protect acetylcholine and stop it breaking down. You might have noticed in Figure 6 (*page 12*), that acetylcholine is high during theta-wave activity in dreaming.

These critical phospholipids, while making up a large part of your brain, have until recently been sidelined because they are 'semi-essential', meaning we can make them to a limited extent but don't make enough, hence they are, like vitamins and essential fats, an essential part of our diet. The phosphatidyl part is easy to make; it's the other part, choline, serine, etc., that we have to eat.

'Choline crisis in the UK?'

This was the title of a report in the *British Medical Journal*,[50] pointing out that choline is an essential nutrient, much like omega-3 fats, and that it is vital for health, especially for the brain, but it is not sufficiently supplied in many people's diets, especially those who are largely vegan.

While the body can make a little, it does not make enough, and thus choline is being reclassified as an essential nutrient, with an adequate intake defined as between 400mg and 520mg a day, the latter for pregnant and breastfeeding women. But these levels don't relate at all to brain function. Research on the brain's need for choline has not been considered by the European Food Standards Agency, who did, however, allow the claims that 'choline is needed for lipids metabolism', 'maintaining healthy liver functioning' and 'reduction in homocysteine levels'. (We also need choline to do the right thing with cholesterol in the liver.)

But choline's role in building and maintaining a healthy brain is even more important. A pregnant woman's intake defines the cognitive abilities of their child. Twenty years ago, we knew that pregnant rats fed choline halfway through their pregnancy had more connections between their brain cells, plus improved learning ability and better memory recall. Now we know it's true for babies. In fact, a lack of choline can lead to a shrinking of a woman's brain as the foetus robs it to build its own – a case of 'Mummy, I shrank your brain.' Babies are born with blood choline levels three times higher than those of their mother, illustrating how vital this nutrient is for building neuronal connections, which newborn babies do at a phenomenal rate. An optimal choline intake for brain function is likely to be a lot higher than the 400mg recommended for adults.

This is suggested by a study in which women in their third trimester of pregnancy were given either 480mg of choline or almost double this – 930mg.[51] The researchers then tested the babies' information-processing speed at four, seven, ten and thirteen months. Not only were the babies of the mothers given the higher dose faster, but also the longer the mother had been given even the lower dose, the faster the child's reactions. The authors concluded that: 'Even modest increases in maternal choline intake during pregnancy may produce cognitive benefits for offspring.' Seven years later, the children whose mothers had had extra choline during pregnancy still had memory advantages.

Of course, we do not know if a non-pregnant person needs quite this much for optimal brain function or if those with cognitive problems need more. But this kind of intake is more consistent with what our ancestors would have eaten in their marine-food-rich diet.

Without choline, omega-3 doesn't work. The attaching of the two depends on methylation, a process dependent on B vitamins, as we have seen. (*More on this synergy in the next chapter.*) Choline helps methylation, and healthy methylation, indicated by a low homocysteine level, helps synthesize choline. It's a 'win–win' if you have both enough choline and enough B vitamins, plus omega-3.

The reason the title of the *British Medical Journal*'s report says 'crisis' is that more people are eating a plant-based diet and shunning eggs, fish and meat, which are the best sources of not only choline, but also B12. There's a tiny bit of choline in broccoli and in nuts, but not enough. An egg provides around 120mg, a 50g beef or salmon steak around 50mg. The same amount of almonds or broccoli gives about 25mg. Cow's milk has a little, but just a fraction of that found in human milk. Beef liver is the richest source. Eggs are by far the best source.

Twenty years ago, I found the evidence sufficiently compelling to recommend eating an egg a day, three servings of fish and one of meat (or another portion of fish) a week, and a handful of nuts a day, plus daily supplementation of circa 100mg, which is what I do in my daily 'Brain Food' formula (*see Resources*). If you also ate a serving of broccoli a day, you'd be achieving something like 2,100mg a week, or 300mg a day – still short of daily requirements for the body (circa 450mg), let alone the brain. So you really have to be 'on it', eating eggs, fish, broccoli, almonds, or some meat or liver if you're that way inclined, to get your choline levels up to optimal.

Plant-based diets fall short on choline

If you don't eat eggs, fish or meat and don't supplement, there's no way of getting even close. That's why it's time to add choline, along with omega-3 DHA and B12, to the list of nutrients that must certainly be supplemented by those eating a vegan diet, but probably us all. Lecithin granules and capsules are the richest vegan source of choline, derived from soya.

Here's a list of the best plant-based food for choline,* compared to egg and fish as a yardstick and listed in order of how much you could get in a reasonable serving:

Food	Choline per serving	per 100g
An egg (all in the yolk) (50g)	113mg	226mg
Fish e.g. salmon (100g)	90mg	90mg
Soya milk (250ml)	57mg	23mg
Shiitake mushrooms (145g)	54mg	37mg
Soya flour (12.5g/standard cake slice)	24mg	192mg
Peas (160g)	47mg	30mg
Quinoa, raw (60g)	42mg	70mg
Beans, raw e.g. black, white, pinto, kidney (60g)	40mg	67mg
Broccoli, cauliflower or sprouts (91g)	36mg	40mg
Tofu (125g)	35mg	28mg
Hummus (112g)	34mg	28mg
Chickpeas (¼ can)	33mg	33mg
Baked beans (¼ can)	31mg	31mg
Flaxseeds (small handful)	22mg	78mg
Pistachios (small handful)	20mg	71mg
Pine nuts (small handful)	18mg	65mg
Cashews (small handful)	17mg	61mg
Wholegrain bread (50g/2 slices)	17mg	34mg
Avocado (½)	14mg	28mg
Almonds (50g/small handful)	12mg	42mg
Peanuts (small handful)	12mg	42mg
Wheatgerm (7g/tbsp)	12mg	178mg
Almond or peanut butter (tbsp)	10mg	61mg

Source: USDA choline content database and nutritiondata.self.com.

* Many foods have not been analysed for choline, and measurements do vary, so this is a guide rather than a definitive list.

A vegan would have to be very committed to maximize their choline intake, and they'd still not get enough. Here's an example of a vegan diet maximizing choline in foods, that would achieve a total of 332mg, perhaps a third of the optimal intake for the brain, and certainly below that required during pregnancy to build a healthy baby's brain.

Breakfast: 250ml soya milk (57mg); a small handful of nuts or
    seeds – flax, chia, almonds, etc. (20mg)
Lunch: 185g cooked quinoa, or 60g raw (43mg); a 100g serving of
    either broccoli (36mg), cauliflower or Brussels sprouts; half an
    avocado (14mg)
Snacks: a tablespoon of almond or peanut butter (10mg); half a cup
    of hummus (34mg); two slices of wholegrain bread (17mg)
Dinner: a 125g serving of tofu or beans (35–40mg); 72g of shiitake
    mushrooms (27mg); a 100g serving of either broccoli (36mg),
    cauliflower or Brussels sprouts
Total: 332mg

All this is the equivalent of three eggs. So, if you ate six eggs a week and four servings of fish, or perhaps three and some servings of meat, plus some of these more choline-rich foods such as nuts and broccoli, you'd also achieve over 300mg a day – still a bit short.

Therefore, most people, especially those not eating eggs or fish, must supplement choline, ideally as phosphatidyl choline. The most direct source of choline is from soya-derived lecithin granules and capsules. A flat tablespoon of lecithin granules (7.5g), which has a neutral and pleasant taste and can be sprinkled on cereals, or in shakes and soups, or eaten as is, provides 1,500mg of phosphatidylcholine and around 200mg (13 per cent) of choline. Some 'high-phosphatidyl choline' lecithin, sometimes called 'high-PC lecithin' is 18 per cent choline, thus you need less – approximately a flat dessertspoon.

One tablespoon of lecithin granules equals three 1,200mg lecithin capsules (if 'high-PC', two capsules would suffice). I suggest that this is a sensible addition to a completely plant-based diet. (If you aspire to be plant-based most but not all of the time, the addition of two eggs, or an egg and a fish serving, would achieve 500mg a day of choline.)

You can also find 'brain food' supplements providing a combination of different kinds of phospholipids, not just choline, but it's hard to get enough choline from these if your only other food sources are plant-based. I supplement an additional 100mg a day of choline in my 'Brain Food' supplement or two lecithin 1,200mg capsules a day, which give over 1,600mg of phospholipids including 250mg of phosphatidyl choline.

In summary, we need both omega-6 and omega-3 fats, as well as phospholipids.

If you are not vegan, the best food source for phospholipids and choline is eggs. Eat six eggs a week. The choline is in the yolk. The advice regarding omega-3 – eat three servings of fish a week – is good for choline too, but it is present in all fish, not just oily fish high in omega-3 fats. Putting all this together, the advice is:

- Eat oily fish three times a week or any seafood four times a week, with at least two servings of any of the seafood sources above the dotted line in the chart on page 111.
- Take a DHA-rich omega-3 fish-oil capsule daily (or two if you don't eat fish).
- Eat six eggs a week.
- Consider supplementing additional choline in a brain-friendly supplement or lecithin.

If strictly plant-based:

- Have one or two servings a day of dark green, leafy veg, especially those that grow in colder climates, such as kale, broccoli and Brussels sprouts, or a serving of seaweed, as sources of both choline and omega-3, in addition to omega-3-rich nuts and seeds (chia, flax, walnut, pecan).
- Have a serving of quinoa, beans or tofu every day, if not two, for choline.
- Have a dessertspoon of high-PC lecithin, or two capsules of high-PC lecithin, every day. These guidelines are especially important if you are planning a pregnancy, pregnant or breastfeeding.
- Supplement omega-3 DHA, derived from algae, plus B12 (*see the previous chapter*).

A word about cholesterol – a brain essential

A quarter of all our cholesterol is in our brain, and 80 per cent of that is in the membranes, where it holds all those phosphorylated omega-3s in place. It is therefore vital for building brain cells and their connections and sending messages between brain cells. Much of this cholesterol is made in the brain but, like choline, it is semi-essential – we can make it, but some comes from our diet, with egg yolks being the richest source. It should therefore be no surprise that having too little (below 4 mmol/l) increases the risk of dementia.

In a study that looked at commonly measured biomarkers to identify who might be at risk of dementia, having a high homocysteine level (i.e. low B-vitamin status) or a low cholesterol best predicted risk.[52]

A major cause of low cholesterol is the inappropriate prescription of cholesterol-lowering statins. The majority of statin trials have failed to show a reduced risk of cognitive decline in dementia.[53]

Earlier we spoke about the ApoE4 gene variation. The ApoE gene makes apo-lipoprotein, which carries cholesterol into those neuronal membranes, building the brain. Those with ApoE4 are *less good* at transporting cholesterol. So, the reason ApoE4 seems to increase risk of brain degeneration is precisely because cholesterol isn't being delivered.

The reason why there was hope for statins helping dementia in the first place was that 'vascular dementia', meaning damaged and narrowed blood supply, hence nutrient supply to the brain, accounted for almost a fifth of dementia. But it is not 'excess cholesterol' that is driving either vascular dementia or Alzheimer's, or indeed heart disease (for more on this, see my book *Say No to Heart Disease* or Dr Malcolm Kendrick's books *The Cholesterol Con* or *The Clot Thickens*, or listen to my podcast with him on podbean.patrick-holford).

In fact, the very same things that drive dementia also drive vascular disease. What is good for the brain is good for the heart. An illustration of this is a recent study that found that having a high homocysteine level increased the risk of cerebrovascular disease by 17 times![54] It also increased the risk of cognitive decline by 10 times.

In the world of nutritional therapy, we do not consider that having slightly raised cholesterol (up to 6mmol/l) is a problem if you eat a low-sugar/carb diet, thus have low levels of blood glucose and low blood fats called triglycerides. We are more interested in your 'good' HDL cholesterol level being high. In another study, having a high HDL level in midlife predicted a significantly lower future risk of dementia, while having a high glucose level (but within the normal range) predicted a significantly greater risk.[55]

In summary:

- It is sugar, not fat, but also raised homocysteine and a lack of omega-3 that are driving cerebrovascular disease.
- It is not cholesterol. Cholesterol is a brain essential, thus eggs are positively good for your brain.

10

Omega-3 and the B Vitamins - a Dynamic Duo

The last two chapters have established that upping your omega-3 and lowering your homocysteine with B vitamins are vital steps for a brain upgrade. Also, that phospholipids are another of your brain's best friends.

You've also learned about the B-vitamin trial by Professor David Smith and colleagues at Oxford that produced 53 per cent less brain shrinkage and nine times less shrinkage of the areas of the brain affected by Alzheimer's, stopping or slowing cognitive decline considerably in those with mild cognitive impairment. This effect was only seen in people whose homocysteine level was above 11mcmol/l, but was better than the amyloid treatments now being touted as the 'turning-point' in dementia treatment.

But I'd be only telling you part of the story if I said that all trials of B vitamins and omega-3 fish oils have worked.

Failed trials of B vitamins and omega-3

Admittedly, some of these trials haven't selected people with raised homocysteine and some haven't given enough B vitamins and some might have just given them too late – in those with Alzheimer's.

An example is a trial that gave B vitamins or placebos to doctors over 65 years old who had no hint of memory problems or associated risk factors[56] – no raised homocysteine levels, for example. They were assessed on a telephone test called TICS, with a maximum score of 40, over an average of 8.5 years. At the start of the study, both those in the placebo group and those in the B-vitamin group scored a healthy 34.3 – no cognitive problems. The vitamin supplement they choose, Centrum Senior, was basically a low-dose RDA multivitamin with a little extra B6 (20mg), folic acid (400mcg) and B12 (25mcg). This is much too low an amount of B12 for someone with high homocysteine. After 2 years, the average in both groups had barely changed – 33.8 in the placebo group and 33.9 in the supplement group. In essence this was a study of a well-educated, reasonably well-nourished group of doctors, not 'at risk' and given relatively low levels of vitamins. The only real conclusion that can be drawn is that giving a multivitamin does not enhance cognition in people without cognitive impairment. But would you realistically expect it to?

However, the B-PROOF trial in Holland gave people with homocysteine above 12 a supplement containing 400mcg folic acid and 500mcg vitamin B12 or a placebo tablet.[57] So that's the right selection of people and the right dose of B vitamins. Two years later, homocysteine had dropped by 5 points in the B-vitamin group, but cognition, as measured by a rather basic memory test called MMSE, had decreased by 0.1 points in the B-vitamin group and 0.3 points in the placebo group. This benefit was positive but not statistically significant. However, an editorial on this study ludicrously concluded that this result provided evidence that 'B vitamins are harmful or ineffective for chronic disease prevention'.

Since then, a recent three-year trial, using the same multivitamin but a more sensitive memory test, has shown benefit, reporting those on the multivitamin becoming the equivalent of three years younger in relation to memory.[58]

What about omega-3? It's a similar story. Studies with too low omega-3 levels, or given too late in the disease process, usually haven't worked. But one study in Sweden, called OmegAD,[59] gave either a placebo or a hefty 2.3 grams of omega-3, providing 1.7g of DHA, which is certainly in the optimal range, and those given the high-dose omega-3 didn't fare better. The 179 participants had mild to moderate Alzheimer's, so perhaps it was too small, too short and probably too late in the disease process?

Why did these well-designed trials fail?

Are omega-3 and B vitamins co-dependent?

As the scientific community unravelled how brain cells worked, and how methylation (dependent on B vitamins) was needed to 'bind' omega-3 DHA to the phospholipid (usually phosphatidyl choline), Professor David Smith and his colleague Dr Frederick Jerneren wondered if the results of their landmark B-vitamin trial would have been better in those with higher omega-3 levels. It was too late to give omega-3, but they could go back to the original blood samples taken at the start of the trial and measure the omega-3 status of the participants.

They split the group into thirds and found that the B-vitamin treatment didn't work at all in the third with the lowest omega-3 status, but in the group with the highest omega-3 DHA, the results were remarkable. The reduction in brain shrinkage wasn't the average of 52 per cent seen in their first study, but 73 per cent less![60] That brought the rate of brain shrinkage down to that which normally occurs in older people with no memory problems at all! (Compare this to the most recent anti-amyloid drug treatment, donanemab, where the rate of whole brain shrinkage *increased* by over 20 per cent.)

The same thing happened to their cognition: those with low omega-3 status had no benefit from the B-vitamin treatment, while those with higher omega-3 levels had a remarkable improvement, with virtually no further memory loss.

That got the B-PROOF trial researchers wondering if their trial had failed because of a lack of omega-3. So they went back to their original blood samples and measured the omega-3 DHA status of the participants. They found exactly the same thing – those with the lowest omega-3 levels had no memory benefits from the B vitamins, while those in the top third for omega-3 DHA had a massive benefit which was statistically significant, so, once again, showing that the homocysteine-lowering B vitamins, which should work by improving methylation in those with raised homocysteine, don't work if you haven't got enough omega-3 DHA to build a healthy brain.[61]

Then in Sweden, the failed OmegAD trial researchers teamed up with the Oxford researchers to reanalyse their results, wondering if the B-vitamin status of their participants who had Alzheimer's might have been the reason for their lack of result. So they went back to their original blood samples, this time splitting the group into those with a homocysteine score below 11.7, meaning better B-vitamin status, those with a homocysteine score above 15.7 and those in between.[62] They found a massive benefit in terms of cognitive improvement in those with the lower homocysteine levels given the omega-3 supplement. The benefit in those given omega-3 with a homocysteine below 11.7 was several times greater than that of any anti-amyloid treatment.

Give a builder a hammer. Do you get a house? No. Give a builder a bag of nails. Do you get a house? No. Give a builder some planks of wood. Do you get a house? No. Give a builder a hammer, a bag of nails and some planks of wood and you get a house. This analogy is pretty much what's going on in your brain. The wood is omega-3, the nail is the phospholipid and the hammer is the methylating B vitamins. You need *both* enough omega-3 DHA and enough phospholipids providing choline (to make phosphatidyl choline), as well as good methylation, meaning a low homocysteine level, which is a result of B-vitamin supply, bearing in mind that some people need a much higher intake of B12 due to poor absorption.

We need a definitive trial on omega-3 plus B vitamins

The discovery of the co-dependence of B vitamins and omega-3 in protecting memory begs for a trial combining the two. This trial was ready to run seven years ago, designed by one of the UK's leading neurologists, Professor Peter Garrard at the University of London's Neuroscience Research Section. It's large enough and long enough to definitely answer the question as to whether giving B vitamins and omega-3 to those with mild cognitive impairment will prevent them from developing Alzheimer's. But no one will fund it.

While the cost of developing Alzheimer's drugs has been estimated at $42.5 billion by 2021,[63] and by now will be much more, both European and British governments and research agencies have so far refused to fund this relatively inexpensive trial costing £3 million. Meanwhile a Department of Health and Social Care spokesperson has said, 'We are working hard to find a cure for dementia, doubling research funding to £160 million a year by 2024–25.'[64]

Two leading Alzheimer's charities are given and spend over £30 million a year on research, but virtually none goes into real prevention – and none into the most promising, evidence-based preventative: B vitamins and omega-3. In the UK, there is a complete blind spot when it comes to non-drug prevention. The most widely used review for dementia prevention, the 2020 report of the *Lancet* Commission,[65] authored by Professor Gill Livingston, fails to even mention homocysteine, despite being sent all the evidence by the Oxford group of the undeniable beneficial effects of homocysteine-lowering B vitamins.

Supplementing B vitamins and omega-3 might cost you £100 a year. The cost of the latest amyloid drug is £20,700, plus all the necessary medical costs and scans to check for the common adverse effects of brain swelling and bleeding. This approach, if rolled out, would cost billions of pounds. The B-vitamin and omega-3 approach would save billions of pounds. Is it any wonder healthcare is failing?

Could omega-3 and homocysteine-lowering B vitamins eliminate half of all Alzheimer's risk?

A risk factor is assessed for its impact using a measure called the population attributable risk (PAR). Professor May Beydoun at the US National Institutes of Health did this for both raised homocysteine (lack of B vitamins) and low intake of seafood or omega-3. For Alzheimer's, the attributable risk or each of these was 22 per cent – that's 44 per cent combined.[66] It's not quite fair to add these two together, though, because there is overlap – someone could have both risk factors. It would be more reasonable to say that these two easily resolved risk factors might account for a third of all risk of Alzheimer's. But now we know that B vitamins and omega-3 are co-dependent, which means that the beneficial effect of B vitamins has been vastly underestimated because omega-3 status wasn't taken into account, and similarly, the effect of omega-3 has been vastly underestimated by not factoring in B-vitamin status.

The best 'meta-analysis' of all risk factors for Alzheimer's, looking at 396 studies in total, concluded: 'Homocysteine-lowering treatment seems the most promising intervention for AD prevention.'[67] This review, in 2020, also didn't factor in what we now know about the dynamic duo of omega-3 plus B vitamins.

The take-home message is to make sure you have both sufficient omega-3 and B vitamins in your diet and supplement programme. In Part 4 I'll put this all together for you in an easy-to-follow brain-upgrade action plan.

In summary, we have learned that:

- Trials giving too few B vitamins to people without raised homocysteine or without sufficient omega-3 or too late in the disease process have failed.
- Omega-3 and homocysteine-lowering B vitamins are co-dependent.
- All trials to date giving either B vitamins to those sufficient in omega-3 or omega-3 to those with a lower homocysteine level, thus better B-vitamin status, have succeeded in reducing brain shrinkage and improving cognitive function far better than any drug treatment to date.
- To keep your brain healthy, you need three nutrients: omega-3 DHA, which attaches to phospholipids (primarily phosphatidyl choline), which is done by the methylating B vitamins – B6, B12 and folate. These are the brain's most essential nutrients.

11

Is Sugar Killing Your Brain? Why Low-Carb Is Brain-Friendly

Sugar and our now standard high-carb diets are a major health problem. To put this in context, more people have died from diet-related diseases, primarily driven by high sugar, ultra-processed foods and refined carbohydrates, than in the First and Second World Wars combined. A big study in the *Journal of the American Medical Association* in 2017 concluded: 'Nearly half of all deaths due to heart disease, stroke, and type 2 diabetes in the USA in 2012 were associated with suboptimal nutrition.'[68] That's hundreds of thousands of deaths in the USA, and over 1 million a year globally, as a result of our cultural shift towards addictive high-sugar foods. Diseases such as diabetes are almost non-existent in cultures which have not been exposed to our fast, highly processed, sugared foods. Sub-optimum nutrition, in this study, also included a lack of seafood, nuts and seeds high in essential omega-3 fats.

Most people know that refined sugar is not good for us, but what is it about sugar that's particularly bad for our brain? My go-to guy on issues of sugar and mental health is Dr Robert Lustig, Professor Emeritus of Pediatrics in the Division of Endocrinology and a member of the Institute for Health Policy Studies at the University of California, San Francisco. He is also a paediatric neuroendocrinologist and an international authority on obesity, diabetes, nutrition and neuroscience. He's our 'sugar man' on the Scientific Advisory Board at Food for the Brain.

Dr Robert Lustig is also known for his hard-hitting books, *Fat Chance*, which lays bare the truth about carbs and how fat has been wrongly demonized, *Hacking the American Mind*, on how our brains have been hijacked, and his latest, *Metabolical*, explaining how almost all of the major diseases of both mind and body are driven by the same underlying problems.

Too much sugar and too many carbs and ultra-processed foods are bad for anyone at any age. They, or a higher glycaemic load, are linked to children's mental health issues relating to symptoms of ADHD[69] and autism and adult anxiety and depression,[70] and strongly linked to increased risk of age-related cognitive decline, dementia and Alzheimer's. Even the glycaemic load of a mother's diet predicts a massive four-fold risk of anxiety in toddlers, with five times more impulsivity in boys, and four times as many sleeping problems, while girls have 15 times the likelihood of anxiety in those in the top third for glycaemic load.[71]

I asked Dr Robert Lustig, 'Why is it essential, not only for brain health at every stage of life but also dementia prevention, to reduce your intake of not only sugar but refined carbohydrates in general?' (By 'refined', I mean those carbohydrates whose fibre has been processed away, leaving them looking whiter, not 'whole'.)

'Let's start at the extreme,' he replied. 'What would happen if you lived at the North Pole, and ate virtually no carbohydrates, or at least so few as to force your body and brain to switch to ketones, a kind of fuel produced from fat? This is often called a "very low-carb, high-fat (LCHF)" or "ketogenic" diet. Would you get sick? This is how Vilhjamur Stefansson lived when his Arctic exploration party was shipwrecked in 1913 and he was forced to live among the Inuit for two years. He noted that there was no diabetes there, no cancer – and no Alzheimer's. In 1928, he and his colleague checked themselves into Bellevue Hospital in New York and ate only meat for one year.[72] By the end of it, they were healthier than the researchers who studied them!'

How sugar damages the brain

The brain can run on either glucose or ketones (*see the film* Fuel Your Brain *at foodforthebrain.org/fuel-your-brain-for-better-memory/*)

and in the next chapter we'll explore the advantages for the brain of switching over to run on more ketones than glucose. (The body always produces a background of glucose, so it's not strictly 'either/ or' but whether ketones or glucose has become your main brain fuel.)

'But what is it about a ketogenic diet that is good for your brain?' asks Lustig. 'Is it the ketones, the lowering of insulin, the type of fat, the elimination of carbohydrate, or specifically the elimination of sugar? We don't yet know – I ask this question of every Alzheimer's and metabolic researcher I know, and no one can tell me – just that it works.

'There are a few possible mechanisms. First, the more carbs and sugar you eat, the more resistant you become to the hormone insulin. Insulin not only drives glucose into cells, including brain cells, but also sends excess sugar to the liver to turn into fat. When a person becomes insulin resistant, ironically, glucose transport is negatively impacted, reducing brain energy availability. Insulin resistance is a major driver of depression.'[73]

A ketogenic diet can reverse that by filling the 'energy' gap in the brain caused by insulin resistance. Ketones don't need insulin to enter cells.

Fructose, which comprises half of sucrose ('white' or 'table' sugar), and half of high-fructose corn syrup (which is added to numerous processed foods), overwhelms our mitochondria, our cells' energy factories, which leads to less brain energy availability.

One study showed that fructose reduced liver mitochondrial function, while glucose stimulated it.[74]

'The most important takeaway of this study is that high fructose in the diet is bad,' said Dr Ronald Kahn from the Joslin Diabetes Center in Boston, Massachusetts. 'It's not bad because it's more calories, but because it affects liver metabolism to make it worse at burning fat. As a result, adding fructose to the diet makes the liver store more fat, and this is bad for the liver and bad for whole body metabolism.'

Eat your fruit – don't drink it

Lustig points out, 'Fructose is the main sugar in most fruit. People then extrapolate, "Oh, fruit must be bad for you." Not true. Whole fruit has fibre, both soluble and insoluble. Together, they slow down glucose and fructose absorption in the gastro-intestinal tract, limiting both liver and brain exposure, and they also help feed the gut bacteria, the microbiome, so actually you get less fructose entering the bloodstream. Juicing the fruit removes the protective fibre, and juice has been shown to be just as dangerous to the metabolism as soda. So, eat your fruit – don't drink it!'

Carbohydrates and fructose age your brain

There's another reason, he says, why sugar, especially fructose, is bad for your brain and body. 'Sugars produce advanced glycation endproducts, or AGEs, which damage the brain. These "oxidize" proteins, as does cigarette smoke, rendering them useless and allowing them to aggregate into clumps and use up valuable antioxidants in your diet such as vitamins C and E.

'Fructose acts on your liver to switch your metabolism away from fat burning to fat making and storing, and inhibits an anti-ageing process called autophagy, which helps clean up and remove damaged mitochondria in order to regenerate new, healthier cells.'

Why sweet foods are so addictive

So far we've only explored why sugar is bad for your 'physical' brain. Knowing this is a good start. But why does your 'emotional' brain keep telling you that you want it? Why do people find it so hard to resist, and so many become sugar addicts?

The answer is that fructose activates the reward system in the brain, causing the release of dopamine, the motivational neurotransmitter associated with 'reward'. As we've already seen, any chemical that does so can be addictive – cocaine, heroin, alcohol, nicotine... The more you have, the more your brain 'downregulates', making you less responsive to your own natural feel-good dopamine, so you end up needing more sugar to get the hit, and in the end you get no hit at all, but feel thoroughly awful without it.

'It's tolerance, or the law of diminishing returns, that leads to addiction,' says Lustig.

Blood sugar control reduces dementia risk

Blood glucose levels in the low–normal range are reflected by a low blood glycosylated haemoglobin (HbA1c) level, which means 'sugar-coated red blood cells'. If your doctor suspects you might be heading for diabetes, they'll measure your HbA1c level, because if over 7 per cent of your red blood cells are 'glycosylated' or sugar damaged, that diagnoses you as diabetic. Having a level above 6.5 is considered pre-diabetic, but really you want your level to be below 5.5. (In the UK this is now measured differently, with above 50mmol/mol as high and below 36mmol/mol as optimal.) Teenagers with an HbA1c above 5.4 show brain shrinkage and cognitive decline similar to that seen in dementia.[75] The youngest non-genetic dementia diagnosis is that of a 19-year-old man in China. A low HbA1c is good and is a proxy for insulin sensitivity, which has been associated with a reduced risk of dementia in several studies.[76]

Type 2 diabetes, the net result of losing blood sugar control, almost doubles the risk of dementia.[77] Diabetes is also associated with more rapid brain shrinkage.[78] Even people in the upper normal blood glucose range have increased brain atrophy, impaired cognition and increased risk of dementia.[79]

For instance, one trial measured HbA1c and glucose levels in several thousand elderly people over the course of almost seven years. In that time, slightly more than a quarter of the participants developed dementia, and the bottom line was that rising glucose levels were associated with increased risk of developing the condition, irrespective of whether the participants also had diabetes. Non-diabetics who experienced a modest increase in blood sugar levels had an 18 per cent increased risk of dementia, as compared with those who already had diabetes at the start of the study or developed it within the trial period, who had a 40 per cent increased risk.[80]

Insulin resistance is strongly related to cognitive decline

Dr Lustig considers that the loss of insulin control is even more important than the loss of glucose control. Back in 2004, researchers at Columbia University showed that people with high insulin levels – the principal hallmark of metabolic dysfunction – were twice as likely to develop dementia as those with healthy levels. Moreover, those with the highest insulin levels had the worst memory retrieval.[81] The same year, an Italian study established a link between heightened insulin levels and declining mental function.[82] Similarly, a Puerto Rican study found that people who consumed large amounts of sugar doubled their risk of suffering poor cognitive function,[83] while another US study discovered a strong correlation between blood sugar level and memory loss.[84]

Two studies – one in Ireland[85] and the other in the United States[86] – established a link between high dietary glycaemic load (GL) and cognitive decline. (GL is the measure of the total glucose load on your bloodstream, which is both how high your blood glucose rises and for how long when you eat carbohydrate.) Indeed, both of these reports suggest that high GL is even more predictive of the pathological changes associated with Alzheimer's than either high carb or high sugar intake. A high-GL diet is also associated with more amyloid plaque[87] and more cognitive decline, especially in those who carry the ApoE4 gene, which helps regulate fat metabolism.[88]

A long-term study found evidence that this sort of shrinkage is more common among people with high blood glucose levels, even when those levels are still within what are considered 'normal' (i.e., non-diabetic) limits.[89]

'This cognitive decline starts young,' says Lustig. 'Cognitive decline in overweight children is associated with a high-GL diet,[90] and adolescents with metabolic dysfunction driven by a high-GL diet have been shown to have shrinkage of the hippocampal area of the brain, as well as other structural changes and cognitive deficits.'[91]

This particular study showed actual shrinkage of the Alzheimer's-associated area of the brain in teenagers with metabolic syndrome as a consequence of too much sugar and 'white' carbs.

Preventative action – how to cut down your sugar load

One of the most obvious indicators that your sugar and/or carb intake is too high is weight gain. Another is sugar cravings. In practical terms, protecting your brain and preventing dementia means avoiding sugar as much as possible. You could even go one step further and go ketogenic (*see the next chapter*). If you're going to eat carbohydrates, eat 'whole' carbohydrate foods such as whole vegetables, fruits (not juice), beans, only wholegrain bread (labelled as '100 per cent wholegrain'), or pasta in small quantities.

Starchy carbohydrates such as pasta, rice and potatoes benefit from being cooked and cooled, then eaten cold or reheated, as that way some of the carbohydrate is converted into resistant starch – a type of fibre we can't digest but which has the added benefit of fermenting and feeding our gut bacteria.

Make sure the carbohydrate comes with its inherent fibre. Oatcakes would be better than bread, since the fibre helps 'slow release' the sugars. Eating white bread is associated with a poorer cognitive test performance, whereas high-fibre bread is associated with better performance.[92] The less squishy, more solid a loaf, the lower its GL. Eating carbohydrate foods with protein, for example brown rice with fish, or porridge oats with seeds, or fruit with nuts, further reduces the glycaemic load. The best fruits in this respect are low-sugar, high-fibre fruits like berries, cherries and plums.

These kinds of foods are consistent with a Mediterranean diet, which has also been shown to reduce risk.[93] Conversely, grapes, raisins and bananas are high-GL.

A study in Finland and Sweden compared those with a healthy versus unhealthy diet, including the above criteria, in midlife for the risk of developing Alzheimer's disease and dementia 14 years later. Those who ate the healthiest diet had an 88 per cent decreased risk of developing dementia and a 92 per cent decreased risk of developing Alzheimer's disease.[94]

The take-home message is, if you are going to eat complex carbohydrates, eat them with fibre, fat and protein, as I'll show you in the Brain-Friendly Diet in Chapter 25.

However, if you want to go one step further, you can switch to eating a ketogenic low-carb, high-fat diet, which we'll explore in the next chapter.

In summary, we have learned that:

- Sugar, and especially high-fructose corn-derived sugar, damages the brain.
- Too much sugar and too many refined carbohydrates, and carbohydrates in general, leads to insulin resistance, which starves the brain of fuel, leading to cognitive decline.
- The best way to measure your sugar status is an HbA1c blood test, with the goal to be below 5.4 per cent, ideally around or below 5 per cent. (*See page 316 for more on testing.*)
- Nature never provides sugar, as in fruit, without fibre, so eat your fruit, don't drink it.
- A low-carb diet is brain-friendly.

Is Fat the Best Brain Fuel? Your Brain Loves Ketones

One of the hottest discoveries in brain health is the positive effect of switching the fuel for your brain from sugar to ketones, derived from fat. High-fat, low-carb diets designed to put you in 'ketosis', with measurable levels of ketones flowing in your bloodstream and consequently brain, have been shown to help memory loss, mood, concentration and more serious disorders, from Alzheimer's to schizophrenia, and also epilepsy and Parkinson's.

All cells in the body can burn either sugar or fatty acids, derived from fat. That fat can come from fat you've eaten or your own fat if you go on a low-calorie diet or fast. However, brain cells cannot. There are so many of these neurons – some 100 billion of them – packed into such a small area that there isn't any free space, so they have to use the cleanest, fastest, most efficient fuel, rather than inefficient fat. Usually this is glucose, but when the glucose 'engine' starts to malfunction, as often happens with diabetics and those with memory decline, ketones, manufactured in the liver from fat, are a terrific alternative source of energy for the brain.

Under these circumstances, the brain often derives a fifth of its energy from ketones. 'Fuelling cells' called astrocytes, which help prep the ketones, are even positioned next to the neurons. Ketones may even be a preferred fuel, especially for those with age-related memory decline.

At the other end of the spectrum, ketones are essential to build babies' brains. Babies are born with 50 trillion brain connections and need to make millions a minute in the first few months, with the brain consuming 75 per cent of all energy from food! There's a limit to how much glucose it can use and the only way it can get all the energy it needs for rapid building is from ketones. That's why human breastmilk is relatively high in medium-chain triglycerides (MCTs). Body fat, or fat we eat, is then turned into ketones in the liver. This is also why babies are born plump, unlike the young of most mammals.

Babies can survive on the ketones that their livers produce from their own fat reserves for as long as 60 days, and interestingly, even a high-carb diet doesn't push them out of ketosis.

You don't have to generate ketones for the brain to work optimally, even though it might help. Normally, the brain uses about a quarter (22 per cent) of the total energy we take in from food. We can get all that from glucose. However, if there are ketones in our system, the brain will use them in preference.

C8 oil

Ketones are only made in the liver from MCTs. The backbone of a fat molecule is a chain of carbon atoms. An MCT is between 6 and 12 carbon atoms long. In contrast, olive oil is a long-chain fat, with 14 carbon atoms. Coconut, palm and olive oil are sources of MCTs. However, recent research as shown in Figure 19 below has proven that almost all ketones are made from a sub-fraction of these fats called C8 (short for carbon 8, or caprylic acid triglyceride, an 8-carbon-chain fat).[95] Coconut oil is only 7 per cent C8, while most MCT oil, which you can buy in a health-food store, is 12 per cent C8. You're better off getting pure C8 oil, which is also available in health-food stores and online (*see Resources*), if you want to supply your brain with ketones. C10 is the next best, but it's not nearly so good for making ketones.

Two breakthrough studies in Canada, by Dr Melanie Fortier and Professor Stephen Cunnane from Sherbrooke University, have established that C8 oil can be extremely helpful as an energy source for those with cognitive decline. Cunnane's research team gave people with either Alzheimer's[96] or pre-dementia[97] two tablespoons of MCT oil (30g of C8 and C10) or a placebo and measured their cognitive abilities, as well as how much energy their brains made.

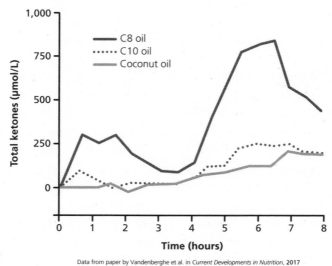

Fig 19. Which types of fat produce the most ketones?

They kept making the same amount of energy from glucose, but had a 230 per cent increase in energy made from ketones. As they started making more energy, certain areas in their brains lit up. These related to functions such as memory and language, and on tests, these improved.

'Measures of episodic memory, language, executive function, and processing speed improved on the C8 versus baseline. Increased brain ketone uptake was positively related to several cognitive measures,' reported Cunnane.

Professor Cunnane is another member of our Scientific Advisory Board at Food for the Brain and holds the chair in ketotherapeutics at the university. His research has shown that Alzheimer's patients start to suffer glucose deficiency in certain regions of the brain even before they start to experience any symptoms. There may be various reasons for this, but the most likely candidate is insulin resistance, which makes it more difficult for the fuel to make its way into the neurons. This makes sense, as diabetics are three times more likely to develop Alzheimer's than non-diabetics.

'We know from our scanning research that the glucose deficit is not due to damage to the neurons, but to insufficient amounts being available as fuel,' explains Cunnane. 'It's safe to treat this deficiency with ketones.'

On the other hand, if the condition remains untreated, the fuel-deprived neurons suffer the sort of damage that ultimately leads to Alzheimer's.

Meanwhile, in New Zealand neurologists decided to test the effects on 26 people diagnosed with Alzheimer's by putting them onto a low-carb ketogenic diet for 12 weeks or a healthy low-fat but not ketogenic diet as the 'control', with each participant following both diets.[98] On the ketogenic diet, there were improvements in their daily function and quality of life measures, which is quite remarkable at this late stage of the disease process.

Mind the brain energy gap with ketones

'People with cognitive decline have an energy gap,' says Cunnane. 'Probably due to insulin resistance, they are not able to make use of glucose. Providing a food source, C8 oil, from which the body can readily make ketones, fills that energy gap, brain cells come back to life and memory and brain function improve as a result. It reminds me of those announcements on the London Underground: "Mind the gap."'

Practically, as in his studies, that means having a couple of tablespoons of C8 oil. The energy effect lasts for a few hours, so this might be best administered by taking a teaspoon two or three times a day, then building up to 2 teaspoons three times a day. It's a pleasant, creamy taste. A few people get gastrointestinal upset from these oils, which is mitigated by emulsifying, for example having the oil in a smoothie, or having it with a meal, or building up the dose slowly over time.

Some people have C8 oil with their coffee, as advocated by low-carb enthusiast David Asprey, apparently inspired by the Tibetans' yak-butter tea. He invented bullet-proof coffee, adding grass-fed butter and two tablespoons of MCT oil to coffee.

My hybrid latte (*recipe on the next page*) combines coffee with carb-free almond milk, almond butter and two tablespoons of C8 oil, plus a teaspoon of unsweetened cacao and half a teaspoon of cinnamon.

Both drinks have the effect of energizing the mind and making you feel full, and many people use them on an 18:6 diet, where you have dinner at e.g., 6 p.m., and don't eat again until 12 p.m., having an 18-hour fast, or carb fast if you have a hybrid latte for breakfast. Even doing this will tip you over into mild ketosis, with your brain deriving some extra energy from ketones.

How to Make a Hybrid Latte

240ml unsweetened no-carb almond milk

120ml filtered coffee

1 tbsp C8 oil (*Ketofast*)

1 rounded tsp cacao powder

1 heaped tbsp almond or peanut butter

Half tsp ground cinnamon

Blend all ingredients

Fig 20. Hybrid latte

Why the military and endurance athletes use ketones

Another good example of ketone power comes from the work of Kieran Clarke, Professor of Physiological Biochemistry at Oxford University. Having been approached by the American Defense Advanced Research Projects Agency (DARPA), she had the opportunity to test ketones as an energy source in combat situations.

'They were looking for an energy source that would improve soldiers' mental and physical performance under battlefield conditions,' she says. 'Troops weren't taking enough rations into action because they filled their rucksacks with extra ammunition instead. As their blood glucose dropped, they became confused, and sometimes ended up shooting their own side.'

She synthesized pure ketones and tried them out on the soldiers. 'We called it DeltaG, which is the biochemical name for energy but also has a military ring to it – Delta Force and all.'

She tried the new compound on rats a few years later and found it boosted their physical and mental performance. Those who got 30 per cent of their diet in the form of ketones ran 30 per cent further on a treadmill and were smarter at finding their way out of a maze.

Most professional endurance athletes supplement pure ketones when they need a boost. These exogenous ketones, called ketone esters, also ketone salts, bypass the liver so it doesn't have to make ketones from C8, so they get into the bloodstream and get you into ketosis fast. They taste pretty disgusting, so are usually taken as shots or disguised with various flavourings.

As far as your brain is concerned, you are unlikely to get the same rise in ketones as you would on a low-carb high-fat ketogenic diet, but the two combined, or C8 oil, would certainly help your brain make more energy from ketones. Is this a good thing if you don't have an 'energy gap', as people do later in life with cognitive decline, or on the road to diabetes? Could this kind of diet help neurological and psychiatric diseases?

A high-fat ketogenic diet can counteract epilepsy

In fact, the ketogenic diet has long been a standard treatment for childhood epilepsy. Indeed, the benefits of this approach have been well known for about 100 years.[99] However, it was 2008 before Professor Helen Cross, a neurologist and expert in childhood epilepsy at Great Ormond Street Hospital, London, ran the first rigorous scientific trial. Unsurprisingly, this proved what many neurologists had known all along: that a high-fat diet is a highly effective treatment for epilepsy.[100] A more recent trial found similar results, with twice as many patients in the ketogenic diet group having a significant decrease in seizure severity.[101]

It's still not exactly clear why this diet is so effective, but it probably has something to do with reducing the activity of glutamate, one of the excitatory chemicals in the brain, while promoting the production of GABA, which calms down adrenal responses, as well as being a fuel source for neurons.[102]

Simply reducing carbs also seems to have an anti-seizure effect, while changes in the neurons' mitochondria, the energy factories, may be involved, too. Moreover, a study in the *Lancet* found that MCT oil, which is often taken as part of the diet, has some significant direct effects, such as blocking glutamate receptors, which would have a calming effect, and increasing the amount of energy that is available to neurons by boosting their mitochondria.[103]

Ketones may help neurodegenerative diseases such as Parkinson's

In light of the profound effect that the ketogenic diet has on the structure and workings of the brain, it is plausible to suggest that it might prove useful in the treatment of neurodegenerative diseases such as Parkinson's. One animal study found giving C8 helped motor neuron disease.[104] All of the studies in this area are still in their early stages, but some of the initial results are promising.

Parkinson's patients have insufficient amounts of the neurotransmitter dopamine, and at present they are routinely treated with an amino acid named L-dopa. However, for it to work, the neurons' mitochondria need to be able to generate sufficient energy to turn it into dopamine. As we know, the mitochondria are usually powered by glucose that is extracted from carbohydrates, but if this process isn't working well – and there is evidence that this is often the case among Parkinson's patients – the ketones produced during ketosis could be extremely beneficial.

One trial placed one group of patients on a low-fat, high-carb diet and another group on a ketogenic diet for a period of eight weeks. Those on the latter diet showed a 41 per cent reduction in shaking, as well as improvements in behaviour and mood, compared with only an 11 per cent improvement among those on the low-fat diet. The high-carb group also experienced more hunger.[105]

Parkinson's experts Geoffrey and Lucille Leader point out that certain amino acids compete for absorption with the standard medication for the condition, so some protein-rich foods should not be eaten within two hours of taking the medication. (The Leaders explain their approach in detail in their book *Parkinson's Disease: Reducing symptoms with nutrition and drugs*.[106]) Therefore, supplementing exogenous ketones or C8 oil either alongside or shortly after medication, while avoiding protein-rich foods, certainly seems to merit a trial.

High-fat ketogenic diet may help depression, bipolar and schizophrenia

Could a ketogenic diet help those with mental illness? A French psychiatrist, Dr Albert Danan from the University of Toulouse, decided to find out by placing 31 adults with severe, persistent mental illness (major depressive disorder, bipolar disorder and schizoaffective disorder) whose symptoms were not responding well to intensive psychiatric management on a ketogenic diet by restricting carbohydrate intake to 20 grams a day.[107] That's about the total carbs you'd get in a small apple.

Three patients quit within the first two weeks, but those who persisted experienced major improvements in their depression and other symptoms of mental illness. An astonishing 42 per cent achieved complete clinical remission of their condition. They also had lots of other health benefits, including losing weight and better blood sugar control. This wasn't a placebo-controlled trial, which is near-impossible to carry out when changing people's diets, but still it was a very impressive result.

It's a bit hard to tease out what caused the beneficial effects. Was it supplying the brain with ketones, or stabilizing blood sugar and reversing insulin resistance, which would unblock the glucose supply to the brain cells, or promoting GABA, the calming neurotransmitter, while calming down glutamate, which overexcites the brain? We don't have all the answers, but there's lots of ongoing research.

Assistant Professor of Psychiatry at Harvard, Dr Chris Palmer, is an advocate of ketogenic diets for those with mental illness. 'I have seen people with severe treatment-resistant psychotic disorders achieve full remission of their symptoms for long periods of time through a ketogenic diet,' he writes in his book *Brain Energy*,[108] which argues that many mental health problems are to do with mitochondria not working properly, and that a ketogenic diet helps to correct this.

Going ketogenic with a high-fat, low-carb keto diet plus C8

Changing your diet to a high-fat, low-carb ketogenic diet takes some commitment. Jerome Burne, a medical journalist, and I wrote about how to do this in our book *The Hybrid Diet*. As far as your brain upgrade is concerned, the consistent findings are that getting into a mild ketosis and/or consuming either some C8 oil or a ketone supplement can help brain function.

There are a couple of caveats. It seems that C8, the gold standard MCT oil, may have benefits in switching off 'stress' in the brain, quite apart from the effects of supplying the brain with a source of ketones. So it would seem there is a benefit in both eating a more ketogenic diet and supplementing it with C8 oil, although some might prefer cutting to the chase and taking exogenous ketones.

While in those with insulin resistance and cognitive decline, where there is an 'energy gap' for the brain, supplementing C8 oil on its own has benefits, those without blood sugar problems would probably have to eat a lower-carb diet to get more benefit from C8 oil.

There are a few ways to do this. The simplest is to not eat for 18 hours by following an 18:6 diet, with an 18-hour gap between dinner in the evening and lunch the next day, and having a hybrid latte containing a dessertspoon of C8 oil or something similar and going carb-free in the morning. This may put you into a mild state of ketosis whereby you could measure up to 1mcmol/l of ketones in your bloodstream. Of course, what you eat for dinner and for your lunch the next day will determine whether you stay slightly in the ketosis zone.

A proper ketogenic diet aims to get your blood ketones, which are otherwise normally under 0.5mmol/l, up to 2 to 5. For maximum fat-burning, and to trigger 'autophagy', the cellular self-repair programme also used to inhibit cancer cell growth, you need to get glucose down and ketones up to about a ratio of 2:1, which is called one's GKI (glucose ketone index). For example, if your blood sugar, which is normally around 6, dropped to 4, and your ketone level went up to 2, 2/4 = 2 GKI. You can measure both glucose and ketones from a skin prick with a device such as Keto-Mojo (*see Resources*). You can also measure ketones in the breath with a Ketoscan Lite device (*see Resources*). It's worth doing so, so you can see what actually works for you.

A great and highly practical book that shows you what to eat to get into ketosis is *Change Your Diet, Change Your Mind* by Dr Georgia Ede.

In summary, we have learned that:

- Your brain loves ketones, derived from fat, and runs better with a supply of both glucose and ketones.
- Ketones are made in the liver, most directly from a kind of medium-chain triglyceride called C8 oil.
- Studies giving two tablespoons of mainly C8 oil to those with declining memory have brought their brains back to life, producing over 200 per cent more energy from ketones.
- You can buy C8 oil, often derived from coconut oil, and add it to foods and drinks.
- Pure ketone esters and salts are used by some to rapidly increase the brain's supply of ketones.
- Giving your brain a break from carbohydrates and going ketogenic for a while helps repair it.

13

Polyphenol Power – Keep Your Brain Young with Antioxidants

Life is a balancing act. We make energy to support life by combusting glucose or ketones with oxygen, but this generates 'oxidant' exhaust fumes which harm the body. Skin goes wrinkly and age spots develop due to oxidation. It's what makes apples go brown and iron rust. All oxygen-based life-forms inevitably age. We all have a finite life.

However, you can not only add years to your life, but also life to your years by improving your intake of antioxidants and polyphenols found in wholefoods, fruits, vegetables, herbs and spices. As mentioned in Chapter 11, a study in Finland and Sweden compared those with a 'healthy' versus 'unhealthy' diet in midlife for the risk of developing Alzheimer's disease and dementia 14 years later. Those who ate the healthiest diet had an 88 per cent decreased risk of developing dementia and a 92 per cent decreased risk of developing Alzheimer's disease.[109] Some of the benefit would have come from low-sugar diets high in omega-3 and B vitamins, and some from foods high in antioxidants and polyphenols, which we will focus on here.

Your intake of these versus your intake and generation of oxidants, for example from smoking and pollution, is a major determinant of brain health. An illustration of this is the fact that both smoking and pollution exposure increase the risk of cognitive decline and dementia, while vitamin C, which is the antioxidant *par excellence*, reduces the risk.

Oxidants vs antioxidants - moving the balance in your favour

Smoking increases risk of Alzheimer's just as much as having low B-vitamin or omega-3 status, according to the US National Institute of Health's analysis.[110] Smoking is something a person can easily change. Air pollution, for many, is not. It is measured in the amount of particulate matter (PM), and people living in polluted cities are exposed to more. A study of women living in cities in the USA found that those exceeding the 'safe' levels (greater than $12 \mu g/m^3$) had 'increased the risks of global cognitive decline and all-cause dementia respectively by 81 and 92 per cent'.[111]

While you may not be able to change where you live, can you mitigate the effects of pollution? The answer is yes, in two ways. First, by increasing your intake of antioxidants and also by improving your B-vitamin status, since the body detoxifies many toxins, including toxic metals from lead to mercury, by methylation. A similar study to the one above found that residing in locations with PM exposure above the safe level was associated with a higher risk of dementia, but only among people with lower intakes of the homocysteine-lowering B vitamins.[112] 'Vitamin C in the diet or taken as supplements might help,' concludes another.[113]

Smokers need at least twice as much vitamin C as non-smokers just to have basic vitamin C levels in their blood. Men do worse than women. Even with an intake of 200mg a day, they don't achieve this basic blood level, which is already two to three times the recommended dietary intake and what you'd get in four oranges.[114] It is certainly wise for any smoker to supplement vitamin C, perhaps adding 50mg per cigarette – 500mg if you smoke 10 a day, although there is a good case for everyone to supplement 1,000mg a day, or 2,000mg a day if over 50. I wrote a limerick to express this:

Nature always provides a solution to help us with our evolution. It seems obvious to me we need vitamin C to combat excessive pollution.

Vitamin C is a keystone nutrient as far as swinging the antioxidant equation in your favour is concerned. It's made in all living things, from animals to plants, from yeasts to fungi. It's probably been the essential 'exhaust recycler' of all oxygen-based life-forms. Production is even activated when oxidants are sensed. Animals also make more when stressed or exposed to viruses. We, and all other primates, are one of very few species who can't make it.

The first non-vitamin C-making animal to be discovered was the guinea pig. That's how it became the 'guinea pig' for research, since, like us, it's dependent every second of every day on vitamin C from diet. Bats, a few birds and the teleost family of fish have also lost the ability to make vitamin C.

You'll see in this figure below (*also watch this film:* Keeping Your Brain Young with Antioxidants *at foodforthebrain.org/keep-your-brain-young-with-antioxidants/*) that vitamin C disarms water-based oxidants, such as smoke, and vitamin E disarms fat-based oxidants such as the burnt fat found in fried food. Then there are other key antioxidant team players that help to neutralize the reactive oxidants that damage our brain and body.

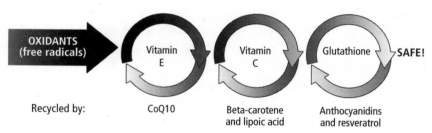

Fig 21. Antioxidants are team players

Your best bet is probably to both eat a diet with a broad spectrum of antioxidants and to supplement them. The older you are, the more you are likely to need.

Key antioxidants are:

- Vitamins A, C and E – associated with reducing Alzheimer's risk
- Lipoic acid[115] – protects the memory-friendly neurotransmitter acetylcholine and dampens down brain oxidation and inflammation

- Glutathione[116] or N-acetylcysteine (NAC)[117] – protects the brain and improves methylation, thus having potential in dementia prevention
- Co-enzyme Q10 – protects the mitochondria in the brain from oxidative stress[118]
- Resveratrol – has antioxidant, anti-inflammatory and neuroprotective properties, and prevents hippocampal brain damage[119]

It doesn't really make a lot of sense to supplement one without the others. Individually, their impact on brain health may be less than when combined. A study of 4,740 elderly residents of Cache County, Utah, found that those supplementing both vitamin E and C cut their risk of developing Alzheimer's by two-thirds. Taking either cut risk by a quarter.[120]

A recent meta-analysis of all studies on factors that could prevent Alzheimer's by one of our Scientific Advisory Board members, Professor Jin Tai Yu of Fudan University in Shanghai, China, shows that 'either a high vitamin E or C intake showed a trend of attenuating risk by about 26 per cent', making these nutrients 'grade 1' top level prevention factors.[121]

All those listed above – vitamins C, E, glutathione and N-acetylcysteine, co-enzyme Q10 and resveratrol – work together and are often found in combined antioxidant supplement formulas (see Resources). At the age of 65, I take a daily antioxidant formula that provides all these.

There are also many other team-player 'cousins', from B vitamins to minerals such as magnesium, selenium and zinc, found respectively in greens, seafood, nuts and seeds.

There are two ways to increase your intake – from food and from supplements. Foods can be measured for their 'total antioxidant capacity', or TAC for short. It's worked out from an equation involving key antioxidants from vitamin A, carotenes (think carrots), lycopene (rich in tomatoes), lutein and zeaxanthin (rich in green vegetables), vitamin E (rich in nuts and seeds), but most of all vitamin C (rich in berries, broccoli, peppers and other vegetables).

There's another good measure, called ORAC (oxygen radical absorption capacity).

The higher the TAC score of your diet, the lower your risk of cognitive and memory decline. This was the finding of a recent study of 2,716 people over the age of 60. The researchers measured the TAC score from their diet, split them into the highest to lowest quarter of TAC score, and compared this to a number of memory tests. Those in the highest quarter, eating the most antioxidant-rich foods, had half the risk of decreasing memory. The higher the TAC score, the better their memory function.[122]

Go rainbow, Mediterranean and eat five or more servings of fruit and vegetables a day

So, what do you need to eat and drink to preserve your memory and protect your brain? Basically, eat a Mediterranean-style 'rainbow-coloured' diet. A Mediterranean diet has more fish, less meat and dairy, more olive oil, fruit and vegetables, including tomatoes and legumes (beans and lentils), and wholegrain cereals than a standard Western diet. It also includes small quantities of red wine. There are variations of this kind of diet, called the MIND diet and the DASH diet, but the core components are the same, and as researchers drill down, we are learning what to eat and drink, and how much, to keep our minds sharp and brains young.

The trick is to really start thinking of the colours you're eating and gravitate to the strong colours:

- *Red:* tomatoes are particularly good for you. Buy seeded, not seedless watermelons. Blend the flesh in a blender, perhaps with some ice. The black husk of the seeds drops to the bottom, and the flesh of the seeds, full of essential nutrients, becomes part of this mouth-wateringly refreshing drink. Great for detox. Red, yellow, green and orange peppers are all rich in vitamin C. Strawberries are a low-GL fruit and are particularly good. According to a study which was part of the Rush Memory and Aging Project at Rush University, Chicago, having a higher intake cut Alzheimer's risk by a quarter. They are high in both vitamin C and flavonoids, a high level of which was also confirmed to cut risk by a third.[123]
- *Orange:* bright oranges include butternut squash, sweet potato and carrots – but do buy organic. Translucent mass-produced carrots are tasteless and have a higher water content, i.e., less actual carrot.

- *Yellow:* mustard and turmeric, for example, are strong yellows. Dijon mustard is great – no sugar. But if you like good old-fashioned English mustard, go for it. Have a teaspoon every other day. Add turmeric to almost any steam-fry, curry and soup.
- *Green:* strong greens are always good for you, from spinach, kale and Brussels sprouts to broccoli, tenderstem broccoli, watercress, rocket, asparagus, artichoke, green beans, peas, kohlrabi and cauliflower (although cauliflower isn't actually green).
- *Blue, indigo, violet:* anything purple, magenta or blue is brilliant for you. From beetroot (eaten raw, grated into salads) to blueberries and blackberries.

Polyphenol power

Some of these foods are particularly rich in polyphenols, a group of health-promoting molecules which also includes flavonoids, sometimes called flavanols. Blue foods such as blueberries contain polyphenols called anthocyanins. Tea, the cacao in chocolate, red wine, red onions, olives and all the blueish berries are rich sources of polyphenols. Many of these polyphenol-rich foods act as anti-oxidants, but they do much more than this. They improve circulation in the brain, lower blood pressure and dampen down the inflammation that lies behind so many conditions, from depression to dementia. Once again, the principle is: what's good for the heart is good for the brain.

One of the first good studies was carried out in Norway more than a decade ago by Eha Nurk and Helga Refsum and colleagues.[124,125] They found that:

- *Tea* – the more you drink, the better. The tea benefit has been confirmed more recently in a study in Singapore, with green tea being marginally better than black tea.[126] However, this benefit was not found in a UK Biobank study, which found tea and coffee-drinking to be associated with worsening cognition compared with abstinence.[127]
- *Chocolate* – benefits peak at 10g, or about 3 pieces; and let's say dark, 70 or more per cent, thus with less sugar, is more likely to be better, as sugar is a strong indicator of cognitive decline. If

chocolate is 80 per cent cacao that means almost 20 per cent will be sugar. More recent studies of people given cocoa, a rich source of flavanols, have shown improved cognition, possibly by improving circulation.[128] This has been confirmed by a big COSMOS trial involving over 20,000 people given a cacao extract supplement rich in flavanols versus a placebo for five years.[129] The reduction in cardiovascular risk was even greater than that of a Mediterranean diet.

- *Wine* – consumption reduces risk of cognitive decline up to an intake of 125ml a day, which is a small glass. A thorough study in the *British Medical Journal* in 2018, which followed over 9,000 people over 23 years, showed that both abstinence and drinking more than 14 units of alcohol a week, which is equivalent to a medium glass of wine (2.3 units) every day, also increases risk.[130] This is consistent with studies showing that a small glass of wine a day decreases the risk of cardiovascular disease. Red wine, high in resveratrol, is likely to be most beneficial. This is medicine. Anything more starts to become a neurotoxin.

All the above are rich in a polyphenol called epicatechin. Jeremy Spencer, a scientific advisor to Food for the Brain, who is Professor of Nutritional Biochemistry and Medicine at the University of Reading, where he specializes in studying the health benefits of polyphenols and other compounds in plants, has shown that these polyphenol-rich plants improve blood flow in specific regions of the brain that govern attention, decision-making, impulse control and emotion, and consequently enhance overall 'executive' function.[131] What's more, the level of flavanols you have in your bloodstream predicts your memory. In the COSMOS study, the biggest impact of increasing flavanols was seen in those in the lowest third for dietary intake specifically seeing improvement in aspects of memory that link to the hippocampus, that central area of the brain that degenerates in Alzheimer's.[132]

The best fruit and veg to eat for your brain

Which vegetables pack the biggest punch as far as polyphenols and antioxidants are concerned and are also low in sugar or low-GL?

Taking all these factors into account, these are the dozen best-rated fruit and veg. Don't think of this list as a definite list, more as a guide, as more and more research reveals the amazing healing power of nature's fruits and vegetables. But these are the kind of foods you want to eat a lot of.

	Lowest GL	Antioxidant	Polyphenol
Olives	★★★	★★★	★★★
Blueberries	★★★	★★★	★★★
Kale	★★★	★★	★★★
Blackcurrants	★★	★★★	★★
Strawberries	★★★	★★★	★★
Broccoli	★★★	★★	★★★
Artichokes	★★★	★★	★★★
Cabbage (red)	★★★	★★★	★★
Asparagus	★★★	★★	★★
Onions (red)	★★	★	★★★
Avocado	★★★	★★	★★
Apples	★★	★★	★★
Beetroot	★	★	★★★
Cherries	★★	★★	★★

The optimal intake for brain protection is five to six servings of fruit and veg a day. Half a plate of a main meal counts as two. A handful of berries would count as one. So, if half your plate for two main meals is vegetables, and you have some berries with your breakfast and another piece of fresh fruit or perhaps some broccoli heads or tenderstem or carrots dipped in hummus as a snack, or half an avocado with some high-polyphenol olive oil, you've had six servings.

The first step is to eat 'whole' foods, especially fresh plant foods, with an emphasis on those listed above. There are some nutrients, such as vitamin C, for which just eating wholefoods doesn't guarantee you are achieving an optimal intake and these are well worth supplementing. My advice is to take 500mg to 1,000mg of vitamin C twice a day and also take an antioxidant formula or antioxidant-rich multivitamin containing vitamins A, C, E, lipoic acid, glutathione or NAC, resveratrol and CoQ10. (*See page 291 for a recommended supplement programme for optimal brain performance.*)

The best way to know that you are doing enough is to measure your glutathione index from a pin-prick blood test. This is part of Food for the Brain's single pin-prick blood test called DRIfT (*see Resources*). It actually measures the ratio between your cells' level of fully loaded (reduced) glutathione and 'spent' or oxidized glutathione. If you eat the right foods, your glutathione index goes up, and if you smoke, it goes down.

In summary, we have learned that:

- Smoking and pollution, which increase oxidant exposure, also increase the risk of cognitive decline. Smokers need more vitamin C to counteract this – at least 1,000mg a day. The best thing is not to smoke.
- Vitamins A, C, E, lipoid acid, glutathione, co-enzyme Q10 and resveratrol protect the brain and are often combined in antioxidant supplements.
- The best foods and drinks for protective antioxidant and polyphenol power are: olives, blueberries, kale, blackcurrants, strawberries, broccoli, artichokes, cabbage (red), asparagus, onions (red), avocado, apples, beetroot, cherries, tea (green may be preferable), low-sugar dark chocolate or cacao (up to 10g a day, which is three pieces of dark, low-sugar chocolate), a small glass of red wine (125ml) (more increases the risk of cognitive decline quite considerably).
- You can test your glutathione index to find out whether you are optimizing your antioxidant potential (*see Resources*).

Your Gut Is Your Second Brain

Where is the barrier between our body and the outside world? We think of it as our skin, but the point at which the food we eat enters our body is through the gut wall. This interface, about as thick as a sheet of paper, with cells that are replaced within four days, is one of the busiest zones of our body. Inside our 10-metre-long gut, which has folds called villi, making the surface area the size of a tennis court, lurk 100 trillion bacteria, weighing about 2kg, with a combination of about 130 different species collectively known as our microbiome.

The health of our gut, and the balance of the bacteria and other microbes that make up its microbiome, are increasingly seen to be playing a role in memory, learning, anxiety, stress, brain growth, and potential protection against neurodegenerative disorders and dementia.

The gut-microbiome-brain superhighway

Rather than thinking of the body and brain as separate from the microbes that live inside us, it seems there is a much more symbiotic relationship between us. This superhighway between our gut and brain, called the gut-microbiome–brain axis, is one of the hottest fields of research, with as many as 30 new studies published every day!

There are millions of nerve connections that run between our brain and our gut, but the main highway is the vagus nerve, the longest nerve in the body, which runs from the brain more or less straight through the body down to the gut. That nervous 'butter-flies in the stomach' feeling is an example of our brain and gut talking.

There are many other nerve connections between the gut and the brain, also communicating to each other with neurotransmitters and other chemicals. Certain undesirable food components, such as gliadins in wheat, if they cross the barrier from gut to brain, can cause brain fog, depression and more serious mental illness.

Often the gut's immune system then learns to attack the offending item, creating a food sensitivity. When this affects the brain and how we think and feel, I call it a 'brain allergy'. These kinds of reactions then crank up systemic inflammation, which is, again, linked to most mental health disorders, from depression to dementia.

My go-to guy for keeping up to date with the science is Associate Professor David Vazour, at Norwich Medical School at the University of East Anglia. He's part of our science squad at Food for the Brain.

'Attention is now turning,' he says, 'to how the microbiota can become the target of nutritional and therapeutic strategies for improved brain health and well-being. However, while such strategies that target the gut microbiota to influence brain health and function are currently under development, with varying levels of success, still very little is yet known about the triggers and mechanisms underlying the gut microbiota's apparent influence on cognitive or brain function.'

How does your gut health affect your brain?

Much of the excitement comes from studies of specific bacteria that appear to be associated with improving memory, learning, stress resilience and mood – and even how our brain develops and degenerates, leading to neurodegenerative disorders such as dementia.[133]

'But the big burning question,' says Dr Vazour, 'is how? How do the gut microbiota influence brain development and function? Are brain disorders potentially shaped by the health of our gut micro-biota? What role does diet play and what is its scope in influencing the gut-microbiome–brain axis? What foods should we eat? What role do probiotic supplements of specific strains of bacteria have on our stress level, mood and memory?'

There are more questions than answers at this time in this emerging field.

The two-way street between our diet, gut health and brain

What we eat is a key determinant of the composition of our gut microbiome, also impacting the time it takes for food to pass through the gut, which is largely a function of the fibre content of our diet. The fibre also slows down the release of the sugars in food, which bacteria then use to nourish themselves and multiply.

Best of all are the soluble fibres found in oats, chia and flax seeds as well as raw or steamed vegetables. Soluble fibre absorbs more water and makes the bowel content lighter and bulkier and easier to pass along. Insoluble fibres such as wheat bran absorb less water and are, consequently, less effective for constipation.

But the important point is that only soluble fibres can be fermented by bacteria making health-promoting short-chain fatty acids (SCFAs) such as butyric acid, which helps to keep the gut wall intact and healthy.[134]

That is why many of the 'probiotic' foods that feed and increase the number of healthy gut bacteria are fibre-rich. These include Jerusalem artichoke, garlic, leeks, onions, asparagus, barley and oats. Supplementing vitamin C also helps cultivate a healthier gut microbiome, promoting two of the most important bacteria for health – *Lactobacillus* and *Bifidobacteria*.[135]

Earlier we learned how medium-chain fatty acids (MCTs) fuelled the brain and how going ketogenic could help mental health. A recent study also shows that a high-fat ketogenic diet has a positive effect on the gut microbiome, thus helping to produce butyric acid and other good gut fats, while simultaneously reducing amyloid markers associated with cognitive decline.[136] These gut-friendly fatty acids produced by bacteria help both the integrity of the gut wall and the blood–brain barrier. This might be one way a ketogenic diet helps, for example, reduce fits in people with epilepsy.[137]

The gut bacteria are thereby acting as the brain's 'bouncers', stopping unwanted particles entering the brain from the gut. A leaky gut–blood–brain barrier is found in those with Alzheimer's disease and is considered part of the problem.[138] It is also found in many children with autistic spectrum disorders.[139]

Is your gut leaky?

Increased gut permeability, called a leaky gut, is hot news in medicine. There's a test a practitioner can give you which involves measuring zonulin, a family of proteins that regulates the barrier between intestinal cells in the digestive tract, hence a marker for gastrointestinal permeability, in either the blood serum or stools (*see Resources*).

Drinking too much alcohol or eating too much wheat makes the gut leakier. Gluten-free foods have great appeal precisely because many people feel better off gluten. What we call gluten is actually a group of proteins called gliadins. These promote something called zonulin in the gut, which opens up a junction between cells and can let gliadins and other incompletely digested proteins through.[140] This promotes food intolerances.

Gliadin intolerance is strongly linked to mental illness. Those with schizophrenia have much higher levels of antibodies against gliadin,[141] indicating that their immune system is designed to attack it when it enters the bloodstream or brain.

An extreme version of gliadin sensitivity is coeliac disease, which can be easily tested with a home-test kit (*see Resources*). It affects less than one in 100,[142] but is much more common in those with mental health problems, from depression to schizophrenia. About one in 30 with gut problems have coeliac disease. Other symptoms include brain fog, headaches and migraines. People with coeliac disease have a higher risk of dementia,[143] but non-coeliacs eating gluten-free don't have a lower risk.[144]

You can be wheat sensitive without having coeliac disease. It's one of the first things I check for in anyone with mental health problems.

I remember a client of mine, Liz:

Liz was diagnosed with schizophrenia in her teens. She tested gluten intolerant, and after an improved diet and supplements, was no longer schizophrenic, went back to school, then university, getting a good job and getting married.

I followed her up three years later. She said, 'I've been fine, but went crazy for a couple of days. I ate a salad at a party and my symptoms came right back. The salad, it turned out, had starch [from wheat] in the salad dressing.'

That was how sensitive she was.

According to the pioneering research of the late Robert Cade, Professor of Medicine and Physiology at the University of Florida, the gliadin by-product gliadorphin, an opioid-like by-product of wheat, was found in very large amounts in 48 per cent of schizophrenics, indicating sensitivity to gliadin, while 86 per cent had higher antibodies to gluten and 93 per cent to the milk protein casein, indicating sensitivity.[145] Cade was perhaps the first to recommend a gluten-free and casein-free diet for those on the autistic spectrum. It helps many, but not all (*see Chapter 24 for more on autism*).

Limiting wheat and/or dairy and increasing your intake of antioxidant and anti-inflammatory foods, which means more fresh fruit, vegetables, herbs, spices and omega-3-rich seafood, and plant food such as walnuts, chia or flax seeds, is likely to be good for both your microbiome and your brain. For some, it is necessary to completely avoid gluten or dairy. Eating fermented foods such as sauerkraut, kimchi, live yoghurt, kefir, kombucha, fermented pickles and some unpasteurized soft cheese is not only good for your microbiome, but should also be good for your brain. The fermented drink kefir, for example, is an anti-inflammatory and an antioxidant and helps control blood sugar.[146]

The immune system starts in the gut

There are more immune cells in our gut than in the whole of the rest of our body. The gut is, after all, as already mentioned, our 'inner skin', the barrier between the outside and inside world. The immune system functions as the bouncers, checking out everything we eat. When the immune system is out of whack, chronic low-grade inflammation develops. This is inevitable if we have a leaky gut.

Low-grade inflammation is found in most neurological conditions, including Alzheimer's and cognitive decline,[147] autism spectrum disorder, depression, epilepsy, Parkinson's disease and cerebrovascular diseases such as strokes.[148] There's a blood marker called C-reactive protein (CRP), which, if raised, indicates inflammation. Your doctor can measure it. The higher your level, the greater your risk of cognitive decline. Just about every brain-upgrade recommendation is associated with lowering inflammation. Inflammation is a mechanism that tips mental health in the wrong direction. Once you are in a state of inflammation, perhaps with a degree of leaky gut, the likelihood is that you'll start to develop food intolerances, if they weren't the cause of the leaky gut and inflammation in the first place.

Is food triggering brain fog, low mood and lethargy?

Have you ever wondered if what you eat has anything to do with your mood, energy levels and ability to concentrate? Do you ever experience 'brain fog' and tiredness and wonder why you feel anxious and low when others seem to cope, yet sometimes you're just fine? Have you ever considered that you might have a food intolerance?

The ability of foods to trigger mental health issues has been known for a remarkably long time. Back in 1980, Dr Joseph Egger, writing in the *Lancet* medical journal, reported: 'The results showed that allergies alone, not placebos, were able to produce the following symptoms: severe depression, nervousness, feeling of anger without a particular object, loss of motivation and severe mental blankness.'[149] But why certain foods in certain people could produce mood changes and brain fog wasn't known.

Researchers in the USA,[150] China,[151] Poland[152] and the UK[153] have found out why, and it's all to do with 'food intolerance' that is unique to the individual. While classic allergies cause the body to product IgE antibodies that attack the offending allergen, depression, brain fog and even schizophrenia, according to research at the Johns Hopkins University School of Medicine in the USA, can occur when a person's immune system produces a different kind of antibody, IgG, which attacks their offending foods.

Stephanie, Wanita and Nicola were part of research that has involved thousands of people, all having an IgG food intolerance test administered via a home-test kit provided by the YorkTest laboratory and then avoiding their 'reactive' foods:

Stephanie, a 28-year-old lawyer: 'After a week, the brain fog and tiredness were significantly better and then after a few weeks, all of my symptoms had gone!'

Wanita, 41, who was signed off work, had complete relief from her anxiety and fatigue and she was then able to return back to work. Her doctor had recommended anti-depressants.

Nicola, 51, had constantly felt tired and lethargic, with brain fog and an inability to concentrate. 'If I didn't eat regularly, I felt worse, so I was constantly grazing on food. I know now I was eating the wrong foods, which didn't help.' Now she says, 'I feel so much better in myself and have a lot more energy. The best thing is to not have brain fog.'

What they all had in common were specific food intolerances whereby their gut and immune system reacted, creating a kind of inflammation and reactivity that can both cause gut issues such as IBS, pain and bloating, but also psychological issues such as brain fog, anxiety and depression.

The scientific director at YorkTest, Dr Gill Hart, is one of the top experts on food intolerance. She told me, 'YorkTest pioneered food IgG testing, developing our first food intolerance test back in 1998 in collaboration with scientists from the University of York. Since then, YorkTest has provided over half a million tests. The tests are accurate, have been shown to be effective and have demonstrated >98 per cent reproducibility. For those with high food IgG reactivity, the pattern of IgG trigger foods is unique to each individual. The tests provide valuable information, and with nutritional advice provided as part of the food intolerance test, people feel fully supported in making the required dietary changes. The good news is that food intolerances aren't necessarily for life, and those taking the test and changing their diet have reported improvements over a relatively short period of time.'

Unlike conventional IgE allergies, which can last for life, IgG antibodies 'die off', so, theoretically, if you avoid the offending food for at least three months, you may be able to reintroduce the food without reacting. However, it is worth doing this systematically, because some people do continue to react.

Nine in ten people having the test and avoiding their offending foods report improvement in mood, brain fog and lethargy.[154] The table below shows the percentage of self-reported benefit for a variety of mental health-related symptoms from a survey of over 3,000 people from YorkTest's research. (*See Resources for details on their food intolerance tests.*)

Symptoms (3,026 subjects)	Benefit per cent	Low or no benefit per cent
Anxiety (40)	77.5	22.5
Autism (1)	100.0	0.0
Bad moods (15)	93.3	6.7
Behavioural problems (3)	100.0	0.0
Fatigue (436)	86.9	13.1
Hyperactivity (3)	100.0	0.0
Insomnia (12)	83.3	16.7
Mental fog (24)	87.5	12.5
Nausea (61)	90.2	9.8
Panic attacks (15)	100.0	0.0
Tension (9)	66.7	33.3

Unpublished data, reproduced with permission from the study published as G. Hardman and G. Hart, 'Dietary advice based on food-specific IgG results', *Nutrition and Food Science*, 37 (2007), 16–23

Neurotransmitters are made in the gut

Earlier, we learned about neurotransmitters, the chemical messengers of the brain, including dopamine, which is key to the 'reward' system of the brain, linked to addiction and which is the precursor for adrenalin; serotonin, often called the mood hormone; and GABA, which switches off the adrenal stress-hormone response. These neurotransmitters are made in the gut as well as the brain.

GABA, for example, is produced by some *Lactobacilli*[155] and specific strains of *Bifidobacterium*.[156] Low GABA levels are associated with mental health problems, including schizophrenia, depression and even anxiety associated with autism.[157] Promoting GABA is key to reducing anxiety.

Serotonin is involved in mood, cognition and sleep, as well as appetite control.[158] It is estimated that 90 per cent of the body's serotonin is made in the digestive tract.[159] You might think this is a good thing, but you want more in your brain and less in your gut. Too much in the gut can even promote inflammation. This may be why some people get gut discomfort when supplementing 5-HTP (5-hydroxytryptophan), the mood-boosting precursor for serotonin.

Having good vitamin D levels, which is a vital part of your brain upgrade, helps optimize your brain's serotonin levels. That's because a vital enzyme called TPH, which converts the amino acid tryptophan into serotonin, is enhanced in the brain by vitamin D and selectively shut down in the gut.[160] So, with sufficient vitamin D, you get higher brain levels of serotonin, promoting good mood, and lower serotonin levels in the gut, protecting against gut inflammation.

Your gut microbiome is key to programming your brain in early life

One of the most intriguing areas of microbiome research concerns the lifelong influence of the gut microbiota on brain health. Human studies would take a lifetime so, admittedly, much of the research is on shorter-living creatures, such as mice.

I asked David Vazour about this research frontier.

He replied, 'One review ranks the gut microbiota as the fourth key factor in early-life programming of brain health and disease, alongside pre-natal and post-natal environment, and genetics.[161] The scientific challenge is to identify ways to alter and fine-tune the microbiota and, through that, enhance brain health and well-being.

'Many scientists now believe in the close relationship between microbial diversity and healthy brain ageing. Studies in mice have shown that faecal microbiota transplantation from young to old mice can correct age-related defects in immune function and key functions of the central nervous system and brain.[162] These and other findings highlight the importance of the gut-microbiome–brain axis during ageing and raise the possibility that a "young" microbiota may maintain or improve cognitive functions in life's later years.[163] We have shown this already in animals transferring young microbiota with faecal transplants into older animals, reversing hallmarks of the aging gut, eye and brain.[164]

'Since neurological research suggests the microbiota also play a role in neurodegenerative diseases, this supports the idea that ageing gut microbiota could be linked to immune and neuronal dysfunction in Alzheimer's disease.'

What exactly is a healthy microbiome?

While great advances are being made, this field is in its infancy. The definition, that is, the characteristics and function of a 'healthy' gut microbiome, are still unknown. Generally, studies have found less diversity of bacteria species associated with more health disorders.[165] As yet, there is little understanding of how the microbiota change over time and may reflect the impending onset of disease. Recent data from more than 9,000 adults of different ages show that, as individuals age, the gut microbiome becomes increasingly unique, increasingly different from others, starting in mid-to-late adulthood.

Microbes, gums and your brain

Growing evidence suggests that undesirable microbes – bacteria, viruses, fungi and protozoa – could all contribute to the development of Alzheimer's disease.[198] The strongest evidence for this so far relates to gum disease. Those who have had gum disease for ten or more years have a 70 per cent increased risk of Alzheimer's.[199, 200] Also, the more teeth you've lost in adulthood the higher the risk is for dementia.[201] There's a particular bacteria called P.gingivalis (Porphyromonas gingivalis) which is found in both the mouth and the brains of those with Alzheimer's. Given that a third of the bacteria in your mouth is between the teeth, flossing and brushing twice a day for two minutes is an easy habit to help protect your brain.

Are probiotic supplements a daily essential?

Several studies, and reviews of studies, have investigated the effects of probiotic (live friendly bacteria) and prebiotic (nutrients that feed bacteria) supplements, and even fermented foods, on symptoms of depression, anxiety and mood, as well as on cognition. The majority of studies did conclude that dietary interventions or supplements had some positive effects on depression and anxiety symptoms,[166] though in one review the effects were only seen in those with mild or moderate depression.[167] In another, the effects were not significant, but trending in the right direction.[168] It is therefore not possible to conclude that a daily probiotic supplement is a brain health essential for all, but may be for those with depression (*see Chapter 17*). Many studies are underway.

My view is that there may be benefit, and certainly no harm, in taking a daily probiotic supplement, powder or drink containing, at least, some of the *Lactobacillus* and *Bifidobacteria* strains. Also, if you have a gut infection or take a course of antibiotics, it is essential to replenish your microbiome by then supplementing probiotics for several weeks.

Whenever a person is found to be food intolerant, ideally with a reliable IgG test (*see Resources*), I recommend they supplement both probiotics and glutamine, which is an amino acid that promotes gut wall integrity and helps repair a leaky gut, and digestive enzymes (*see Resources*) for a month, alongside avoiding the identified food intolerances.

The optimal diet for your gut-microbiome-brain axis

Putting all this together, eating wholefoods rich in fibre and soluble fibres, such as oats and oatcakes, beans, nuts, seeds, whole fruit and vegetables, is gut-friendly, as is eating prebiotic foods such as Jerusalem artichoke, garlic, leeks, onions, asparagus, barley and oats, and fermented foods such as sauerkraut, kimchi, live yoghurt, kefir, kombucha, fermented pickles and some unpasteurized soft cheese. Since the integrity of the gut barrier is negatively affected by alcohol,[169] the gliadin in wheat,[170] and a lack of antioxidants and anti-inflammatory omega-3 fats, I recommend drinking less alcohol, eating less wheat and ensuring a good intake of omega-3 and antioxidant-rich foods. It also makes sense to supplement with vitamin C.

If you suspect you have a food intolerance, having an IgG test is likely to help. If you have significant gut problems, ruling out coeliac disease with a coeliac test is a wise move. If you choose to take probiotics, make sure they include the *Lactobacillus* and *Bifidobacteria* families and 'billions' of viable organisms, which will be shown on the product label.

In summary, we have learned that:

- Our gut and brain are inextricably linked, mainly via the vagus nerve.
- A diet high in soluble fibres, especially high in oats, chia and flax seeds, is gut-friendly.
- Supplementing vitamin C promotes healthy gut bacteria, as do a more ketogenic diet and C8 oil.
- Wheat, containing gliadin, tends to make the gut wall 'leakier' and encourage food intolerance and coeliac disease, which may induce mental health problems from depression to schizophrenia.
- Fermented foods such as sauerkraut, kimchi, live yoghurt, kefir, kombucha, fermented pickles and some unpasteurized soft cheese are not only good for our microbiome, but should also be good for our brain.
- Testing for and eliminating food intolerances help both the gut and the brain.
- Vitamin D, probiotic and prebiotic supplements may help. It is too early to say whether they are needed on a daily basis by all.
- Increasing omega-3, vitamin D, vitamin C and antioxidant-rich foods, while reducing or eliminating wheat and alcohol, is gut-friendly and likely to be best for the brain too.

Use It or Lose It – Why an Active Lifestyle Is Essential

What is the point of upgrading your brain anyway? To ensure you are mentally sharp, emotionally happy and feel in the flow of life's rich tapestry, sleeping well and not feeling stressed, anxious or overwhelmed, right?

Many of the secrets for brain health we've explored so far affect the structure and the function of the brain and the neural network. But a vital piece of the jigsaw is utilization – 'use it or lose it'. The exercise and stimulation your brain gets from an active physical, social and intellectual lifestyle are a vital part of what keeps your brain healthy. It's that flow of activity that keeps your brain healthy, in the same way that your body needs movement and exercise. You also need to recover, which is why sleep is important, and keep your stress levels low, which is the subject of the next chapter.

How all these pieces fit together is shown in the figure on the next page.

Our active lifestyle expert at Food for the Brain is Assistant Professor Tommy Wood, from the University of Washington. He's advised Formula 1 drivers, Olympians and world champions on how to maximize their performance, both mentally and physically. I asked him what was his top tip for keeping your brain sharp.

'In short,' he replied, 'use it or lose it. The brain is an amazing organ, and it's more resilient and adaptable than we've been led to believe. I'm sure you've heard that adults have a fixed amount of brain cells. Then, as we get older – or every time we take a sip of wine – we lose some of those brain cells as part of an unstoppable decline towards dementia or Alzheimer's disease. That's not necessarily true.

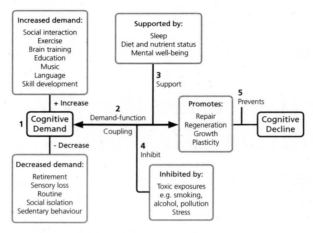

Fig 22. The Demand Coupling Model; used with permission of Dr Tommy Wood and Henry Turkel

'I like to think about the brain like I think about muscles. In order to grow our muscles, we need to provide a stimulus – like lifting weights in the gym – followed by a period of rest. The opposite also happens – if we stop going to the gym or if we stop using a limb after breaking a bone – our muscles get smaller. Most have experienced this personally, and there's every indication that your cognitive "muscle" behaves in the same way.'

A classic example of this is a study of London taxi drivers in training who have to learn 'the Knowledge'. Many spend three years on the 25,000 streets of London, logging up tens of thousands of miles, on foot or a scooter. Not all pass first time. Katherine Woollett at University College London decided to find out if acquiring the Knowledge actually changed a person's brain by measuring the density of grey matter as an indicator of brain volume. About half of her group of training taxi drivers passed first time and the other half failed. She also had a control group of people of the same age, most in their late thirties, with similar other demographics such as IQ. Sure enough, those who passed the Knowledge had increased their brain density of grey matter, and specifically in that central hippocampus area most associated with cognitive resilience.[171]

Keep cognitively active

There's a pattern in our society: we are meant to learn every day as we go through school in our childhood and teenage years, then acquire a job, which, past a training phase, may not require much more learning, then around 65 we are meant to retire, with no more 'need' to work or learn.

Every indicator that you can think of – leaving school early, having a lower educational standard[172] or retiring early[173] – has been associated with increasing risk of cognitive decline.

When Professor May Beydoun, at the US National Institutes of Health, did a comprehensive study of the biggest risk factors for developing Alzheimer's, she attributed 24 per cent of risk to educational status (you'll recall that omega-3/seafood accounted for 22 per cent, homocysteine-lowering B vitamins also 22 per cent, physical activity was 32 per cent and smoking was 31 per cent).[174] So, utilization of the brain, reflected in educational and physical activity, is a big part of keeping your brain healthy.

Think about how you use your mind. How much time do you spend stimulated, learning something? How much time do you spend engaged in relatively mindless mental activities? According to Fred Luskin at Stanford University, 'The average person has about 12,000 to 60,000 thoughts per day. Of those, 80 per cent are negative and 95 per cent are exactly the same repetitive thoughts!'

Television can be stimulating or mind-numbing – engaging your attention but not really making you think. Social media activity, like scrolling through TikTok or Instagram, can be mind-numbing, while digital engagement with others can be stimulating. A simple yardstick is to ask, 'Am I learning anything? Am I using my mind?' Complex 'whodunnit' dramas might engage your mind in working out who did the deed, while 'reality TV' may not.

You might think that all of these activities are keeping your mind busy, but what you really want is to be engaged in learning or working something out, ideally without too much stress. As you'll see in the next chapter, prolonged stress actually shrinks the brain. Many films are designed to engage you by stimulating a stress response, so you're kept on the seat of your pants, so to speak. On the other hand, doing Wordle or a crossword, or playing a game of backgammon or chess involves concentration and thinking without cranking up your stress response. Gambling, while engaging, is also cranking up that stress response and leading to addictive behaviours and brain degeneration, as we saw earlier.

There are lots of apps designed to improve your mind. Two that have high ratings are Brain HQ and Lumosity. Brain HQ (www.brainhq.com) adapts according to your needs – do you want better memory, better attention or faster processing? The recommendation is to do at least 60 to 90 minutes of training a week, perhaps in three 20-minute sessions. Lumosity (www.lumosity.com) is also adaptive and achieves much the same improvement in cognition. In just the same way as you become physically fitter by increasing the duration or intensity of an exercise, the same is true with your mind.

Reading books or listening to podcasts can also be great ways to stimulate your mind, but it depends entirely on what you read or listen to. Again, ask yourself, 'Am I learning anything from this?' Even better, join a book club so you have the social stimulation (*see below*) of sharing your views, hearing others and working out where you stand.

Learn by failing

Tommy Wood encourages failing. 'Failure constitutes protective cognitive demand,' he says. 'Activities that provide the greatest cognitive stimulus involve learning and skill development. That means we're initially bad at them and occasionally fail before we get better. This is the real sticking point for improving brain health – as adults, we hate the feeling of being bad at something. Failing is, however, when the magic happens.

'A fascinating study looked at the brains of musicians.[175] While both professional and amateur musicians' brains looked younger than those of non-musicians of the same age, the benefit was greatest in amateur musicians. The researchers suggested that playing music was more of a cognitive stimulus for amateurs – it was harder, so they got more benefit. The cocktail of hormones released as we try, fail, repeat and learn provides the ideal environment for the brain to grow and adapt.'

He recommends picking an activity that's truly challenging. 'Cognitive demand requires failure, so pick something you'll be bad at initially. What's cognitively challenging is personal, but learning a new language is better than sudoku, building model airplanes is probably better than reading the news, and playing chess is definitely better than scrolling through Instagram. As you get better, add challenge to keep stimulating your brain.'

Two big brain pluses are learning a new language or learning to play a musical instrument. It's challenging and can take a long time to become completely proficient. But every step along the way – learning new words, processing the grammar, learning chords and finger positions – is a significant mental challenge. Even if you spend just a few minutes a day learning, you're making new brain connections. There are many language-learning apps, like Duolingo, that will keep you cognitively engaged.

Speaking two languages is not only associated with less risk of cognitive decline but, according to one study, 'the neuroprotective effects of lifelong bilingualism act both against neurodegenerative processes and through the modulation of brain networks' connectivity.'[176]

So, your brain ends up more connected – literally hard-wired for brain health.

Keep physically active

You'll note that in the National Institutes of Health study above, being physically active was the single greatest predictor of the risk of cognitive decline. The brain works hard in exercise, especially if it involves complex movements and learning, such as learning to dance, or doing different movements in a yoga or *t'ai chi* class or running or walking on uneven surfaces. The brain is processing a lot of information, triggering patterns of muscle movement and keeping you in balance. You want a bit of both movement and balance. Just working out on a fixed machine or walking on a flat, straight, tarmac path is not nearly as challenging as hill-walking up an uneven path, cycling, surfing, skateboarding or anything where your body is micro-adjusting to keep you in balance.

If you're in a challenging environment, for example hill-walking, or learning something new, your brain is not only getting more exercise, it is positively growing and making new connections. One study of retired people assigned to walk briskly for 40 minutes three times a week showed increased hippocampal brain volume.[177] Another showed benefits from doing one or two sessions of resistance or strength training twice a week.[178]

There may be more benefit to building muscle, which is what resistance training does, than just the stimulation of the exercise. After all, just doing one repetitive exercise might not appear so mentally challenging. Yet of all the measures relating to how fit or fat you are – your weight, body mass index (calculated from your bodyweight and height), fat mass or muscle mass – it is your muscle mass, or how much muscle you have compared to fat, that best predicts both your brain volume and risk of cognitive decline in later years. Less fat and more muscle is what you want. One big study from the UK Biobank data found that those with a lower fat-to-muscle ratio (FMR) in their legs had around 40 per cent less risk of dementia later in life.[179] Muscle uses energy and 'soaks up' glucose. This helps keep your blood sugar stable and prevent insulin resistance. Often, as people age, they gain weight but swear they aren't eating any more than they used to. This is often simply because they've lost muscle mass. If you don't use it, you lose it.

If you can find an activity that engages both mind and body and is not too repetitive, all the better. As an example, I've taken up paragliding, and qualified at the age of 65. I had to pass an exam on meteorology, aerodynamics and air law, and failed first time, but now have to think about these things before and during flight. Then there's the exercise of carrying an 11kg pack up a mountain, and the balance and strength and adjustments my brain is having to make to keep the canopy stable even before take-off. This may not be your thing, but it shows how one constantly challenging activity can tick so many brain boxes. It is good to learn new sports for this very reason.

Step it up

A good general guideline is to aim for 30 minutes of brisk walking per day. Some days you may do none and others twice this, but this is a good weekly average to shoot for. Over time you can step it up by walking faster, jogging or including some hills in your circuit.

But don't limit yourself to 'exercise'. You could be gardening, mowing the lawn, playing a sport, doing vigorous cleaning, clearing out a yard – anything that gives you a faster heart rate and a bit of sweat and engages different sets of muscles, thus including 'resistance'.[180] A good trick is to use these kinds of activities as exercise and do them faster or more vigorously, trying to expend, not save, energy.

Another way to monitor and up your exercise level is to count your steps. Smartphones and watches have apps that do this for you. Shoot for increasing your daily steps by a minimum of 10 per cent a week, or a maximum of 20 per cent. If you start at 2,000 and add 200 steps per day each week, that's great. If you're at 4,000 steps already, then getting up to 4,400 in this week is also great. While 8,000 steps a day is considered optimal, what's much more important is to make sustainable improvements as you 'activate' your lifestyle.

If you do something that involves coordinated movement and hence both engages your mind and your need to keep adjusting for balance, that is an added bonus.

Aerobic plus resistance anti-ages your brain

Including something that helps build and maintain muscle tone correlates most strongly with brain health. Perhaps you are a member of a gym, go to a Pilates or yoga class or have some equipment at home for your own workout. Whatever you do, a good weekly guideline is to include two resistance training sessions a week.

If you're not sure where to start, I wrote a book with exercise guru and former Gladiator (Zodiac) Kate Staples called *Burn Fat Fast*. I did the diet and she devised the exercises, including an excellent set of strength-building exercises that anyone can do at home in eight minutes, three times a week. The exercises include beginner, intermediate and advanced versions. To do them, if you are a beginner, you need nothing other than a water bottle, while if you are doing the 'intermediate' or 'advanced' workout, you'll need a mat and a pair of dumbbells (free weights) (*see below*), which you can get in any major supermarket or sports equipment shop.

You can see Kate Staples demonstrating each exercise at www.patrickholford.com/kate-staples-burn-fat-fast-videos/. The sequence of the exercises is shown in the table below, starting with the beginner sequence, then building up to advanced as you get fitter. Do make sure you warm up with a few minutes of anything that increases your heart rate, so that you will avoid any strains or injury. This could be jumping or running on the spot, dancing or a quick hill walk, but should only take you about five minutes.

Beginner	Intermediate	Advanced
Wall sit	Squat shoulder press	Jumping squats
Modified box press	Box press with alternate leg lift	Full press-up
Plank step-outs	Plank jacks	Mountain climbers
Alternate reverse lunge	Reverse lunge with tricep kick-back	Pendulum lunge

- In the *beginner* sequence each exercise takes 45 seconds and you repeat the entire sequence twice.
- The *intermediate* exercises take 60 seconds and you repeat the entire sequence twice. You will need a mat and dumbbells (women 2kg; men 3–4kg).
- The *advanced* exercises take 60 seconds and you repeat the entire sequence three times. You will need a mat and dumbbells (women 2–5kg; men 4–6kg).

Be social

A lack of meaningful social interaction is also a major driver of both low mood and cognitive decline later in life.[181] As water is to fish, social interaction is to humans. We are social beings and we need that exchange with others.

How often do you go to social gatherings, meet new people, have engaging conversations? This could be meeting friends, going to the movies, a museum, a gallery, a show, church or temple or a restaurant – anywhere you exchange ideas with others. When was the last time you met new people?

There are times in life where you might find yourself more isolated. For example, if you split up with a partner and lose connection with 'their' friends, or if your partner dies and most of your social interaction was with them. These are extremely challenging times, but remember that seeing a friendly face will help you through.

Unset your mind

Later in life, as you inevitably lose more friends, it's important to find ways to expose yourself to new ideas, new ways of seeing or thinking, and have the opportunity to discuss these with others. It is all too easy to get set in a particular mindset and way of living, doing the same things and only interacting with people who, essentially, agree with you about most issues.

So, get out there. Wherever you are, there are many opportunities, for example, to volunteer, perhaps helping others, planting trees or supporting the local arts club. It's quite good to be a bit out of your comfort zone, joining a group of new people engaged in an activity you might like but don't normally do. Take a risk.

Do something different. If you think of yourself as not creative, do something creative. Join a writing or art class or course. If you think of yourself as not 'intellectual', do something that engages your intellect. If you think of yourself as not social, do something social.

Check out what's on near you. Your local bookshop will know about book clubs. Your local arts centre will know what's happening in that arena. Your local allotments will know about gardening groups.

Perhaps call up someone you haven't seen in ages. When you were a teenager, you'd explore and exchange new ideas, try new things and have that exchange with your peers. Who did you hang out with? Who challenged your thinking? Get in touch with them.

If you walk in the park, or walk your dog if you have one, say hi to people. Make the effort to make a connection. Drop in on a neighbour. Invite them round for a cup of tea. Get involved in what's going on around you. Be inquisitive.

It's all too easy to get locked into a way of living that removes any form of challenging social interaction, yet this is not only how we learn, it also nourishes the social aspect of who we are. So, make sure you have a significant social event or interaction every week, starting with this week.

Travelling and exploring other cultures also broadens your mindset. Where would you like to go?

As Tommy Wood says, 'The key is to push right at the boundaries of what you're capable of – with occasional failure showing that you're at the right level of difficulty. Keep at it, and you'll be more likely to be healthy and sharp for decades to come.'

In summary, we have learned that these kinds of activities support brain health:

- Spending at least 20 minutes doing activities such as walking, gardening, light housework or repairing things – anything that gets you moving.
- Building in two hours or more a week of energetic activity such as dancing, cycling, swimming, playing tennis/squash, gym or exercise classes, running, hill-walking or a competitive sport.
- Being social. Aim to spend two hours a week or a couple of days spending time with other people in a social (not work) setting – groups, friends, family, etc.
- Keeping your mind active by learning something new and challenging and practising a new skill – learning a new language, sport, musical instrument, etc.

16

How Stress Ages the Brain and Why Sleep Is Essential

What does a dog do after going for a walk? Sleep. Sleep is how the brain recovers. There is overwhelming evidence that it is a brain essential, and if we get too much or too little, our risk of cognitive decline goes up.

The optimal amount of sleep for brain health is seven hours in total, though there is some debate about whether it needs to all be in one go. One study found a nap after physical exercise reduced the risk of cognitive impairment.[182]

Those with problems sleeping, or getting consistently less sleep than this, may literally double their risk of age-related cognitive decline.[183] A UK study of Whitehall civil servants, starting in the 1980s and examining their health from the age of 35 onwards, found that 'Persistent short sleep duration at age 50, 60 and 70 compared to persistent normal sleep duration was also associated with a 30 per cent increased dementia risk.'[184] But it's not just the future risk of dementia that lack of sleep cranks up, it's the ability to function the next day and to feel good. Lack of sleep decreases empathy and cranks up negative emotions.[185]

If sleep is a problem for you, I'll give you some top tips on how to get a good night's sleep in Chapter 19. But first, why do we sleep and why is it a brain essential?

Why sleep is a brain essential

All mammals sleep, and without it, things start to go very wrong in the brain. It helps repair the brain from its daily activities and damage induced by things like too much sugar, lack of omega-3, antioxidants, smoking and pollution.

What is it that stimulates us to sleep? As nightfall approaches, the brain starts to convert the neurotransmitter serotonin, made from the amino acid tryptophan, into melatonin. This largely happens in the pineal gland in almost the exact centre of the brain, in from between the eyebrows. It correlates to the 'third eye' or the *ajna* chakra in yoga, and is what the philosopher René Descartes thought was the seat of the soul. In most animals, it is light sensitive. It is in us too, but not directly so. We make more melatonin as the day ends and night begins, and exposure to light suppresses its production.

You can think of melatonin as the neurotransmitter that keeps you in sync with the day–night cycle. An example of how melatonin works is jet-lag. When we fly to a different time zone, our brain is still stuck in a cycle telling us it's night-time when it isn't in the new time zone. If we supplement melatonin, it helps our brain adjust more quickly to the new time zone, giving us a better night's sleep.[186] I'll explain how to make use of this in Chapter 19, if sleep is a problem for you. A loss of this natural circadian rhythm, and lower brain levels of melatonin, are found in those with cognitive decline. But, other than keeping us asleep, what is melatonin actually doing?

Sleep can be thought of as the brain's housekeeper, and one of the key players that helps clean up our brains while we sleep is the increased level of circulating melatonin. During sleep, blood and cerebrospinal fluid circulation improves and waste products of brain metabolism get removed.[187] These waste products include both oxidants and amyloid protein, associated with Alzheimer's and brain inflammation, which starts to accumulate after just one night of sleep deprivation.[188] That's a big reason why the brain needs this downtime.

Although there are many by-products of all the day's brain activity, one big slice of the toxins that accumulate in the brain is made up of various oxidants. Apart from all the antioxidants and polyphenols we can eat to keep our brains young, the melatonin that gets released into the brain's circulation is perhaps the most important antioxidant helping to disarm these oxidants and restore the mitochondrial energy factories to full function. Melatonin is made in the body from a type of tryptophan, 5-HTP, which is an effective anti-depressant. One study found it was even more effective at mopping up these dangerous oxidants than melatonin or vitamin C.[189] Melatonin is also a powerful anti-inflammatory, and supplementation has been used to speed up recovery from cancer, Covid and cardiovascular disease.[190]

Why dreaming is important

But there's something else going on while we sleep, and particularly as we dream, that helps discharge the negative emotions of the preceding day.

All being well, after about 30 minutes we enter a period of deep sleep when our heart rate reduces, our blood pressure drops and our breathing becomes slower. This is the most restorative stage of sleep, when tissue repair and regeneration occur. After around 90 minutes, we shift to a period of REM (rapid-eye-movement) sleep, which is when most dreaming occurs. This stage is believed to be particularly important for our psychological health and well-being. Then we move back and forth between deep sleep, lighter sleep and REM, with the REM stage ideally accounting for around 25 per cent of our overall sleep time.

During the night, especially during the deep and REM sleep phases, the brain also produces higher levels of growth hormone. This hormone helps with the repair and regeneration of the body's tissues while melatonin helps clear out the waste products of metabolism.

When we're stressed, the high levels of the stress hormone cortisol suppress growth hormone and REM sleep, diverting energy away from repair into coping with the energy demands of a stressful situation. This impedes tissue repair, effectively speeding up the brain's ageing process.

As far as the mind is concerned, the most critical phases of sleep are the bursts of REM sleep. These tend to last for about 30 minutes, occurring on average between three to five times a night. If we are deprived of REM sleep, we don't feel fully rested on waking and are more likely to get depressed. When we do get a chance to sleep, we have longer periods of REM sleep, all of which suggests that our minds need to have this time while we're asleep to process what's been happening in our lives. One theory is that negative emotions such as anger, fear, sadness and frustration that were triggered in the preceding day but couldn't be fully expressed and released, get experienced and hopefully discharged during dreaming. To test this theory, when you have a strong negative emotion in a dream, track back to the experiences of the day before when you felt a similar emotion.

Stress ages the brain

As William Shakespeare so aptly said, 'There is nothing good or bad but thinking makes it so.' The state of stress is how we react to the circumstances of our lives. That being said, when bad things happen, it is not so easy to 'look on the bright side'. Later, I'll share some secrets for building stress resilience and deprogramming anxiety, which is so often a consequence of past negative experiences that haven't been let go of, leading to fear for the future.

What is clear is that major stresses and perceived and prolonged stress age the brain and increase the risk of cognitive decline and dementia. This has been shown by tracking people who have had two or more major stressful events, such as the death of a spouse, child or grandchild, divorce, financial or health problems, and also perceived psychological stress in adulthood and levels of neuroticism.[191]

Stress has a lot to do with control. This was shown by a study that assessed people's work based on two criteria: high or low psychosocial demands (i.e., a demanding job) and having high or low control. Those who did worse both for depression and cognitive decline had both high demands and low control over the circumstances.[192]

For example, a classic example of high stress might be caring for a parent with dementia and dealing with various NHS and social service bureaucracies. Another would be a stressful job where you don't have the power, or the budget, to make the necessary changes.

Having too many unfinished things is also a classic source of overwhelm.

But what is stress actually doing to the brain? The best way to understand this is to talk about cortisol.

Cortisol

There are two main stress hormones – adrenalin and cortisol. Adrenalin is short-acting, kicking in in under a second and lasting for up to an hour, but usually less. As we learned earlier, it is made from dopamine, which is made from the amino acid tyrosine, itself made from phenylalanine, an amino acid in food protein.

Cortisol is long-acting and its level cycles throughout the day. In the evening, and as we approach sleep, our level should be reducing. In the morning, cortisol levels need to increase to kick-start our day. In the first hour of waking there's a cortisol peak to get us going.[193] That is why it is probably better not to have coffee, which further promotes adrenal hormones, for at least an hour on waking. You may stop producing enough of your own cortisol and become dependent on the caffeine hit.

If your cortisol level is high at night, you'll have difficulty getting to sleep and if it's low in the morning, you'll have difficulty waking up.

These hormones are 'stimulating', so you do need them for activity. At the other extreme, if you are completely burnt out, sometimes called 'adrenal burnout', you can have low cortisol, reflecting an inability to function or cope with life's inevitable challenges. But this is not so common and represents the final step on a long road of prolonged stress.

Stress makes us stupid

Much more common is to get locked into a high-stress state, reacting stressfully, waking up with stressful thoughts and operating with a background level of anxiety.

At an evolutionary level, the stress reaction programmes us both for reward and aversion as part of learning how to survive. We learn what to like and what to avoid. It's all part of the 'fight or flight' reaction that has us fleeing from situations we perceive to be dangerous or reacting in an aggressive way to threatening situations.

If we get stuck in reacting stressfully, though, we have continuous elevated cortisol as a result, and many studies have linked this excess cortisol with worsening overall cognitive functioning, memory, the ability to get things together, slower thinking and worse social skills. Ultimately, this leads to a greater risk of dementia and Alzheimer's in later years.[194]

What's actually going on in the brain is that cortisol is triggering these stress responses in the limbic brain, which includes the hippocampus. This part of the brain then feeds back to put the brakes on further cortisol release. But with prolonged stress, the brakes don't get fully applied, so we get into a negative loop of continued cortisol leading to increased hippocampal brain shrinkage.

The negative loop of sugar, alcohol and stress

But this isn't the only negative feedback loop that reacting stressfully can get you stuck in. When we feel overwhelmed and are having difficulty dealing with circumstances we consider stressful, there is a natural tendency to want to let off steam, or dissipate energy. The psychologist and philosopher Oscar Ichazo calls these energy-dissipating behaviours the 'doors of compensation'. There are quite a few. Toximania, such as drinking alcohol, smoking or taking other drugs, is a common choice. This is largely because alcohol causes an immediate increase in the calming neurotransmitter GABA by opening up GABA receptors, and the increased GABA then switches off adrenalin, at least for an hour or so. That's a main reason we use alcohol to relax. But there are two problems with this. First, the effect wears off, and drinking too much in the evening actually shuts down the GABA receptors the next day, so we get into a cycle of feeling more anxious and stressed. Secondly, alcohol is a neurotoxin and ultimately contributes to a brain downgrade, increasing the risk of dementia.

Another favourite 'door of compensation', especially among those who don't drink, is sugar. This is partly because of the 'feel-good' effect of glucose stimulating the brain's reward system, but an over-load of sugar can be quite intoxicating and, in a way, numbing. But what makes the combo of sugar and stress particularly insidious is that glucose cranks up the adrenal system, magnifying the response to stress and the corresponding cortisol levels.[195] Just in case you're wondering, foods high in protein or fat don't do this. It is specific-ally sugar or glucose.

Stimulants containing caffeine do, of course, increase adrenal hormones such as cortisol, as we saw earlier, so if we 'cope' with stress by drinking alcohol or eating sugar or both, then the likeli-hood is that the next day we'll feel more dopey and anxious or stressy on waking, due to the lack of GABA receptors and lower blood sugar levels. So we'll be inclined to have a caffeinated drink and want to eat something sweet. This then sets us up for more cortisol release, which makes us more stressed, so by the evening we need more alcohol. This combo increasingly shrinks our hippocam-pus, which then no longer gives the full feedback signal to switch off cortisol. So we start living in a constant state of stress.

If this is you, read on – in Chapter 18 I'll give you some top tips for getting out of this cycle.

Balancing hormones for mind and mood

Women have a higher risk of dementia than men. There is some debate about how much this is simply to do with women living longer and to what extent the drop in hormones, both progester-one and oestrogen, have to do with it.

Once a woman stops ovulating (and many women start to have anovulatory cycles in their forties), progesterone levels crash. Oestrogen, in essence, make things grow, while progesterone – pro-gestation, prepping the womb for fertilization – keeps tissue healthy. It is also anti-inflammatory and calms down the stress response, counteracting adrenalin by promoting GABA.

So, when progesterone levels fall pre-menopause, a woman become 'oestrogen dominant'. This is why the breast and ovarian cancer risk goes up – too many growth signals.

This oestrogen dominance continues during and after the meno-pause, although oestrogen levels halve post-menopause. Oestrogen is also made in fat cells and is present in meat and milk. So, being menopausal, overweight and eating meat and milk is a recipe for oestrogen dominance. This situation is made worse by oestrogen-based hormone replacement therapy (HRT).

The medical establishment is, however, obsessed with oestrogen and largely ignores progesterone, which, as you'll shortly realize, is the real hero.

While there is dubious evidence that those using HRT might have a lower risk of dementia and Alzheimer's, studies do not actually show benefit, according to the most comprehensive recent review.[196] This doesn't surprise me.

As we saw above, too much of the stress hormone cortisol leads to brain shrinkage. Progesterone dampens down the stress response. This is why many women find themselves more on edge, moody, stressed, anxious and sometimes even aggressive during the menopause. It is also why bio-identical progesterone cream can switch off a panic attack (*see page 217*).

The rationale for bio-identical progesterone cream is that it is given in low, physiological doses straight into the bloodstream, thus mimicking the normal levels found in pre-menopausal women. Unlike oestrogen, it is also anti-cancer, because it doesn't stimulate the growth of cancer cells. In fact, it opposes oestrogen, because they share the same receptors, thus it can reduce cancer risk. Most anti-breast cancer drugs work in the same way, blocking oestrogen receptors.

Too much oestrogen also interferes with the reception of thyroxine, the thyroid hormone that energizes us. Post-menopause, many women develop an underactive thyroid, which has symptoms similar to those of dementia.

The biggest problem with progesterone is that, being natural, it is not patentable. To make matters worse, pharma have invented messed-up progesterone molecules, called progestins, which *can* be patented and hence are profitable, and do create problems, increasing, for example, the risk of ovarian cancer. Lots of studies and articles mistakenly call these synthetic lookalikes 'progesterone', when they aren't the same thing at all. This also means that very little money is available for progesterone research, especially large-scale randomized controlled trials, which cost an average of $7 million.

Why progesterone is brain-friendly

What actually happens when you go into a state of stress is that you produce cortisol, which is made from progesterone, which is made from pregnenolone (*see figure below*). So, the more cortisol you make, the less pregnenolone is available to make progesterone, so that plummets. So, too, do the healthy stress hormone DHEA and testosterone. This leads to low drive, less desire for sex and generally not feeling good and happy.

Progesterone deficiency also promotes glutamates, which increase anxiety. Giving progesterone cream reverses all this, promoting GABA, which helps turn off adrenalin. Your whole system calms down, including your metabolism, so you feel calmer. If oestrogen also drops, you get hot flushes.

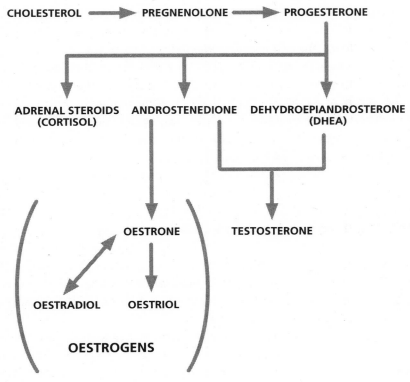

Fig 23. The sex hormone family tree

If you've experienced cognitive decline with the menopause, you might want to consider using bio-identical progesterone cream (*see Resources*). The Marion Gluck Clinic is a centre of excellence for this approach, headed by their clinical director, Dr Ghazala Aziz-Scott.

She says, 'I see many women in the peri-menopausal and menopausal period who complain of memory problems, low mood and increased anxiety. From the pattern of symptoms and confirmatory testing, I inevitably see low progesterone levels and often treat with transdermal progesterone cream. If the woman is also low in oestrogen and testosterone, we make a personalized cream to address these imbalances.

'Most women notice a considerable improvement within a few weeks and report feeling like their old self – better moods and concentration, with the anxiety levels dialled down.'

Liz, age 45, is a case in point. She presented with 21-day cycles, previously 28-day cycles for the last year, with heavier cycles. She was emotional, tearful and very irritable. Sleep was disrupted and she had brain fog and poor retention of memory. She was also having extreme panic attacks, with her GP giving her propranolol, and had been in bed for three days. She had catastrophic thinking, being convinced she was going to crash on the motorway.

Bloods showed good levels of oestrogen, but low progesterone and low testosterone. She was started on progesterone 50mg transdermal cream twice daily and testosterone 0.5mg cream and had a huge improvement in symptoms such that she could function.

Testosterone for men is brain-friendly

A similar story exists for older men when testosterone levels fall. Again, too much 'stress' demand for cortisol leads to low testosterone. Low testosterone levels increase the risk of dementia, with the lower the level, the greater the risk.[197]

Some studies giving testosterone, but not all, show improvement in cognitive function. Much like progesterone, if bio-identical testosterone is given and a person reduces stress, eats a low-GL diet and supplements omega-3 and B vitamins, replacing testosterone is, in my opinion, more likely to be effective.

For those wanting to explore the 'male menopause', called the andropause, the best book is *Testosterone Resistance* by Dr Malcolm Carruthers. He set up the Centre for Men's Health (*see Resources*). Reg is a case in point:

Reg was in his mid-forties when he first started feeling irritable much of the time. Over the next few years things got worse – he began having night sweats, his memory became poorer, he had outbursts of irrational anger and his libido plummeted.

'I no longer felt like myself,' he said. 'I went right off sex, I had no energy whatsoever and my memory was so bad I had to write simple instructions on my hand, such as "Lock office door."'

Blood tests revealed his testosterone level was less than 10 pg/ml of 'free' testosterone – half the normal level for a 70-year-old.

He was prescribed testosterone capsules. 'Within two days my memory returned, my depression had lifted and my libido had returned. I felt sharp, bright and full of energy.' His other symptoms eventually all disappeared.

In summary, we have learned that:

- Sleep repairs the brain. We need about seven hours a night.
- Melatonin, made from the amino acid tryptophan, is a powerful brain antioxidant. Supplementing either melatonin or tryptophan or 5-HTP helps if you suffer from insomnia.
- Stress ages the brain and inhibits brain repair. Don't get stuck in a stress cycle, using alcohol to unwind.
- The natural amino acid GABA helps turn off stress. So do HeartMath exercises (*see page 280*).
- A deficiency in progesterone in women and testosterone in men later in life can lead to cognitive decline. There's a good case for giving bio-identical progesterone to post-menopausal women and testosterone to older men who are struggling with memory if their level is tested and found to be low.

PART 3

Reclaim Your Brain

Applying the brain-upgrade essentials, this part shows you how to resolve specific mental health issues and reclaim your brain health – your good mood, calm mind, sharp memory, great sleep, freedom from anxiety, stress and addiction, and connection with your purpose. It also includes guidance for building healthy young brains in children.

Improve Your Mood

If you find yourself becoming enthusiastically negative, not happy most of the time, stuck in a black hole, not enjoying your life and not seeing a way forward, read on to discover the seven essentials to improve your mood.

A staggering and increasing number of people feel like this, with one in six being prescribed anti-depressants. I strongly believe a combination of psychological and nutritional solutions is the way up from down, not drugs. The biggest problem with anti-depressants, apart from their poor effectiveness compared with some of the natural agents I'll be discussing, is you can't get off them. According to Professor John Read from the International Institute for Psychiatric Drug Withdrawal, up to 86 per cent of people experience withdrawal effects, half of which are severe, and not uncommonly for several months – and GPs have no idea how to help them.[1]

Professor John Read has a simple explanation for much of the depression we experience: 'Bad things happen which make you depressed.' There's a lot of truth in this. But some people bounce back and others don't.

Psychologists also point out that depression is often anger without enthusiasm, and it is important to examine if you are living your life true to yourself and what you believe in. If you are stuck in a circumstance – a job, relationship or situation – that doesn't support your growth towards your full potential, no amount of omega-3 or B vitamins is going to change that. I often recommend people read the book *Lost Connections* by Johann Hari,[2] which explores very well all the psychological and social avenues that lead to feeling down. However, it completely ignores nutrition and its profound impact on the chemistry of mood. Having rightly dissed anti-depressants as the answer, Hari then dismisses the whole idea that brain chemistry has anything to do with depression, throwing the baby out with the bathwater.

As I will show you, brain chemistry, and what you eat, have everything to do with how you feel and both your physical and mental energy and ability to think straight. In fact, you cannot separate psychology from brain chemistry. Social media addiction, for example, which can be a cause of depression, with everyone creating a 'false self' that looks fantastic, reinforcing the idea that you are a loser, and cyber-bullying are extreme examples, both of which deplete the reward system of the brain, which runs on dopamine. When you run out of dopamine, you feel down. And dopamine is made directly from the amino acid tyrosine.

At the Brain Bio Centre, which is part of the charitable Food for the Brain Foundation, we've helped many people come out of a low mood by tuning up their brain chemistry, not with drugs, but nutrients.

Gabrielle, who had been suffering from extreme lethargy and mood swings for decades, was a case in point. 'I've been trying to feel like this for 25 years – I'm over the moon!' she told me.

Fran, who had suffered from debilitating depression, lack of confidence and fatigue, and was unable to work, turned around in a few months on the nutritional programme. 'I am back in work, feeling my old self again – feeling fantastic,' she said. 'Your approach has genuinely saved and transformed my life.'

Holly, who had been plagued by anxiety, low moods and indecisiveness for years, derived clear benefit from a nutritional upgrade. 'It's made a substantial difference,' she said. 'I feel much more balanced and have a much more positive outlook on life.'

How did these people turn around? By correcting one of the most commonly critical factors. Please don't assume they all apply to you, because they are unlikely to, but the great news about these nutritional approaches is that they tend to work fast, within 10 days, and aren't harmful or addictive, so even if you try one approach and it doesn't work, there's no harm done.

You can hone in on what's likely to help by testing, for example, your omega-3, vitamin D, HbA1c (blood sugar) and homocysteine level to see if you have room for improvement. These tests are available with home-test kits (*see Resources*).

Omega-3 – a proven anti-depressant

As we have learned, omega-3 fats literally built our *Homo sapiens* brains, and the higher our intake, the better our mood. Omega-3 fats affect both the structure and function of our brains, improving the communication of neurotransmitters and reducing inflammation, which is a hallmark of so many mental health problems, whether as a cause or a consequence.

Omega-3 fish oils contain both DHA and EPA fatty acids. DHA is structural, building in the brain. EPA is more functional, helping brain communication. The science shows, beyond a shadow of doubt, that they work for depression. Back in 2014, the most comprehensive study of all 19 studies up to that date concluded: 'The use of omega-3 fats is effective both in patients with major depressive disorder and milder depression.'[3] By 2019, there were 33 such meta-analyses showing that omega-3 EPA at doses up to 4,400 mg/day (with an average therapeutic dose of 1,000–2,000mg of EPA per day) were significantly effective in depression.[4] The lowest level of effect was in supplements providing 300mg of combined EPA and DHA.

One of the first placebo-controlled trials, by Dr Andrew Stoll from Harvard Medical School back in 2002, gave 40 depressed patients either omega-3 supplements or a placebo and found a highly significant improvement in the patients on supplements.[5] In the next study, 20 people suffering from severe depression who were already taking anti-depressants but were still depressed were given either a concentrated form of omega-3 or a placebo.[6] By the third week, the depressed patients on an EPA-rich fish oil supplement were showing major improvement in their mood, whereas those on the placebo were not. So you don't have to wait long for a result.

It also works for bipolar. Dr Sophia Frangou from the Institute of Psychiatry in London gave an EPA supplement or a placebo to 26 depressed people with bipolar disorder and again found a significant improvement in those taking the supplement.[7]

If any drug had this kind of consistent, positive evidence over 20 years of research, it would be a blockbuster. Yet few doctors even mention it, let alone assess their depressed patients' blood levels of omega-3 or ask about dietary intake.

But omega-3 fish oils aren't just a mood improver. Study after study has shown that the combination of EPA and DHA means less aggression, fewer emotional and physical outbursts and, generally, a calmer and more content outlook. There may be other benefits too. Psychiatrist Joe Hibbeln told me, 'My patients, on 4 grams of EPA and DHA a day, tell me that they feel an emotional state of content accompanied by better skin, hair and a better sex life.'

As we saw earlier, you have to be eating oily fish at least three times a week to have a chance of getting 1,000mg of EPA. My recommendation is you do both this and supplement 1,000mg a day to achieve closer to 2,000mg a day, which is probably the most effective amount if you're feeling depressed. Some people may need more.

By the way, the conversion of the type of omega-3 in plant foods such as chia and flax, called ALA, into EPA is about 5 per cent and into DHA is about 0.05 per cent, so there is no possibility of reaching these levels on a plant-based diet, without supplements.

Serotonin and 5-HTP – the enlightener

How does omega-3 improve your mood? One likely mechanism is that it improves how brain cells communicate and improves sensitivity to serotonin, the brain's feel-good neurotransmitter. Serotonin is what's called a tryptamine. From it, we make melatonin, another tryptamine, which, as we have seen, controls the sleep–wake cycle. But what are serotonin, melatonin and all the brain's tryptamines made from? The answer is the naturally occurring amino acid tryptophan, which is then converted into 5-hydroxy-tryptophan, or 5-HTP for short, and 5-HTP is the most potent form of tryptophan, readily converting to serotonin.[8] Animals given tryptophan show a clear increase over the next few hours in brain levels of both 5-HTP and serotonin.[9] People with a prior history of depression, deprived of tryptophan, tend to become more depressed within 24 hours,[10] and depressed people given 5-HTP get significant relief, usually more than from anti-depressants in head-to-head trials, but with few of the side-effects and no withdrawal problems.

The first study proving the mood-boosting power of 5-HTP was carried out in the 1970s in Japan, under the direction of Professor Isamu Sano of the Osaka University Medical School. He gave 107 patients 50–300mg of 5-HTP per day, and within two weeks, more than half experienced improvements in their symptoms. By the end of the four weeks of the study, nearly three-quarters of the patients reported either complete relief or significant improvement, with no side-effects.[11]

There have been 29 studies using 5-HTP for the treatment of depression, involving 1,050 people to date, most of which proved to be effective.[12]

Unfortunately, there is no reliable and easily available test to measure your serotonin level. The ideal place to measure it would be in the brain's cerebrospinal fluid (CSF), but that would require a lumbar puncture! Some labs measure serotonin in blood plasma or its breakdown product, 5-HIAA, in urine, but neither correlate well with CSF serotonin.[13] The only measure I know of that reflects brain levels is measuring platelet serotonin, where serotonin is stored before transferring across into the brain. Platelet serotonin tests are unfortunately not readily available (*see Resources*).

Why not take 5-HTP instead of anti-depressant drugs? Why not, indeed. As a nutrient, it is not patentable and hence not profitable. However, a pharmaceutical review suggests adding it to patentable drugs (the combo could be patentable) to increase the effectiveness of anti-depressants.[14]

Holly's case shows what can be done. She felt that anxiety, depression and indecision were ruining her life. She constantly felt stressed, had frequent mood swings, would cry for no reason and was finding it hard to think straight. A platelet serotonin test showed her serotonin levels were rock bottom. She was also very low in magnesium, which is an important mineral for mental health. One study gave 248mg to 126 adults and reported,

'Magnesium is effective for mild-to-moderate depression in adults,'
with improvements in both depression and anxiety.[15]

Holly was recommended a supplement programme to increase
her serotonin, including 5-HTP, B vitamins and 300mg of
magnesium. Very quickly, she began to feel much better. She started
sleeping well, her anxiety reduced and her mood lifted. Her
serotonin level normalized and she was amazed at the reduction in
anxiety, and said it had made a substantial difference and that
she felt much more balanced and could see the positive side of life,
rather than the negative.

Are there any downsides to this kind of approach? Most serotonin
is made in the gut from tryptophan, or 5-HTP, and a few people
experience mild to moderate nausea or stomach cramps when starting to take 5-HTP. This often resolves if they continue or lower the
dose. Two studies report that enteric-coated or slow-release 5-HTP
capsules substantially reduce gastrointestinal adverse events.[16] The
slow-release form has the added advantage of increasing the length
of time 5-HTP is effective.[17] Vitamin D may also have something to
do with this, since it encourages the conversion of tryptophan into
serotonin in the brain, where you want it, and suppresses it in the
gut.[18] So make sure you have enough vitamin D (*see page 206
below*).

The other concern has been the theoretical possibility of 'serotonin syndrome' – an overload of serotonin – if 5-HTP is taken with
anti-depressant drugs. But, according to the most recent comprehensive review, '5-HTP has never been associated with serotonin syndrome
in humans' and 'Even in combination with anti-depressants it has
a low propensity to cause severe adverse events in humans.'[19] In
fact, if anything, long-term anti-depressant use is likely to deplete
serotonin,[20] in which case 5-HTP could help lessen withdrawal
symptoms.

Even so, I generally advise people not to take 5-HTP with anti-
depressants, but certainly to start weaning in 5-HTP when weaning
out anti-depressants, under the guidance of a doctor, and to take a
decent dose (200 to 300mg daily) on stopping an anti-depressant,
since it is highly likely that long-term anti-depressant use will have
depleted serotonin. The lowest viable amount is 100mg, and I
recommend taking 50mg in the morning and evening. Since 5-HTP

helps make melatonin, which helps you to sleep, there is a good reason to take it an hour before bedtime if you have difficulty sleeping or don't appear to dream. There is some debate about whether it is better absorbed on an empty stomach, as are other amino acids, so I would say take the first supplement at least 15 minutes before breakfast and the second an hour before bed.

Tyrosine – the motivator

The reason the new generation of SNRI anti-depressants are serotonin *and* noradrenalin reuptake inhibitors is that when noradrenalin (norepinephrine in the US), made from dopamine, becomes depleted, you lose motivation or drive. While low serotonin is associated with the 'black hole' of depression, low dopamine or noradrenalin is associated with the lack of drive to do something to make yourself feel better.

We know that almost any addiction – social media, gambling, sugar, alcohol, sex, cocaine – is associated with dopamine depletion, because it targets the brain's 'reward' system to make you feel good about yourself. Eventually, the receptors for dopamine, and noradrenalin, start to shut down. This also depresses serotonin. That's why marketing is aimed at triggering this response. Overuse, as in too much sugar, alcohol, caffeine, social media engagement and so on can lead to a burnt-out reward system like this, life seems pointless, nothing floats your boat. I believe this scenario is a major driver of the big increase in teenage suicide, although we do also know that suicidal ideation is a not uncommon side-effect of anti-depressant drugs.

Instead of blocking the noradrenalin reuptake channel with an SNRI drug, which is likely to lead to even less noradrenalin/dopamine being available, and consequently even worse withdrawal effects, why not provide the nutrient from which dopamine and noradrenalin are made? Why not, indeed. This is the naturally occurring amino acid tyrosine. While I love the combo of 5-HTP with tyrosine, I want to emphasize that there's not a lot of point taking tyrosine if you keep eating loads of sugar, drinking loads of coffee, being addicted to social media and using alcohol to calm down and numb out in the evening. So, step one is to wean yourself off caffeine and alcohol dependency and start eating a low-GL diet (*see chapters 11 and 23*).

The recommended amount of tyrosine to supplement daily, ideally with 5-HTP, is 750mg to 1,500mg, taken twice a day away from food, either 15 minutes before or two hours after a meal. Some supplements combine tyrosine with 5-HTP (*see Resources*).

Chromium and your blood sugar balance

Not only do diabetes and depression go hand in hand, with depression often preceding a diabetes diagnosis by two years, but HbA1c, the long-term measure of blood sugar control, predicts both. HbA1c is a simple blood test which doctors routinely measure and is also available as a home-test kit (*see Resources*). It's not just a black or white test, as in diabetic or healthy; there's a grey zone with a score less than 6.5 per cent and greater than 5.5 per cent (or between 48 to 37mmol/mol), which means you're starting to lose blood sugar stability, which is an important factor to consider, given that dips in blood sugar levels are a known promoter of low mood. The diabetes zone is above 6.5 per cent or 48mmol/mol.

So, a major mood essential is to substantially reduce the sugar in your diet and reduce your overall intake of carbs, especially refined, white carbs. Instead, either eat a low-GL diet or go one step further and try out a ketogenic diet (*see Chapter 23*), which has also been shown to be effective for depression.

The trace mineral chromium, if supplemented, might both help cravings for sugar and improve your mood. While chromium supplements are known to improve metabolic syndrome and help stabilize blood sugar levels, reducing HbA1c in people with type 2 diabetes,[21] chromium's effect on mood is little known, and was discovered in an interesting way.

Malcolm McLeod, Professor of Psychiatry at the University of North Carolina, had a patient, George, who had been severely depressed for several years, then suddenly got completely better after taking a nutritional supplement. McLeod thought it was a placebo effect and, since the supplement contained ephedra, a potentially dangerous herb, he asked George to stop taking it. What happened in the following week amazed him.

'It was unbelievable. I didn't believe it at first, but without the supplement, his depression returned.'

He couldn't ignore the rapid change and concluded that it might be to do with one of six ingredients in the supplement. So, he gave George an envelope containing one unidentified ingredient to take for the next week. Six weeks later, having ruled out the other ingredients, he'd determined that it was the chromium in the supplement that had relieved George's depression.

He then set up a randomized controlled trial of patients with the same kind of depression George had, and six out of ten got completely better on chromium.

The classic picture of what's called melancholic depression is someone who doesn't eat enough, doesn't sleep enough and loses weight. But many people suffering from depression, like George, are gaining weight, feel tired all the time, crave carbohydrates and could sleep forever. People with this kind of 'atypical' depression often get instant relief by taking 400 to 600mcg of chromium a day, which is also the effective dose to help control blood sugar in diabetics.

Check out these questions to see if this might apply to you:

Do you crave sweets or other carbohydrates or tend to gain weight?
Are you tired for no obvious reason, or do your arms and legs feel heavy?
Do you tend to feel sleepy or groggy much of the time?
Are your feelings easily hurt by rejection from others?
Did your depression begin before the age of 30?

If you answer 'yes' to even one of these questions and you often feel low, the chances are chromium and a low-GL diet will help you.

Up to a third of those diagnosed with depression fulfil the criteria of atypical depression.[22] A survey of several hundred depressed patients, conducted by Andrew Nierenberg, MD, Associate Director of the Depression and Clinical Research Program at Massachusetts General Hospital, found that 'atypical' depression affected one in five diagnosed with major depression and an even higher percentage of younger women also with anxiety.[23] A study in China of over 1,000 depressed patients identified 15 per cent as 'atypical'.[24]

McLeod went on to test his theory by running a double-blind study of 15 patients with atypical depression. Five were given a placebo and ten were given 600mcg of chromium picolinate. At the end of eight weeks, seven out of the ten patients on chromium had had major improvement, compared to none on the placebo.[25]

A larger trial has confirmed McLeod's discovery. Professor of Psychiatry John Doherty, at Weill Medical College of Cornell University gave 113 patients with atypical depression either chromium 600mcg or a placebo for eight weeks and measured their mental state using the Hamilton Rating Scale of Depression. At the end of the eight weeks, 65 per cent of those on the chromium had had a major improvement in their depression, compared with 33 per cent on the placebos.[26]

Chromium is particularly helpful for pre-menstrual mood disorders. A study gave chromium to women with pre-menstrual mood disorders and found significant mood improvements,[27] and a placebo-controlled study reported those on chromium having 'greater reductions in bingeing, weight, and depression'.[28]

Another, longer trial tested the effects of chromium on bipolar disorder over two years. Almost one-third of patients reported a great decrease in depressant symptoms.[29]

Chromium is a remarkably safe mineral, even at amounts several times higher than 600mcg long term. George, the original patient, has been on chromium for over a decade and it has positively transformed his life.

McLeod recommends taking chromium twice a day, although you should take it in the morning (at breakfast and lunch), as it can cause insomnia and vivid dreaming. If it is going to work, it often works within two to three days. In McLeod's studies with chromium, many of his patients obtained complete relief in a matter of weeks. The Hamilton Rating Scores of Depression of several patients dropped below 5 within two weeks, which means they no longer had depression. You don't see this on SSRIs.

Chromium levels decline with age, so the older you are, the more you need. Our diets are, generally, very deficient anyway, but the more fast-releasing carbohydrates you eat, the more chromium you lose. Stress also depletes chromium.

These results with chromium fit in well with other promising frontiers in the nutritional treatment of depression. 5-HTP, the precursor of serotonin, needs insulin to get from the blood into the brain. So, chromium may help in this way. Omega-3s also improve serotonin's ability to bind to receptors.

Given the role that stress, highly refined and high-sugar diets and caffeine have on blood sugar, and the lack of chromium and omega-3s in most people's diets, it isn't perhaps so difficult to comprehend why the incidence of depression is on the increase in the 21st century.

The lowest amount of chromium I'd recommend is 200mcg, which is what you'll find in most supplements, although most studies have given 400–600mcg in the morning and 200mcg at lunch.

Think zinc

Zinc is another essential mineral that is vital for the brain. It's found in protein-rich foods, such as nuts and seeds, and the richest food source is oysters.

Zinc is one of the most commonly deficient minerals in a junk-food diet. You can even go crazy without enough of it (*see page 253*). Those with depression are often deficient in it and, especially in such people, supplementing at least 15mg of zinc (you can safely take twice this) is effective, with a combined effect from all studies of reducing the risk of depression by more than a quarter (28 per cent).[30]

A good multivitamin should provide at least 10mg. Zinc is also important for lowering homocysteine, so you may find a homocysteine-lowering supplement will provide a little more.

Methyl magic, SAMe and B vitamins

The word you often hear in relation to feeling down is 'disconnected' – in terms of social connection, love connection, spiritual connection and meaning of life connection. The biochemical equivalent of connection is methylation.

B vitamins

You'll recall that methylation is dependent on B vitamins, especially B6, B12 and folate, and a deficiency is associated with a greater risk of depression.[31]

Healthy methylation, indicated by a low plasma homocysteine level, is essential for making all the key neurotransmitters, including serotonin, dopamine and noradrenalin, and those suffering from depression have higher homocysteine levels.[32] This relationship is particularly strong for men.[33]

While I've spoken a lot about raised homocysteine predicting cognitive decline and dementia later in life, methylation is vital for all, at every stage of life. An example of this relates to a study of 89 children and adolescents with depression compared with 'control' patients of the same age. The depressed patients had much higher homocysteine, indicating worse methylation, and clearly lower B12 and vitamin D levels, with the levels predicting the severity of their symptoms.[34]

Not all studies giving people with depression B vitamins (usually B12 or folic acid) have worked. This is not surprising, since you only need larger intake of these vitamins if you have a raised homocysteine level or low level of the vitamins.

A UK study tested the effects of adding folic acid to anti-depressant treatment. Depressed people were either given an SSRI anti-depressant with 500mcg of folic acid or the SSRI with a placebo. Nine out of ten of the women taking the SSRI with folic acid had at least a halving of their depression rating.[35]

A study in Pakistan selected 199 depressed patients with lowish B12 (190–300pg/ml) and gave them anti-depressants either with or without a weekly B12 injection (1,000µg). Those given B12 did much better, with all on B12 reducing their HAM-D depression rating by at least 20 per cent.[36] What's interesting about this study is that in the UK the 'reference' range for B12 that is considered normal is anything above 180pg/ml. This study in Pakistan, which has more vegetarians, found a quarter of those with depression have low levels of B12, below 200pg/ml. This study used 300pg/ml as the cut-off point for inclusion in the study. In the EU and Japan, the lower end of the reference range is rightly 500pg/ml (*see page 293*). I would not be surprised if at least a third of those with depression were found to be low in B12.

The moral of this story is that if you are suffering from depression, especially if this is accompanied with any cognitive issues such as feeling disconnected or having memory concerns, it's worth testing both your homocysteine and B12 levels and supplementing accordingly. If your homocysteine is high, take a homocysteine-lowering formula (*see Resources*). If your serum B12 level is below 500pg/ml, take 100mcg, and if below 300pg/ml, take 500mcg.

> *Amanda-Jane is a case in point. She was suffering with chronic fatigue and low mood, so she decided to check her homocysteine level. She was shocked when she found her H score was 26 mcmol/l (it should be below 7).*
>
> *She followed the diet and supplements I recommend in the book, and almost immediately her sleep improved. Within four weeks, she had much more energy.*
>
> *Two months later, she retested her homocysteine level and found it had dropped to 9 units. That's a 64 per cent decrease.*
>
> *Here's what she said: 'I feel much better. My mood is very positive – no panic or depression. I feel buoyant, energetic and enthusiastic. I'm sleeping much better and my PMS has disappeared.'*

SAMe – the master methylator

The purpose of optimizing methylation is to produce S-adenosyl methionine, or SAMe (pronounced Sammy), as Figure 16 (*page 104*) shows. In the USA, SAMe is available over the counter and can be bought online for personal use. In the EU, it is not, however, as it has been classified as a medicine. This is a classic 'catch-22' – as a natural substance, it can't be patented, hence is not inherently profitable, but as it works, it is classified as a medicine, so can't be sold without a medical licence. But the process for obtaining such a licence, especially without the monopoly of a patent, is too expensive for anyone to foot the bill for a natural substance. Therefore, there is less appetite for doing research on this safe and effective anti-depressant, no budget to promote it and few doctors know about it.

A thorough Cochrane review of eight trials involving almost 1,000 people shows SAMe has surpassed SSRIs in all trials,[37] with minimal adverse effects – and no withdrawal effects.

It also works fast. In one trial with people who hadn't responded to SSRI anti-depressants, supplementing 800mg of SAMe twice a day produced a big 5-point improvement in HAM-D scores within a week.[38] A recent trial, using a lower 200mg dose of SAMe given with a probiotic, *Lactobacillus plantarum*, showed improvement in those with mild to moderate depression within two weeks.[39]

I recommend taking 400mg SAMe in an enterically coated capsule twice a day as an alternative or adjunct to lowering homocysteine with B vitamins, especially if you find it difficult to bring your homocysteine level down. It can be very effective together with 5-HTP.

Also, bear in mind that omega-3 and B vitamins are co-dependent, as Chapter 10 explains, so some studies giving B vitamins may not have worked in those low in omega-3. An example of this, given in this chapter, was the B-PROOF study, giving a decent amount of B vitamins (B12 100mcg, folic acid 500mcg) to older adults and monitoring depression. They didn't appear to deliver any benefit in preventing depression or improving mood, or with memory, until they looked at the difference between those with good or bad omega-3 status. In those with good omega-3 status the B vitamins worked.[40] So, I recommend you always make sure you have both enough omega-3 and enough B vitamins, if you're feeling down.

Vitamin D – the sunshine vitamin

Vitamin D is an all-rounder as far as your brain and mental health are concerned. It helps neurotransmission and has anti-inflammatory and neuroprotective effects on the brain by reducing both inflammation and the oxidative stress.[41]

Generally speaking, the lower your vitamin D, the worse your mood, which makes it especially important to supplement vitamin D from October to March if you live in the UK or at a similar latitude in the northern hemisphere, for during those months the angle of the sun is very low and you're also less likely to get outdoors and expose your skin to sunlight. It's best to assume that we are all vitamin D deficient in winter, unless we travel to the sun, and need to supplement at least 15mcg (600iu), although twice this may be necessary to correct deficiency.

The lower your vitamin D level, the more depressed you are likely to feel. If your mood takes a dip in winter months, this is a key sign that you might need more. That's what researchers at the University of Tromsø in Norway found on testing 441 volunteers who were given a test for depression and also a test for blood levels of vitamin D, then given either a vitamin D supplement or a placebo. Tested one year on, those given the vitamin D had substantially lower depression ratings.[42]

However, you don't have to wait for a year to get a lift in mood. An eight-week study in Australia found that some of those given vitamin D supplements had an improvement in mood in only five days.[43] Another study, in Iran, gave a single vitamin D injection and reported an improvement in depression when measured three months on.[44]

Since vitamin D is stored in the body, there is no need to supplement daily. You can take a weekly dose. In the Norwegian study, they gave 20,000iu or 40,000iu weekly. Both worked and there wasn't a big difference in the effect on mood. So, you can assume that 20,000iu weekly or 3,000iu daily would likely be sufficient.

However, the yardstick for what you need is really whatever gets your blood level into the optimal range. In the study above, those given 20,000iu a week averaged a blood level of 88nmol/l, while those given 40,000iu averaged 111nmol/l. It is now well recognized that levels above 75nmol/l correlate with good health for many health measures, while levels above 100nmol/l might be even better is some respects. My recommendation is to test yourself and consider anything below 50nmol/l to be deficient, and above 75 nmol/l to be sufficient, with an optimal level being closer to 100nmol/l. If you then supplement 3,000iu daily, or seven times this weekly, especially from October to March, retest yourself against these yardsticks.

But it isn't just vitamin D we need, it's sunlight. During the summer months, if you are spending half an hour outdoors in the sun in short sleeves or shorts or with even more skin exposure, even a multivitamin that provides you with 800iu (just a quarter of what you need in the darker months) might be sufficient.

The other way to boost your light exposure is with light therapy. Canadian researchers compared the effects of an anti-depressant (fluoxetine), a placebo and 30 minutes daily of light therapy as soon as possible on waking on people with major depression. Light therapy was both superior to the placebo and the anti-depressant, which was no better than the placebo.[45] I have a full-spectrum light (*see Resources*) in my study, which I put on in the winter when I'm writing in the early morning, before the sun comes up.

The best food sources of vitamin D are oily fish and eggs. A serving of salmon or mackerel is likely to give you 400iu. Two eggs will provide about 130iu. In some countries, though not the UK, milk is fortified with vitamin D, but otherwise it is not a great source. Some mushrooms are purposely fortified with vitamin D by exposing them to UV light.

Daryl, a patient at the Brain Bio Centre, was suffering from what he described as 'brain fog' and he felt very low, irritable and angry, particularly during the winter.

His blood tests showed very low levels of both vitamin D and essential fats. We gave him supplements of both vitamin D and omega-3, and recommended eating more oily fish.

He quickly noticed what he described as 'a massive improvement' in his symptoms. For the first time in six years, he was no longer waking with headaches, instead feeling thoroughly refreshed.

In summary, the way up from down is to:

- Eat a low-GL diet, with plenty of oily fish and eggs.
- Avoid sugar.
- Cut back on stimulants and alcohol.
- Make sure your daily supplements include omega-3, B vitamins (with extra B12 if your homocysteine level is high), vitamin D, zinc, magnesium and chromium, plus the amino acids 5-HTP and tyrosine.

18

Deprogram Anxiety and Build Stress Resilience

Stress is often expressed emotionally as anxiety, which affects many people to varying degrees. In my '100% Health' survey of over 55,000 people, two in three (66 per cent) said they got anxious or tense easily, and 39 per cent said they often felt nervous or 'hyperactive'. For some people, extreme anxiety and panic attacks can become so frequent as to be debilitating and life limiting.

As well as feelings of fear and an inability to think straight, the symptoms of stress can include a pounding heart, a dry mouth, excessive perspiration, insomnia, fatigue, headaches and muscle tension. Dealing with the normal challenges of daily life can be a trigger – walking into a room of people, getting stuck in traffic, travelling to an unfamiliar place, having to talk at a meeting, for example. But anxiety can also occur with no obvious cause, leaving sufferers feeling frustrated that they cannot control these reactions.

However, as we'll see, will-power alone is not the answer. Researchers working in the field of neuroscience have found that emotions operate at a much higher speed than thoughts and can frequently bypass the mind's linear reasoning process entirely.[46] The part of the brain involved in emotional processing – the amygdala – also evolved before the cognitive, i.e. thinking, part of the brain, and is highly attuned to potential danger, so is hypersensitive to possible threats.

What this means in practice is that a past event, which at the time seemed threatening, can set a pattern for future reactions. And because this trigger is often held in the subconscious, it can be hard to identify. So, for example, witnessing an angry exchange between your parents as a young child may then make you terrified of anger and confrontation. Also, if you experience a particularly challenging period that causes you to feel extreme stress or anxiety, your amygdala can become hyper-reactive, so will be looking for other potential triggers. This means you can find yourself in panic mode before your rational brain can evaluate a situation to see if such a response really is necessary. This state is referred to as 'emotional hijacking'. One of the best approaches for dealing with this is HeartMath (*see page 280*).

But there's a lot you can do with your nutrition and lifestyle. While you are working towards adopting a consistently calmer way of being, steer clear of activities that significantly raise your heart rate, as these may confuse the brain into thinking you're in an emergency situation. Opt instead for activities like yoga, meditation or *t'ai chi* that help you to relax and raise your natural energy levels. Likewise, avoid stimulants that get your heart racing – coffee, tea, cigarettes, colas, energy drinks, chocolate and caffeine pills.

The state of anxiety is synonymous with raised levels of the stress hormones adrenalin and cortisol. When your blood sugar dips (often a rebound from a blood sugar high), this promotes the release of adrenal hormones, as do stimulants such as caffeine and nicotine. So, the first step towards reducing anxiety is to balance your blood sugar by eating a low-GL diet containing slow-releasing carbohydrates eaten with protein, and avoid, or at least considerably reduce, your use of both stimulants and alcohol (*see below*). This alone has a major effect in reducing anxiety.

Managing a chain of supermarkets had left Andrew very stressed. In the day, he'd drink coffee, and in the evening, he'd relax with a beer or some wine, as otherwise he would experience difficulty sleeping. He was also gaining weight.

He went on my low-GL diet, quit drinking coffee and booze, and took my recommended supplements. Three weeks later he said, 'My energy is through the roof, I don't feel stressed and I have no problem sleeping and am waking refreshed.'

Pursue GABA: the antidote to anxiety

Most people, when faced with an intense or constant feeling of anxiety, will 'self-medicate' with either alcohol or cannabis. Or, if the anxiety is more extreme and they consult their doctor, they will possibly be given a prescription for a tranquillizer, now also called a 'mood stabilizer'. In one week in the UK, we pop something like 10 million tranquillizers, puff 10 million cannabis joints and drink 120 million alcoholic drinks.

The choice of these three drugs is no coincidence. They all promote GABA, which is the brain's peacemaker, helping to turn off excess adrenalin and calm us down. That's why that beer or glass of wine makes us feel sociable, relaxed, happy and less serious, at least for an hour, as GABA levels rise. But after that, GABA starts to fall and we feel irritable and disconnected, so we have another drink, and another one. The trouble is that after a session of drinking, GABA levels become very suppressed, leaving us grumpy and irritable. Most of us avoid this by drinking in the evening and going to sleep under the influence. What we don't realize is that alcohol also disturbs the normal cycle of dreaming, and it's dreaming that regenerates the mind. So, when we wake up in the morning, we're mentally tired, grumpy and irritable because of the low GABA, and also dehydrated and sluggish as our body detoxifies the alcohol from the night before. The net effect is that in the long run, alcohol makes us more anxious, not less. The same is true for cannabis, which, if habitually smoked, also reduces drive and motivation.

Supplement GABA and taurine

There are alternatives. GABA (gamma-aminobutyric acid) is not only a neurotransmitter, it's also an amino acid. This means it's a nutrient, and by supplementing it, you can help to promote normal healthy levels of GABA in your brain.

There is one problem, however. In the EU, GABA has been classified as a medicine, meaning it is no longer available over the counter in the UK. In some countries, including the USA, it is available in health food stores. GABA is made from taurine and glutamine, and some 'chill' supplements contain these GABA promoters.

If you can get hold of GABA, supplement 250mg to 500mg, taking it once or twice a day as a highly effective natural relaxant. But note that while it is not addictive, that doesn't mean there are no side-effects. Up to 2g a day has no reported downside; however, if you go up to 10g a day, this can certainly induce nausea or even vomiting, and a rise in blood pressure. So use GABA wisely, especially if you already have high blood pressure, starting with no more than 1g a day, and do not exceed 3g a day. If you take it in the evening, it also helps you get to sleep.

Taurine is another relaxing amino acid, similar in structure and effect to GABA. Many people think it is a stimulant because it is used in so-called 'energy drinks', but it is not. It helps you relax and unwind from high levels of adrenalin, much like GABA. It's also often recommended as an anti-ageing supplement, as supplementation slows the key markers of ageing.[47]

Taurine is highly concentrated in animal foods such as fish, eggs and meat. Vegetarians are therefore more likely to be at risk of deficiency. Try 500 to 1,000mg of taurine, taking it twice daily. There are no known cautions or adverse effects at reasonable doses.

Taurine and the amino acid glutamine help to make GABA, so you may find these in 'chill' supplements (*see Resources*).

Take B vitamins and vitamin C

B vitamins also help with anxiety. Vitamin B6 supplementation increases GABA, and supplementation of 100mg reduced self-reported anxiety in a recent study.[48] Another study found that higher vitamin B6 intake was associated with lower depression and anxiety risk in women but not in men.[49] A combination of B6 and magnesium has proven particularly effective in reducing pre-menstrual anxiety.[50,51,52] A higher intake of B vitamins is associated with lower levels of both anxiety and depression.[53] A review of all the evidence on nutrients concluded: 'Magnesium and vitamin B6 may be effective in combination in reducing pre-menstrual stress, and vitamin B6 alone may reduce anxiety effectively in older women. High-dose sustained-release vitamin C may reduce anxiety and mitigate increased blood pressure in response to stress.'[54]

Vitamin C, which is made in all animals bar a few, including primates, acts like a stress hormone. It is stored in the adrenal cortex, along with cortisol, and released into the blood, raising blood levels several-fold under conditions of stress. It actually helps cortisol to work, such that animals who make vitamin C don't have to produce so much of it. It is logical that our evolutionary loss of the ability to make vitamin C has made us more prone to stress and anxiety.

A number of studies show that increasing vitamin C reduces anxiety. A 14-day trial of 500mg of vitamin C versus a placebo, given to high-school students, found exactly this.[55] Another, giving 500mg twice a day, improved 'mental vitality' and attention and reduced fatigue.[56] Vitamin C's energy-increasing effects have been known since the 1970s, when Dr Emanuel Cheraskin at the University of Alabama showed much lower levels of fatigue in those with an intake of vitamin C above 400mg a day.[57] I recommend 1,000mg, taken twice a day, especially when you are under stress or feeling anxious.

Try relaxing herbs – valerian, hops, passion flower and ashwagandha

Valerian

Valerian (*Valeriana officinalis*) is an excellent anti-anxiety herb. As a natural relaxant, it is useful for several disorders, such as restlessness, nervousness, insomnia and hysteria, and it has also been used as a sedative for 'nervous' stomach. It acts on the brain's GABA receptors, enhancing their activity and thus offering a similar tranquillizing effect as the Valium-type drugs but without the same side-effects. To use it as a relaxant, you need 50 to 100mg twice a day, and twice this amount 45 minutes before retiring for a good night's sleep.

Since valerian potentiates sedative drugs, including muscle relaxants and antihistamines, don't take it if you are on prescribed medication without your doctor's consent. Valerian can also interact with alcohol, as well as certain psychotropic drugs and narcotics.

Hops

Hops (*Humulus lupulus*) is an ancient remedy for a good night's sleep and was probably included in beer for that reason. It helps to calm the nerves by acting directly on the central nervous system, rather than affecting GABA receptors. You need about 200mg per day, but the effect is much less than valerian, and most effective when taken in combination with these and other herbs, such as passion flower.

Passion flower

Passion flower (*Passiflora incarnata*) was a favourite of the Aztecs, who used it to make relaxing drinks. It has a mild sedative effect and promotes sleep, with no known side-effects at normal doses. It can also be helpful for hyperactive kids. You need around 100 to 200mg a day.

Combinations of these herbs are particularly effective for relieving anxiety and can really help break the pattern of reacting stressfully to life's challenges.

Hops and passion flower are best if you don't want to be zonked out.

Ashwagandha

There is good evidence for ashwagandha, an Ayurvedic herb, reducing anxiety. A randomized control trial comparing 240mg with a placebo showed a reduction in anxiety and stress and reduced cortisol. In men, testosterone levels increased.[58] It appears to help regulate the hypothalamus–pituitary–adrenal axis, balance the brain and the adrenal glands, and switch off background anxiety.

A recent review of 12 studies concluded: 'The current systematic review and dose-response meta-analysis of RCTs [randomized controlled trials] revealed a beneficial effect on both stress and anxiety following ashwagandha supplementation.'[59]

Holly is a case in point:

I had a significant relationship breakdown which left me feeling very anxious. I had heard about ashwagandha and took 500mg organic ashwagandha for a month. I felt a definite but subtle difference in my baseline anxiety levels, which also had a positive impact on physical symptoms such as IBS and muscular aches and pain.

Increase magnesium

Magnesium is another important nutrient that helps relax both our muscles and our mind. It is often included in sleep formulas (*see page 224*) for this reason. It is also a potent antioxidant and helps stabilize blood sugar. It works together with zinc and B vitamins, especially B6, in many key enzymes in the body.

The worst diet for magnesium is one that is high in meat, milk, refined foods and sugar. Not only is such a diet deficient in magnesium, but also high in calcium. The body needs the right balance of these 'push-me-pull-you' minerals that control brain, nerve and muscle function. Too much calcium in relation to magnesium can cause muscle cramping, irregular heartbeat, high blood pressure, nervousness, irritability, insomnia and depression. Stress, coffee and alcohol also deplete magnesium.

A study giving stressed but otherwise healthy adults either just magnesium or a combination of vitamin B6 (30mg) and magnesium (300mg) reported significant improvement in both anxiety and depression, with the combination being more effective.[60] The study was eight weeks long, but most improvement occurred within four weeks. Another, giving 248mg of magnesium, reported improvement in depression after six weeks.[61]

Most people eat about 270mg, but need closer to 500mg. Eating a diet rich in vegetables, nuts and seeds can get your intake up to 500mg but, much like omega-3, our ancestors would have been eating twice as much as we do today. A small handful or heaped tablespoon of chia or pumpkin seeds (28g or 1 ounce) will give you in excess of 100mg. A similar amount of almonds, peanuts or cashews will give you 80mg. A serving of oats, brown rice, potato or beans, black beans being the best, delivers about 50mg. Another great food for magnesium is wheatgerm.

The best vegetables for magnesium are greens, especially spinach, kale, chard, green beans and peas in that order. A decent serving – think half a plate – can easily deliver 100mg. As part of your brain-friendly diet (*see Chapter 25*), I encourage you to have at least two if not three servings of green veg a day, with half a plate counting as two servings, plus a small handful of nuts and seeds and one other magnesium-rich food source, such as a serving of oats, brown rice or beans. This will get you close to a daily intake of 500mg.

If you do all this and take a multi giving you 150mg of magnesium (very few provide more than 50mg), you should be in the optimum zone. But if you are especially anxious, depressed or can't sleep, supplementing 300mg of magnesium in the evening may help calm your mind.

Nutritional therapists know to supplement around 300mg of magnesium to anyone who needs more, for example, for sleep, anxiety, depression, muscle cramps or heart disease. Magnesium is also a potent antioxidant. Very few multis contain more than 50mg, the best providing up to 150mg.

Theanine: why tea is better than coffee

In studies when caffeine levels are matched, the effects of tea and coffee on mood are very different.[62] This may be because tea also contains the natural amino acid L-theanine, a relaxant. Research suggests that 50mg L-theanine naturally stimulates alpha brain waves, which are associated with a relaxed but alert mental state.[63]

Supplements containing L-theanine and GABA can help to make you feel more relaxed and less 'edgy'. A trial of 400mg of theanine has been shown to help boys with ADHD get to sleep.[64] Supplements providing combinations of GABA or its precursors, theanine, magnesium and relaxing herbs are most effective (*see Resources*).

Don't panic – nothing is under control

Some people experience panic attacks, characterized by extreme feelings of fear. Symptoms often experienced include palpitations, rapid breathing, dizziness, unsteadiness and a feeling of impending death. Those who suffer from agoraphobia, a fear of being alone or in public places, often know that they can go out or can be alone, but are afraid of having a panic attack.

As 'psychological' as this sounds, there is a biochemical imbalance behind many people's anxiety attacks, apart from, or as well as, any psychological factors. It's too much lactic acid.

When muscles don't get enough oxygen, they make energy from glucose without it. The trouble is, there's a by-product called lactic acid. As strange as this might seem, giving lactic acid to those prone to panic attacks can induce one.[65]

One way to increase lactic acid levels is to hyperventilate. Many people will do this when they're experiencing a panic attack. Hyperventilation changes the acid level of the blood by altering the balance of carbon dioxide. The body responds by producing more lactic acid. The solution is to breathe into a paper bag during a hyperventilation attack and concentrate on breathing deeply for a minute. This helps redress the balance.[66]

Moments of blood sugar dips can also both bring on hyperventilation and increase lactic acid. So, keep your blood sugar level even by eating little and often.

A more advanced and highly effective breathing technique is Buteyko breathing (*see Resources*). It is good for general anxiety, but especially good for those who often hyperventilate and have panic attacks, which can be exacerbated by the lack of CO_2 induced by over-breathing. Buteyko breathing can be taught in a workshop or one-to-one session.

The other main driver of panic attacks is just too much adrenalin. Many people don't realize that the hormone progesterone is anti-adrenalin. When levels fall low, commonly in the peri- and post-menopausal phases, women often become more anxious and prone to panic attacks. Simply rubbing natural (bio-identical) progesterone cream (*see Resources*) on the inner arms, where it is easily absorbed, can literally stop panic attacks in a few minutes.

An instant way to switch off anxiety

If you experience a panic attack or extreme anxiety, dipping your face into a basin of very cold water for 30 seconds (while holding your breath of course) can instigate what's called the diving reflex, which has a rapidly calming effect. This is because cold water stimulates the vagus nerve, which is a key part of the para-sympathetic nervous system (PNS). The PNS works in partnership with the sympathetic nervous system (SNS), which is involved in the stress response. So after a stressful event has passed, it's your PNS that takes over to calm you down and restore your body to business as usual. But triggering the diving reflex activates the PNS immediately, so you feel calmer and less stressed in a matter of seconds. Splashing your face with icy water, or pressing your face onto a plastic bag filled with ice, can have the same effect for some people, and works better if you also lean forward and hold your breath for 30 seconds. The only word of caution is that this procedure should not be attempted by anyone with a slow heart rate or low blood pressure, as it slows your heart rate.

Emily illustrates the point:

'I recently started getting panic attacks after an unpleasant week of events in which future life as I knew it became uncertain. On returning to normality, panic attacks began. I was never sure what set them off, but was in a constant state of shaky nerves, high heart rate, no appetite and feeling hot and sweaty for a month, and I couldn't work out why.

'I can happily say it's now been a three-week panic-free period. I learned about progesterone cream and the diving technique, which both dramatically helped stop the panic attacks in the moment, from a 12-hour panic to nothing. Stopping the onset of them came from a trip away, when I had time to breathe and get to know my non-panicky self, with the knowledge that I could stop them at any time if they returned.'

Stress-reduction techniques

Some people need a little extra help to learn how to switch out of the adrenalin state. There are breathing and meditation techniques for this, as well as psychotherapeutic avenues to explore, and many of them can be extremely helpful. I have been particularly impressed by HeartMath techniques (*see page 280*).

If you believe the root of your anxiety is embedded deep in your subconscious, there are also psychotherapeutic approaches that can help you to access and release negative programming, such as

Emotional Freedom Technique (EFT) and EMDR (Eye Movement Desensitization and Reprocessing) (*see Resources*).

An integrated approach works best

While the causes of high levels of anxiety are often psychological, by balancing blood sugar, reducing stimulants and ensuring optimum nutrition, plus judicially using these natural anti-anxiety herbs and nutrients, you can break the habit of reacting with fear and anxiety to life's inevitable stresses. Addressing the potential underlying triggers for anxiety is also important.

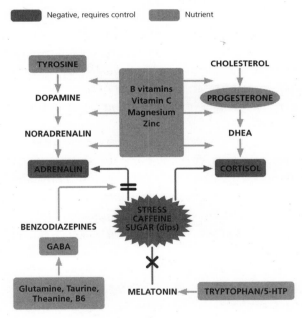

Fig 24. How nutrients help control the stress hormones adrenalin and cortisol

In terms of supplements, often a combination of relaxing amino acids and herbs is the most effective for reducing high levels of anxiety. The synergistic action of nutrients and herbs such as GABA or its precursors taurine, glutamine plus B6, magnesium and 5-HTP and either valerian or hops and passion flower, also means the doses for each can be lower. Vitamin C and B vitamins, plus zinc, are also needed for adrenal support (*see figure above*). These are my favourite 'chill' food ingredients, taken in the evening, or an hour before bed.

If you are also exhausted and unable to cope with stress, try an 'awake' formula containing tyrosine, plus adaptogenic herbs such as ginseng and Reishi in the morning (*see Resources*). Two of these before breakfast, and two chill supplements in the evening, for one month, is a great support to get yourself back on track.

In summary, we have learned that:

- Practising HeartMath is a great way to deprogram emotional hijacking.
- It's good to opt for activities like yoga, meditation or *t'ai chi*.
- Cut right back on coffee, tea, cigarettes, colas, energy drinks, chocolate and caffeine pills.
- Eat a low-GL diet (*see chapters 11 and 23*).
- Supplement B vitamins and extra vitamin C when under stress (2 grams a day).
- Supplement 300mg of magnesium and eat magnesium-rich foods such as greens, chia and pumpkin seeds.
- Consider supplementing GABA (500mg), or its precursors, glutamine and taurine, as well as theanine.
- Also try relaxing herbs – valerian, hops, passion flower and ashwagandha. You may find these kinds of 'chill' nutrients in combination formulas.
- If you're prone to panic attacks, learn the 'diving' technique; or learn Buteyko breathing (*see Resources*).
- Also explore other stress-reduction techniques such as EFT and EMDR (*see Resources*).

19

How to Get a Good Night's Sleep

Researchers tend to agree that you need up to nine hours of largely uninterrupted sleep as a teenager, decreasing to around seven hours as an older adult,[67] although some suggest doing this in two 'sittings', as in siestas. We are all different, and whatever amount of sleep leaves you feeling awake and rested the next day is right for you.

Insomnia is defined as 'difficulty falling asleep (on average taking more than 30 minutes to fall asleep); waking up frequently during the night and having difficulty getting back to sleep; waking up too early in the morning and being unable to return to sleep; waking up tired or exhausted, which can persist through the day, making you feel irritable, anxious or depressed'.

About a third of people suffer from some level of insomnia. In my '100% Health' survey, 55 per cent of the population had difficulty sleeping or had restless sleep, while 43 per cent woke up feeling tired. If this sounds like you, you have a sleeping problem. So, what can you do about it?

There are two dynamics at play. More often than not, the inability to get to sleep is an inability to 'switch off' the adrenal stress response. Many people use alcohol to do this, but if you go to sleep under the influence of alcohol, it disturbs the normal sleep cycle, which can promote low moods. The net consequence of regular alcohol consumption is GABA depletion, which leads to more adrenalin, anxiety and emotional oversensitivity and less good-quality sleep. One study found that men who drank more increased their risk of sleeping problems by 25 per cent.[68] The less sleep you get, the more potent and dangerous the effects of alcohol; not only does it suppress dreaming, which is called REM (rapid eye movement) sleep, but it also decreases deep sleep.[69]

If you follow an undisturbed sleep pattern, when you first drift off, you enter a period of light sleep as you disengage from your surroundings. Your body temperature starts to drop a little and your brain waves slow down. All being well, after about 30 minutes you enter a period of deep sleep when your heart rate slows, your blood pressure drops and your breathing becomes slower. This is the most restorative stage, when tissue repair and regeneration occur. After around 90 minutes you shift to a period of REM sleep, which is when most dreaming occurs. We have already discussed why dreaming is important for your psychological health and well-being. Then you move back and forth between deep sleep, lighter sleep and REM, with the REM stage ideally accounting for around 25 per cent of your overall sleep time. If you don't dream, or don't remember your dreams, there are a few possible explanations. Acetylcholine levels are especially high during REM, so make sure your choline levels are sufficient (*see page 117*). Also, optimize your intake of B6 and zinc.

The last chapter showed many ways to switch off in preparation for sleep, from HeartMath techniques (*see Chapter 24 in Part 4*) to nutrients that promote GABA. The inability to stay asleep is often due to a lack of the neurotransmitter melatonin, made from serotonin, which is itself made from tryptophan. Chapter 17 explained how to support having a healthy serotonin level which is important for mood. Key brain essentials such as omega-3 and B vitamins help to promote healthy neurotransmitter function (*see chapters 8 to 10*).

Why not sleeping pills?

If you can't sleep and you go to your doctor, the chances are that you will be prescribed sleeping pills, also known as hypnotics. They all promote GABA (*see page 9*). The first generation were benzodiazepines (think Valium, Librium), and highly addictive. The next generation are called non-benzodiazepines. With names such as zopiclone and zolpidem, collectively, they are often called 'Z' drugs. These drugs regularly feature in the top 20 most-prescribed drugs both in the UK and the USA, despite having a long charge sheet of side-effects.[70] Not only that, but they aren't actually very useful, according to a report in the *British Medical Journal*.[71] Just how marginally effective they are was vividly illustrated by a 2007 study by the American National Institutes of Health, which found that the newer drugs, like Ambien (zolpidem), made you fall asleep only 12.8 minutes faster than with a fake pill, and sleep for just 11 minutes longer.[72]

Nutritional solutions to sleep problems

Nutrients play a key role in producing the hormones that aid sleep, and also ensuring the body is able to calm down. Those that calm us down are the same as those that reduce anxiety, so please read the last chapter.

The ability to stay asleep and not wake up too early is largely dependent on melatonin. Natural sources of melatonin include porridge oats, sour cherries (e.g., as the juice concentrate Cherry Active), bananas, peanuts, grape skins, walnuts and liquorice, although I'd avoid liquorice in the evening, as it stimulates the adrenals. And it is also concentrated in herbs such as St John's wort, sage and feverfew. Avoiding caffeine, at least after midday, is a no-brainer, because caffeine suppresses melatonin for up to 10 hours.[73]

You can buy melatonin as an over-the-counter medicine in the USA, or on prescription from a doctor in the UK. You can alternatively supplement 5-HTP, an amino acid which, as we have seen, the body uses to make melatonin. There's evidence that supplementing 200mg of 5-HTP half an hour before bed improves sleep.[74,75] Melatonin is both safe and effective if 1 to 10mg is taken an hour before intended sleep. Doses above 5mg do not seem to be more effective. A usual dose is 3mg. For example, a four-week study giving 3mg or a placebo to adults with insomnia showed that they woke up later.[76] It is also not addictive, so you don't keep needing more or suffer withdrawal effects if you come off it. If your doctor is going to prescribe you a sleeping pill, this is the one to go for. But few do, recommending the non-benzodiazapine drugs instead. One study found that this class of drugs 'was an independent risk factor of cognitive impairment in middle-aged and older patients with chronic insomnia' and concluded that 'Due to the addiction and tolerance, Z drugs should also be prescribed with great caution in middle-aged and elderly patients.'[77]

The combo of 5-HTP and melatonin may be even more effective. A study in Mexico on depressed patients gave 100mg of slow-release 5-HTP and 10mg of melatonin versus a placebo and found clear improvements in mood, sleep and cognitive function.[78]

The combination of GABA and 5-HTP is even better. In a placebo-controlled trial, supplementing GABA and 5-HTP cut the time taken to fall asleep from 32 minutes to 19 minutes and extended sleep from five to almost seven hours.[79] That's much better than sleeping pills. (*See page 165 for more on GABA and its precursors.*)

L-theanine, the amino acid found in tea, can help to make you feel more relaxed and less 'edgy'. Research suggests that 50mg naturally stimulates alpha-wave activity in the brain, which is the relaxed brain wave pattern you need to be in to get to sleep.[80]

Magnesium is particularly important both for anxiety and insomnia. Having a higher intake, whether from food or supplementation, is associated with better sleep.[81]

Another way to both potentially up your magnesium intake and relax in the process is to have an Epsom salts bath. Epsom salts are magnesium sulphate. There is some evidence that a small amount of magnesium is absorbed through the skin,[82] but I wouldn't rely on this as a replacement for upping your dietary or supplementary intake.

Omega-3 fish oils may also help. In a study comparing the effects of either higher-dose EPA (900mg) or a combo of lower-dose EPA (270mg) with 900mg of DHA, both worked in improving aspects of sleep in otherwise healthy adults.[83]

Once again, it is combinations of these nutrients, plus a low-GL diet, that can make the difference. It is especially important to eat a low-GL meal in the evening with enough protein (meat, fish, pulses, tofu, etc). If you find you frequently wake between 2 and 3 a.m. with a pounding heart or in a sweat, you may be experiencing a low blood sugar dip. Eating a small protein-rich snack such as an oatcake and nut butter before you go to sleep might alleviate the problem. Don't start eating sweet foods in the middle of the night.

The sleep hygiene approach

Essentially common-sense advice, sleep hygiene forms part of most good sleep regimes. The idea is to create regular sleep-promoting habits on the grounds that the less successful you are at getting to sleep, the more you are going to worry about it. So you are advised to keep the bedroom quiet and dark, to have comfortable clothing, to avoid having a big meal before bed, or coffee or alcohol, and to exercise regularly but not within three hours of bedtime. If you do drink caffeinated drinks, research shows that consumption within six hours of bedtime can have significantly disruptive effects on sleep.[84]

Although sleep hygiene is widely recommended, there have been very few studies of it as an individual treatment, and those have only found a limited improvement. Good results have been reported, however, for something similar known as 'stimulus control therapy' which essentially involves ensuring that the bed is only associated with sleeping. Patients are advised against having naps (although there may be some health benefits to napping; *see below*), to go to bed when sleepy, to get up within 20 minutes if they haven't fallen asleep and do something relaxing till they feel drowsy, then try again, but to get up again if it fails. Keep artificial light to a minimum in the bedroom, because being exposed to bright light can turn off the production of melatonin, which peaks at around 1 a.m. If you need to get up in the night, only use low-wattage bulbs.

I consider the HeartMath approach a vital part of sleep hygiene. Once you are in bed, spending a few minutes doing a simple Heart-Math Quick Coherence® exercise (*see page 284*) is great for falling asleep. It's also a really good thing to do to get back to sleep if you wake in the early hours of the morning.

Switch your phone off

There is also a growing body of evidence that suggests electromagnetic radiation from mobile phones and wireless internet connections can interfere with melatonin production. For example, in one small study, melatonin levels were 44 per cent lower at 2 a.m. in those exposed to mobile phone signals, compared to those who weren't.[85] So it may be worth experimenting to see if turning off your mobile and any Wi-Fi connections at night aids your sleep quality. Melatonin may even protect against the negative effects of electromagnetic radiation exposure.[86]

Have a siesta

Having a nap in the day may also reduce some of the health risks of poor sleep. Scientists from the University of Athens and the Harvard School of Public Health studied 23,681 healthy adults aged between 20 and 86 for an average period of six years. They found that those who napped for at least 30 minutes three times a week had a 37 per cent lower risk of coronary mortality than those who did not sleep during the day.[87] Doing HeartMath exercises (*see page 280*) or listening to Silence of Peace (*see below*) can help you switch off at siesta time.

Psychotherapy

Otherwise, the most likely root of poor sleep is psychological – stress, anxiety or depression. Therapy such as Cognitive Behavioural Therapy (CBT) is able to help by encouraging patients to acknowledge the stress that is preventing them from sleeping and then helping them to deal with it. This might be by identifying negative or unhelpful thoughts – 'I just can't sleep without my pills', for example – and changing them.

A review in the *Lancet* medical journal found that various forms of counselling and psychological help were not only the most effective, but also the safest way to tackle chronic insomnia.[88] For example, a study compared CBT with one of the 'Z' sleeping pills (zopiclone). While CBT improved the percentage of time spent asleep from 81 per cent to 90 per cent after six months, with zopiclone actually slightly less time was spent asleep.[89] In a proper evidence-based medical system, we'd have most people being referred to counsellors and few getting drugs, instead of the other way round.

Sounds of sleep

New York psychiatrist Dr Galina Mindlin uses 'brain music' – rhythmic patterns of sounds derived from recordings of patients' own brain waves – to help them overcome insomnia, anxiety and depression. The recordings sound something like classical piano music and appear to have a calming effect similar to yoga or meditation. A small double-blind study from 1998, conducted at Toronto University in Canada, found that 80 per cent of those undergoing this treatment reported benefits.[90]

Another study found that especially composed music induced a shift in brain-wave patterns to alpha waves, which are associated with the deep relaxation before you go to sleep, and that this induced less anxiety in a group of patients going to the dentist.[91] Many of my clients have also reported excellent results listening to the alpha-wave-inducing music of John Levine called *Silence of Peace* as they go to sleep (*see Resources*).

> Sue, an insomniac, and Olga, who suffered from post-traumatic stress disorder, listened to Silence of Peace *before bed. Olga said, 'It was a miracle. After 15 minutes I experienced a miracle! I received the rest that I was desperate for!'*
>
> Sue said, 'I used to sleep for about three hours and wake every 45 minutes. The improvement happened from Night One, and now, just one week later I am sleeping for six to seven hours. If I wake – which is becoming rare – I simply tune in again! I haven't heard the end of the CD yet.'

In summary, to help yourself get a good night's sleep:

- Prioritize relaxing activities in the few hours before you go to bed, so you reduce your stress levels and get your body into a calm state ready for sleeping.
- Avoid alcohol before bed and limit any caffeine intake after midday.

- Aim to follow a soothing bedtime routine, such as having a warm bath with Epsom salts and lavender or listening to soothing music, such as *Silence of Peace*, or practising HeartMath's Quick Coherence technique.
- Follow good sleep hygiene, ensuring your bedroom is quiet and dark and you are comfortable. Also, turn off mobile phones and Wi-Fi connections at night.
- Once in bed, do some simple relaxation exercises to get yourself ready for sleep.
- If you have difficulty sleeping, consider taking melatonin and/or 100mg of 5-HTP half an hour before bed or a sleep formula containing both of these, plus GABA or GABA precursors (taurine and glutamine) and theanine.

20

Free Your Brain from Addiction

Every addictive substance or behaviour is, in effect, mimicking or hijacking one of our brain's natural feel-good neurotransmitters. As we have already learned, the reason we end up addicted is that with overuse of the addictive substance, the brain stops making enough of its own feel-good chemicals and we feel we 'need' the outside agent to make us feel good or to relieve abstinence symptoms as the drug effects wear off.

We often start using addictive substances to cope with difficult feelings or circumstances, or because we are already in a state of 'reward deficiency' (*see Chapter 4*). When we find a substance that makes us feel good, and our brain gives us a reward, we're going to use that substance again. This applies to mild addictions, such as the coffee we use to wake up or the sugar we use for an energy kick or the alcohol we use to relax, but also to major addictions to heroin, cocaine or alcohol.

As we have already learned, however, whatever the substance, the more we consume, the more our brain adapts to the presence of these large quantities, until we must use larger and larger quantities to get the same effect. Eventually, the brain shuts down its production of neurotransmitters and becomes reliant upon the mood-altering substance.

It's important to recognize that whatever psycho-social issues might have led you to use numbing and addictive substances, once your brain is addicted to them, you are dealing with a biochemical

Name: _____

Gender: M F (Circle one) Date of Birth: _____/_____/_____ Today's date: _____

Circle the number that best indicates the severity of each symptom you are experiencing today (zero indicates the absence of the symptom, 10 represents an extreme, intolerable intensity level). **Answer each question as honestly as possible.**

		LOW LEVEL								HIGH LEVEL		
1.	Craving or drug hunger	0	1	2	3	4	5	6	7	8	9	1 0
2.	Craving for sweets/sugar/bread	0	1	2	3	4	5	6	7	8	9	1 0
3.	Craving for salt	0	1	2	3	4	5	6	7	8	9	1 0
4.	Loss of appetite	0	1	2	3	4	5	6	7	8	9	1 0
5.	Overeating/always hungry	0	1	2	3	4	5	6	7	8	9	1 0
6.	Bloating or sleepiness after eating	0	1	2	3	4	5	6	7	8	9	1 0
7.	Sense of emptiness/incompleteness	0	1	2	3	4	5	6	7	8	9	1 0
8.	Anxiety	0	1	2	3	4	5	6	7	8	9	1 0
9.	Internal shakiness	0	1	2	3	4	5	6	7	8	9	1 0
10.	Restlessness	0	1	2	3	4	5	6	7	8	9	1 0
11.	Impulsiveness/act before thinking	0	1	2	3	4	5	6	7	8	9	1 0
12.	Difficulty concentrating/focusing	0	1	2	3	4	5	6	7	8	9	1 0
13.	Fuzzy thinking/head cloudy/brain fog	0	1	2	3	4	5	6	7	8	9	1 0
14.	Memory problems/memory loss	0	1	2	3	4	5	6	7	8	9	1 0
15.	Depression	0	1	2	3	4	5	6	7	8	9	1 0
16.	Mood swings	0	1	2	3	4	5	6	7	8	9	1 0
17.	Negative self-talk	0	1	2	3	4	5	6	7	8	9	1 0
18.	Irritability/impatience with people	0	1	2	3	4	5	6	7	8	9	1 0
19.	Daytime sleepiness/drowsiness/doze off	0	1	2	3	4	5	6	7	8	9	1 0
20.	Problems getting to or staying asleep	0	1	2	3	4	5	6	7	8	9	1 0
21.	Fatigue/lack of energy/worn out	0	1	2	3	4	5	6	7	8	9	1 0
22.	Hypersensitivity to stress	0	1	2	3	4	5	6	7	8	9	1 0
23.	Hypersensitivity to sound or noise	0	1	2	3	4	5	6	7	8	9	1 0
24.	Hypersensitivity to pain	0	1	2	3	4	5	6	7	8	9	1 0
25.	Dry mouth/dry eyes/dry skin	0	1	2	3	4	5	6	7	8	9	1 0
26.	Achiness/muscle or joint pain/headaches	0	1	2	3	4	5	6	7	8	9	1 0

Add up Your Total Score: _____

Fig 25. The Scale of Abstinence Symptom Severity

dependency that needs to be broken. Joan Mathews-Larson, who ran the highly successful Health Recovery Centre, made this point by saying, 'When you've scrambled your brain, sitting around and talking about it isn't going to unscramble your brain.'

This chapter is neither about the life issues that lead people into addiction, nor how to detox if you have a serious addiction, as there are support groups for this and for staying clean or sober, but rather how to free your brain from addiction, which I believe is the prerequisite to staying clean or sober.

The paradox of addiction is that in order to break free from addiction, you need abstinence. But abstinence-based symptoms interfere with the ability to stay clean or sober, and some of these symptoms last months or years into sobriety. Or may never go away.

Dr Jim Braly and David Miller, Associate Professor of Addiction Studies at Graceland University in Missouri, with whom I co-wrote *How to Quit without Feeling S**t* taught me this and how they could predict who would start re-using a drug after quitting based on completing the Scale of Abstinence Symptom Severity that you can see, and complete, on page 230. The way you can use this is to score yourself now, score yourself a few days after you've quit your addiction(s), then take all the nutrients recommended and score yourself every two or three days thereafter.

Addiction recovery nutrition

David Miller was himself an alcoholic 'in recovery' who had struggled to stay sober with the support of Alcoholics Anonymous and the 12-Step programme, which he represented, running local groups. But years after quitting drinking, he was still experiencing abstinence symptoms. The turning-point came when he discovered amino acids and how supplementing them unaddicted his brain. He was one of the first to experiment with intravenous amino acids.

David Miller and Jim Braly went on to pioneer giving addicts a personalized cocktail of amino acids and support nutrients intravenously for up to a week after quitting, having tested their neurotransmitter levels (*see Resources*). In one treatment centre called

Neurotransmitter	Amino acid it's made from	What it does	Symptoms of deficiency	Substances used to compensate for deficiency
Adrenalin, noradrenalin	L-phenylalanine L-tyrosine	Arousal, energy, stimulation, mental focus	Lack of energy, depression, poor concentration	Caffeine, cocaine, amphetamines, tobacco, marijuana, alcohol, sugar
Dopamine	L-phenylalanine, L-tyrosine	Good feelings, satisfaction, comfort, alertness	Emptiness, lack of pleasure and reward, fatigue, depression, lack of motivation, over-eating	Alcohol, marijuana, cocaine, caffeine, amphetamines, sugar, tobacco
Endorphins, enkephalins	D-phenylalanine, DL-phenylalanine	Physical and emotional pain relief, pleasure, good feelings, euphoria, sense of well-being	Hyper-sensitivity to emotional and physical pain, inability to feel pleasure, feeling of incompleteness, craving for comfort or pleasure, craving for certain substances, feeling down	Heroin, alcohol, marijuana, sugar, chocolate
Serotonin	L-tryptophan or 5-HTP	Emotional stability, self-confidence, pain tolerance, quality sleep	Depression, worry, obsessiveness, compulsiveness, low self-esteem, sleep problems, craving for sweets, irritability, fearfulness, tantrums, violence, sexual promiscuity	Alcohol, sugar, chocolate, tobacco, marijuana
GABA	GABA, L-glutamine	Calming, relaxation	Anxiety, panic, tenseness, insecurity, sleeplessness, seizures	Valium, alcohol, marijuana, tobacco, sugar
Taurine	L-taurine	Calmness, promotion of sleep and digestion, seizure control	Tendency to seizures, sleeplessness, anxiety, poor digestion	Benzodiazepines, alcohol

Fig 26. Actions of neurotransmitters and amino acids

Bridging the Gaps, they ran a point of principle trial giving a group of addicts, many of whom had been 'in recovery treatment' more than once, intravenous amino acids for five days, followed by nutritional supplements for a month, and compared them with other people in the treatment centre. Everything else stayed the same – counselling, good diet, exercise and the 12-Step meetings. The deal with the treatment centre was to follow up these people one year later to see how they had done. On average, one in five of the centre's addicts was clean or sober one year on and half had relapsed within 90 days of leaving. But of those given the nutritional boost, 21 out of 23 were clean or sober one year later, and 16 had had continuous sobriety, with not one relapse.[92] This showed how, with the right nutritional support, a person could go from a symptom score in the 70s to under 10 within two weeks.

In the chart on page 232 you can see what each neurotransmitter does, how it makes you feel, how you feel in a state of deficiency and which drugs compensate for the deficiency. If you highlight the symptoms you feel and the drugs you use to compensate, it will help you understand which amino acids are likely to help you.

Sadly, hardly any drug treatment recovery centres use this approach, or intravenous nutrient therapy. Oral supplementation does also work, but not quite so fast.

Addiction recovery isn't just about amino acids, though. In our *How to Quit* book we cover 12 keys to recovery, eight of which are essentially the same as the eight brain-upgrade essentials. So, the background to freeing your brain from addiction includes ensuring you have enough essential fats and B vitamins to bring your homo-cysteine level down to around 7mcmol/l; balancing your blood sugar; upping your intake of antioxidants; having a healthy gut; exercising; building stress resilience and getting a good night's sleep (*see Chapters 18 and 19, and Part 2*).

The 'add-on' is supplementing the amino acids that help unaddict your brain, depending on which substance you've become addicted to.

There are also other nutrients and amino acids that generally help all addictions. These include:

- the vitamin B3 family – niacin, niacinamide, NAD and NMN (nicotinamide mononucleotide), NR (nicotinamide riboside)
- N-acetylcysteine
- vitamin C
- vitamin D

as well as other B vitamins and omega-3 fats, which have been shown to reduce addictive cravings and drug use in animals.[93]

Vitamin B3

Vitamin B3 is called niacin. The niacin form is a vasodilator and makes us blush. The blushing may help get toxins out of cells, so is useful in a detox. The non-blushing form is called niacinamide, although there is also a 'no-blush' form which attaches niacin to a phospholipid. These get turned into a vital body chemical called nicotinamide adenine dinucleotide, or NAD for short. One step closer to NAD is NMN (nicotinamide mononucleotide). Supplements exist for all these forms and are promoted both for their anti-ageing[94] and anti-addiction[95] properties. Some treatment centres give intravenous NAD injections.

I'm a great fan of niacin in any form, and at quite high amounts. In fact, the late Bill Wilson, who founded AA, became convinced that nutritional therapy was the missing piece of the puzzle when he first encountered the nutritional approach through meeting my mentor Dr Abram Hoffer back in the 1960s. Dr Hoffer pioneered the treatment of addiction with high doses of vitamin B3 and vitamin C, and wrote it up in his book *The Vitamin Cure for Alcholism*.

He gave, and I recommend, 500mg twice a day of a non-blushing or extended-release form of niacin. However, those wishing to detox may get better results with the blushing form, taking 100mg with meals, three times a day, and gradually building up to 1,000mg. After several days, the blush, which lasts for up to half an hour, subsides. It helps cut cravings not only for alcohol but also for nicotine, which shares the same receptors as niacin, which is also called nicotinic acid.

Niacin can also be very helpful for schizophrenia (*see page 96*) and lowers cholesterol. Ironically, it went out of favour both in psychiatry and for lowering cholesterol as pharmaceutical drugs took over, with erroneous claims of liver damage. Ironically, it is now being reconsidered for the treatment of non-alcoholic fatty liver disease, due to its effects on reducing liver fat accumulation, a product of eating too much sugar and too many carbohydrates, as the liver has to convert the excess into fat.[96]

N-acetylcysteine (NAC)

N-acetylcysteine is the precursor for one of the body's most important antioxidants, glutathione, but it also has very interesting effects on addictive cravings. It is used to reload the liver's capacity to detoxify in cases of liver failure due to alcohol and paracetamol overdose. NAC has been shown to have promise in treating cocaine,[97] alcohol,[98] gambling,[99] probably digital media and maybe cannabis addiction. It promotes the GABA–glutamate pathway and thus may help satisfy anxiety related to GABA deficiency. It is effective in reducing reward-seeking behaviour and a recent randomized controlled trial confirmed the efficacy of NAC augmentation of behavioural therapy in the treatment of pathological gambling.[100] This is a great example of how a nutrient changes a psychological addiction.

You need at least 1 gram, best taken as 500mg twice a day, although twice this amount may be more effective and is quite safe. NAC also helps to lower homocysteine, so you may find significant amounts in some homocysteine-lowering formulas (*see Resources*).

Vitamin C

Vitamin C is another tremendous support nutrient for anyone dealing with addiction. Like NAC it is liver-friendly, hence most important for alcoholics.

Back in 1977, Dr Alfred Libby and Irwin Stone pioneered a detoxifying treatment for drug addicts using mega-doses of vitamin C. In one study, involving 30 heroin addicts, they gave 30 to 85 grams a day and reported a 100 per cent success rate. Dr Abram Hoffer reported similar results in one week with 10 heroin addicts, using 50g of vitamin C combined with high-dose niacin.[101]

If you take too much vitamin C, you get loose bowels. My advice, if you are withdrawing from almost any drug, is to take vitamin C up to your bowel-tolerance level, starting with 1 gram three times a day. One you reach 'bowel tolerance', you can add in liposomal vitamin C (*see Resources*), which uses fat channels for absorption and avoids the loose bowel effect, so you can go higher.

A small study giving heroin addicts around 20 grams a day reported a massive reduction in withdrawal symptoms compared with those not given vitamin C.[102]

Vitamin D

Vitamin D, as we learned earlier, helps to promote serotonin in the brain. Interestingly, vitamin D deficiency is associated with greater opioid addiction,[103] suggesting the need to up vitamin D intake to reduce cravings. Sun exposure, which raises vitamin D levels, reduces opioid addiction.

There's something else interesting about vitamin D, sun exposure and addiction: people can become addicted to sun-beds!

Supplementing amino acids for your addiction recovery

Supplementing the right amino acids rapidly reduces cravings. Most aminos are best taken away from a protein meal, ideally with a carb snack. But they should always be taken with multivitamins/minerals concurrently, as these help amino acids work.

You don't need to supplement aminos forever, just until abstinence symptoms are relieved.

Occasionally, people experience mild nausea when supplementing amino acids. If this happens, and persists, lower the dose.

Your addiction support regime

Since every addiction requires its own focused support programme, which is beyond the capacity of this book, I've created pages on my website – patrickholford.com/how2quit/ – to give you support advice for quitting the following:

- alcohol
- anti-depressants
- caffeine
- cannabis
- cocaine
- nicotine
- opioids (incl. heroin)
- sleeping pills
- sugar

In summary, the key points are:

- To put into effect as much as you can of the eight essentials in Part 2.
- To eat a low-GL diet.
- To increase antioxidants and essential omega-3 fats.
- To supplement according to your addiction, but in all cases include more B vitamins and vitamin C.

Which amino acids will help free your brain from addiction depends very much on your addiction. Think in terms of a three-month comprehensive supplement programme to allow your brain and respective neurotransmitter levels to fully recover. You may wish to consult a registered nutritional therapist (*see Resources*) to help you work out your brain recovery plan.

21

Recovering Your Memory and Rebuilding Your Brain

Are you worried about your memory? Whether your concern is to prevent it from getting worse or enhance or to optimize your mental acuity, the starting point is the 'eight essentials' in Part 2, bearing in mind that optimal cognition depends on having the best 'structure', that is, building brain cells and their connections; the best 'function', as in fuel supply; and 'utilization' – having an active physical, social and intellectual lifestyle.

The thing about memory is that it is very subjective. Many people, later in life, think their memory is getting worse. For others, it clearly is, but they deny it, often for years, probably subconsciously fuelled by the fear of getting Alzheimer's. Yet the specific aspects of cognition that decline on the road to dementia can be objectively measured decades before any diagnosis might occur and, most importantly, improved if we take the right actions soon enough. That is why I strongly recommend taking, at any age, our objective, validated Cognitive Function Test (*see Resources*). Many people who worry their memory is getting worse find that they score well into the healthy green zone. Only by having enough people of different ages can we explore what is optimum, and possible to further improve, and discover what people with higher scores are doing differently from those with lower scores to stay in the green zone.

For example, if a person is aged 50 to 70, a score of 54 is the average expected score, and we expect most respondents to score between 43 and 65. Scores below 43 and above 38 we classify as amber, or 'at risk'. Below 38 is in the red zone and is consistent with mild cognitive impairment.

Jan is a case in point. He had monitored his cognitive function every year since retiring and had seen his scores steadily decreasing, from 53 in 2019, to 48 in 2020, then 40, entering the amber zone, in 2021. Then he joined our COGNITION programme and started to make the changes I recommend in this book, and his cognitive score steadily improved to 50 by 2022, then 59, and now 63 in 2023, at the high end of normal for his age and well into the green zone.

What did he do to achieve this steady improvement in memory? He followed the educational advice, one step at a time, in the COGNITION programme.

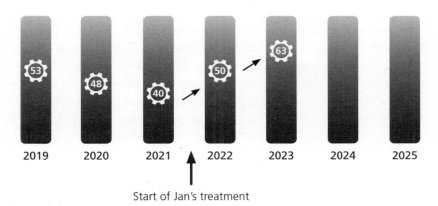

Start of Jan's treatment

Fig 27. Jan's cognitive function changes

Here's what he says: 'Food for the Brain's COGNITION programme has really helped to focus my mind on key changes, a step at a time. Since following their advice, I'm delighted to report that my cognitive function, which was close to the red after 17 months of decline, has returned into the green, better than the average for my age. I had lost my job and my ability to have a productive life, even my ability to speak without long pauses, and any hope of recovery. Food for the Brain's educational support through COGNITION has demonstrated the potential for recovery such that I now have confidence and increasing hope for the future. Food for the Brain has been my lifeline.'

So, the first step to improving your memory is to take the Cognitive Function Test, and then complete the questionnaire that follows to find out your 'weakest links', then act on them, which is what the COGNITION programme is all about.

There are also a few quick wins and avenues you can explore to improve your memory.

The B-vitamin/omega-3 dynamic duo

The first, relating to how we build neurons and their connections, is the dynamic duo of homocysteine-lowering B vitamins and omega-3 fats, especially DHA. This was the subject of Chapter 10, where I showed you that those already with memory problems in the top third for DHA in their blood, given homocysteine-lowering B vitamins, had a massive 73 per cent reduction in the annual rate of brain shrinkage compared with those on a dummy placebo pill. I also showed you a trial giving 2.3 grams of omega-3 fish oils, which produced a halving of the participants' clinical dementia rating (CDRsob), and an improvement in their memory on the mini-mental state exam (MMSE) in those with lower homocysteine (below 11.7), thus adequate B-vitamin status.

But I want to emphasize here that a homocysteine of below 11.7 is not 'optimal'. It is above the level where you can measure brain shrinkage. It is certainly better than average for those over 70. But it is not optimal.

Also, 2.3 grams of fish oils may not be optimal either. Psychiatrist Joe Hibbeln often gives 4 grams, four large fish oil capsules, a day. That is why measuring your homocysteine and getting it down certainly below 9, if not below 7, is more likely to be optimal for your mental acuity. Likewise, measuring your omega-3 index and getting this above 8 per cent by whatever means it takes, whether eating fish or supplementing omega-3 fish oils or both, is more likely to be optimal.

On the homocysteine front, if yours is raised (above 10 mcmol/L), it is better to take a homocysteine-lowering supplement (*see Resources*) that covers all the bases, including B12, folate, B6, TMG, zinc and NAC.

Up antioxidants

The next no-brainer is to do all you can to up antioxidants. Two of the key antioxidants in the body are glutathione and melatonin. Glutathione is made from NAC (N-acetylcysteine), an amino acid that should be included in your homocysteine-lowering formula. It is also 'recycled' by anthocyanins – that's all those blue/red foods. I aim to have a serving of berries every day for this explicit purpose, but supplement this with glutathione or NAC in an antioxidant, just to cover the bases. Glutathione is also rich in onions and eggs.

Melatonin is a product of your serotonin status, made from tryptophan or 5-HTP. If you have a neurodegenerative disease, cognitive impairment, high stress or poor sleep, and especially if you have more than one of these, supplementing 1 to 5mg of melatonin every night, the higher level being for those with sleeping problems, may have anti-ageing benefits for your brain.[104]

These nutrients are in addition to eating an antioxidant and polyphenol-rich diet (*see Chapter 13 and the Brain-Friendly Diet in Part 4*).

Don't forget niacin

One B vitamin that has a benefit for your memory is niacin, or vitamin B3. In the last chapter I spoke about the cousins of niacin, NMN and NAD, which both help with addiction and have anti-ageing benefits. They are also likely to help memory. In animal studies, the combo of NMN and melatonin helps to protect the central hippocampus area of the brain, slowing down ageing and improving mitochondrial energy production and cognition.[105] These are the hot new nutrients in brain research, with the potential to protect against amyloid and p-tau formation.

In a long-term study looking at nutrient levels in people aged 18 to 30, then measuring their memory 25 years later, niacin intake most predicted better memory, followed by folate, B6, then B12.[106] Another study found niacin intake protected against Alzheimer's. Those with higher niacin intakes had a third of the risk.[107]

A small study giving supplements of niacin at a dose of 141mg, which is almost 10 times the basic 'nutrient reference value' of 16mg, produced a measurable improvement in memory in eight weeks in healthy people without cognitive decline.[108]

I hedge my bets and supplement 50mg daily in my multivitamin.

Fill the energy gap with C8 oil

In Chapter 12 we learned that the brain loves ketones as fuel, primarily derived from a specific type of medium-chain triglyceride (MCT) called C8 oil. C8 oil makes up 7 per cent of coconut oil, from which it is usually derived.

For people with blood sugar problems, such as diabetics, but also many older people who may become less able to get sufficient glucose, which is the other critical brain fuel, into the brain's mitochondrial energy factories within neurons and end up with a brain energy deficit, filling this energy gap with one or two tablespoons (15 to 30g) of C8 oil is a quick win.

This has been proven to increase brain energy in those with cognitive decline, thanks to the excellent research of Professor Stephen Cunnane. Four out of six studies giving MCT oils have shown improvements in memory in those without dementia.[109] But are there any benefits if you're younger and healthier? One study at Liverpool Hope University giving healthy young adults a combination of C8 and C10 found cognitive improvements in three weeks. They gave either 12g, approximately a tablespoon, or 18g, and found little difference between the doses. The oil they used was 60 per cent C8 and 40 per cent C10.[110]

Now we know most of the ketone energy benefit comes from C8 oil, my suggestion is to supplement a tablespoon of C8 oil a day to support memory if you are younger and healthier, and twice this if you have any blood sugar problems, such as an HbA1c level above 6 per cent or 42mmol/mol (*see Resources for tests*), or are older and are already experiencing some cognitive decline. It is an optional extra.

The other way to provide your brain with ketones is to eat a low-carb, high-fat diet (*see page 138*) or do alternate fasting. I recommend two or three days a week doing 18:6 – not eating food between dinner and lunch, but starting your day with a hybrid latte (*see page 273*) containing a tablespoon of C8 oil. Your brain is more likely to convert the C8 to ketones if you are 'starved' of carbo-hydrates in this way.

Vitamin D protects your brain and memory

Vitamin D is an all-rounder as far as your brain and mental health are concerned, and it's worth ensuring your level is optimal, both for brain and body. It helps neurotransmission and has an anti-inflammatory and neuroprotective effect on the brain by reducing inflammation and the oxidative stress,[111] both of which are drivers of cognitive decline.

Vitamin D deficiency increases the risk of Alzheimer's.[112] In a study in France involving 912 elderly patients followed for 12 years, a total of 177 dementia cases occurred. Those with low vitamin D levels had a nearly three-fold increased risk of Alzheimer's.[113] Supplementing 800iu (20mcg) a day for 12 months has also been shown to improve cognitive function.[114]

Supplements may also help ward off dementia, according to a recent large-scale study involving over 12,000 dementia-free 70+-year-olds in the USA.[115] More than a third (37 per cent) took supplements of vitamin D, and those who did had a 40 per cent lower incidence of dementia.

Professor Zahinoor Ismail, of the University of Calgary and University of Exeter, who led the research, said, 'We know that vitamin D has some effects in the brain that could have implica-tions for reducing dementia, however so far, research has yielded conflicting results. Overall, we found evidence to suggest that earlier supplementation might be particularly beneficial, before the onset of cognitive decline.'

You want to get your blood level above 75nmol/l (30 ng/ml), which usually means supplementing 3,000iu in winter and perhaps up to 1,000iu in summer, depending on your sun exposure.

Brain-friendly plants

Mushrooms and your mind

Various plants and fungi have positive effects on memory that are worth knowing about. Those that stand out are the oldest living tree, *Ginkgo biloba*, and the fungus Lion's Mane and the Reishi mushroom.

Ginkgo is a potent antioxidant, anti-inflammatory and neuro-protective compound. The usual doses given are 120 to 300mg of standardized *Ginkgo biloba*. It slightly thins the blood, so should be used with caution for those on blood thinners. It's an optional extra, but a trial giving healthy adults ginkgo for 30 days showed memory improvements.[116]

Lion's Mane (*Hericium erinaceus*) fungus has been shown to improve aspects of memory and cognitive function in three trials: on healthy volunteers,[117] those with mild cognitive impairment[118] and dementia.[119]

The best-researched mushroom, used for thousands of years in Japan for its anti-ageing properties, is Reishi. It is a potent anti-oxidant, thus protects the brain from damage.[120] Many people in Japan take it on a daily basis.

Brahmi for your brain

Brahmi (*Bacopa monnieri*) is an Indian adaptogenic herb that has been used traditionally to boost longevity and enhance cognitive function. Numerous trials conducted on Brahmi extracts, usually giving 300mg a day, have shown beneficial effects on memory retention and cognitive performance versus a placebo. A meta-analysis of nine trials involving 437 older people with memory problems reported improved cognition and better function and better attention.[121] One study also reported improvement in Parkinson's patients.[122]

Other brain-friendly plant remedies

There are other brain-friendly plant remedies that fall more into the 'stimulant' category. Maca root from Peru,[123] ginseng, Siberian ginseng (*Eleutherococcus*) and rhodiola are other potentially brain-friendly plants perhaps best used by those with low brain energy or mental fatigue or high stress, as they have effects on stress hormones and may support stress resilience. Some stimulating supplements (*see Resources*) use combinations of these.

There are others, such as guarana, whose main active ingredient is caffeine. I'm not so keen on these, as caffeine ultimately causes downregulation, making you less responsive to your own adrenal hormones. In this way, the more you have, the more you need (*see Chapter 4*).

Rebuilding the brain

While it is clear that prevention of cognitive decline is achievable, can we actually rebuild the brain? In established Alzheimer's, where there is visible brain shrinkage and loss of brain cells, this is unlikely. But is it possible after stabilizing cognitive decline by doing the right things described in this book? This is also especially pertinent to anyone who has had a brain injury, for example a stroke or transient ischemic attack (TIA), which are often shown in brain scans as tiny injuries or scars.

There are two aspects to rebuilding:

- Making new dendritic connections between brain cells, which is happening all the time. This rewiring is especially important after a brain injury, as the neural network develops 'workarounds'. This is called 'neuroplasticity'.
- Making new brain cells, which is a more challenging task and considered by some to be impossible or at least a very slow process.

Some of the memory enhancers above may help. Having a lower homocysteine level, for example, helps those who've had a stroke recover faster.[124] So, too, does having a higher vitamin D level or supplementing vitamin D at levels above 2,000iu a day.[125] I recommend 3,000iu a day or 21,000iu a week, but most importantly, monitoring your vitamin D level to keep it above 75nmol/l (30 ng/ml). A level of 100nmol/l may be optimal.

Remembering that neuronal membranes are made from phospholipids, eating phospholipid-rich foods such as fish and eggs and supplementing with the phospholipids found in lecithin could help recovery. Lecithin is available in 1,200mg capsules or in granules. Some lecithin granules are 'high-PC'. Combining B vitamins with choline is particularly helpful in stroke recovery, encouraging neuroplasticity.[126]

A precursor of choline, also found in the brain, is DMAE, sometimes sold as Deanol. It helps optimize the production of acetylcholine, the neurotransmitter associated with learning. It has been shown to increase alertness, attention and overall mood improvement,[127] as well as sleep and dreaming,[128] and could help hyperactive children[129] and those with learning and behavioural disorders[130] in a daily amount of 500 to 2,000mg. It is another optional extra 'nootropic'. I used to include it in my 'Brain Food' supplement, but EU regulations no longer allow this.

Of the plants and fungi, Lion's Mane is particularly interesting, as it seems to stimulate neuroplasticity thanks to its two active ingredients, hericenones and erinacines, which enhance the brain's own nerve growth factor (NGF), a hormone which encourages neuronal growth.[131] The usual dose is 500 to 1,000mg a day (*see Resources*).

In California, dementia expert Dr Dale Bredesen, author of *The End of Alzheimer's Program*, has been helping people recover from cognitive decline with a comprehensive approach tailor-made to each individual, covering all the factors in this book – and more. His 'proof-of-concept' trial in the *Journal of Alzheimer's Disease*,[132] involving 25 people diagnosed with various stages of cognitive decline, shows improvement in 84 per cent of those with MCI or early dementia, which is an unprecedented result. When compared with the anti-amyloid antibody injections, these results are very impressive, as shown below.

Dr Bredesen's protocol, while focusing on the importance of diet, brain support supplements and lifestyle, also considers other factors, such as mycotoxins, inorganic toxins (such as air pollution or mercury), chronic undiagnosed infections, sleep apnoea and other risk factors.

'Repeatedly we read that "nothing can be done",' he says, 'and you've pointed out that prevention can in fact be achieved, but our trial shows that it is not hopeless for those with MCI or even early-stage dementia.'

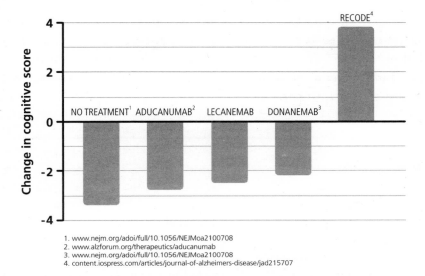

1. www.nejm.org/adoi/full/10.1056/NEJMoa2100708
2. www.alzforum.org/therapeutics/aducanumab
3. www.nejm.org/adoi/full/10.1056/NEJMoa2100708
4. content.iospress.com/articles/journal-of-alzheimers-disease/jad215707

Fig 28. Dr Bredesen's RECODE precision nutrition approach to cognitive decline compared with anti-amyloid treatments; from Dr Dale Bredesen, used with permission

Psychedelics for brain recovery?

One of the hottest areas of brain research is the effects of various hallucinogenic compounds, notably psilocybin, LSD and the Amazonian plant potion ayahuasca, a rich source of DMT, on mental health and brain function. These compounds are tryptamines and share the quality of activating a key brain receptor site, 5-HT2 receptors, for serotonin. As a group, they are all shown to be potential promoters of neuroregeneration and neuroplasticity, helping make neuron connections and perhaps new neurons.[133] They also stimulate brain-derived neurotrophic factor (BDNF), a key brain signaller that stimulates growth.

With many studies now showing the potential of psychedelics to help those with treatment-resistant depression and drug addiction, and also terminal patients with anxiety, much attention is being focused on what they actually do in the brain. On a psychological level, breakthroughs in debilitating depression and anxiety seem to occur through the experience of patients 'exorcising the demons' of early traumas through psychotherapy-assisted trips. But there may be more going on at a biological level.

Also, studies are underway testing less heroic doses, micro-doses, of these agents. It is too early to say whether they could have a helpful role for those with early cognitive decline and brain shrinking, but it is certainly plausible and an area of ongoing research. It's a case of 'watch this space'.

In summary:

- First, do the Cognitive Function Test at foodforthebrain.org to find out what is likely to be driving your future risk of cognitive decline.
- Also test both your homocysteine and omega-3 index blood levels, with a home-test kit provided by the charity. If your homocysteine level is above 10, then supplement B6 20mg, B12 500mcg and preferably methylfolate 400mcg or more.
- Get your omega-3 index above 8 per cent, which is likely to require supplementing 500mg of DHA a day and eating three servings of oily fish a week.
- Ensure adequate phospholipids by supplementing lecithin and eating eggs and seafood. Aim for at least 250mg of phosphatidyl choline.
- Increase your intake of antioxidants, not only from colourful foods and berries, but also by supplementing them, especially NAC or glutathione. Read Chapter 13 to increase your antioxidant and polyphenol power. Melatonin (5mg) may also help, as may niacin (100 to 500mg).
- Take 2 tablespoons of C8 oil and/or go ketogenic for a few days every month or follow a high-fat, low-carb diet and stay in mild ketosis.
- Test your vitamin D level and make sure it's above 75nmol/l (30ng/ml). In the winter you'll probably need to supplement 3,000iu a day to achieve this.
- Try Lion's Mane, Reishi, ginkgo or Brahmi for a memory boost.

Building Young Brains

In recent years the number of children diagnosed with learning, behavioural and mental health problems has escalated. Attention-deficit hyperactivity disorder (ADHD), autistic spectrum disorder (ASD) and other neurodevelopmental disorders, all classifying children as 'neurodivergent', as opposed to 'neurotypical', have rocketed in both the UK and USA. Over the past decade there has also been a steady increase in mental health problems in young people, with four in ten now reporting persistent feelings of sadness or hopelessness and almost a quarter (22 per cent) reporting contemplating suicide.[134]

'Now, one in six children in the USA are classified as neurodivergent and one in 36 as autistic – a fourfold increase in 20 years,'[135] says Dr Allesio Fasano, Professor of Pediatrics at Massachusetts General Hospital for Children, Harvard Medical School.

Rising figures are being reported in the UK. According to Dr Rona Tutt, past president of the National Association of Head-teachers, 'There has been a dramatic increase in the number of people being diagnosed with ASD. Although some of this is due to a broader definition of autism, as well as better diagnosis, it raises the question of whether it may also be the result of environmental changes, which have also been dramatic.' Some UK schools are reporting as many as one in four children having problems.

For clarification, the University of Washington defines a 'neuro-divergent' person as 'a person on the autism spectrum or, more generally, someone whose brain processes information in a way that is not typical of most individuals. These people may have learning disabilities, attention-deficit and anxiety disorders, obsessive-compulsive disorder, and Tourette's syndrome. Through a neurodiversity lens, such conditions reflect different ways of being that are all normal human experiences. Although "neurodiversity" is usually used to describe a group of neurodivergent individuals, it also refers to all of humankind, because everyone has a unique way of processing information.'

For those less desirable uniquenesses that cause individuals difficulty, the question is, why do they occur in some and not others, and can they be prevented?

Making healthy babies

Autistic spectrum disorder has often been positioned as being genetically linked. However, since the genes cannot have changed this rapidly, this suggests the influence of environmental factors, of which diet and maternal nutrition are big contributors.

Brain development starts from conception

Brain development is influenced from the moment of conception. That is why a mother's preconceptional nutrition is so critical.

Nothing can be built without healthy methylation, which means a low homocysteine level. Raised homocysteine is a well-known predictor of miscarriage and pregnancy problems, which is why I recommend no woman attempts pregnancy until her homocysteine level is below 7mcmol/l. While we have learned that a homocysteine level above 11 means increased brain shrinkage, even a homocysteine level of above 9 during pregnancy predicts more problems, specifically withdrawn behaviour, anxiety, depression, social problems and aggressive behaviour in the child at the age of six.[136]

That's why building a healthy child's brain starts with ensuring mothers-to-be are optimally healthy.

We already know that pioneering researcher Professor Michael Crawford, working with Dr Enitan Ogundipe, can predict which babies are going to be born pre-term with greater risk of having developmental problems from the fats in the pregnant woman's blood. But the most convincing evidence comes from a study of 11,875 pregnant women which showed a clear relationship between the amount of seafood consumed by a pregnant woman and their child's development. The less seafood consumed, the worse the child's social behaviour, fine motor skills, communication and social development, and verbal IQ.[137]

Also, a lack of vitamin A during pregnancy can affect brain development and lead to long-term or even permanent impairment in the learning process, memory formation and cognitive function.[138]

Supplementing mothers-to-be with folic acid (400mcg/day) during the second and third trimesters of pregnancy is associated with better cognition in their children at the age of three and better word reasoning and IQ (verbal and performance) at seven.[139]

Nourishing infants with optimum nutrition

Once a baby is born, 75 per cent of all the energy derived from breastmilk goes to build the brain, as brain development continues at the mind-boggling rate of something like 1 million connections a minute. Babies use ketones to power their early brain development, but they also need the raw materials – essential fats, phospholipids and vitamins. Without sufficient omega-3, vitamin A, vitamin D and B vitamins, especially folate and B12, as well as minerals such as iodine, magnesium, iron and zinc, the brain cannot develop optimally.

This means that a breastfeeding mother must, at least, supplement omega-3 fish oils, but many other nutrients are also necessary. Without sufficient nutrients, not only do brain cells not make the connections, but the production and flow of neurotransmitters doesn't happen optimally.

Low vitamin D status in both the mother and newborn baby increases the likelihood of the child developing ASD by 54 per cent.[140]

Bruce Ames, Emeritus Professor of Biochemistry and Molecular Biology at the University of California, thinks that 'serotonin synthesis, release, and function in the brain are modulated by vitamin D and the two marine omega-3 fatty acids, eicosapentaenoic acid, EPA, and docosahexaenoic acid, DHA'. He says, 'Insufficient levels of vitamin D, EPA, or DHA, in combination with genetic factors and at key periods during development, would lead to dysfunctional serotonin activation and function and may be one underlying mechanism that contributes to neuropsychiatric disorders and depression in children.'[141]

We know that a mother's folate intake predicts the child's performance in cognitive tests at the age of nine to ten[142] and the higher a baby's B-vitamin status, the higher their cognitive function at the age of 25.[143]

Nourishing the growing child

In the UK, fewer than 5 per cent of children achieve the basic dietary recommendations for omega-3 and fish.[144] Lower DHA concentrations are associated with poorer reading ability, poorer memory, oppositional behaviour and emotional instability.[145] Several studies have shown increased aggression in those with low omega-3 DHA and EPA, and giving more omega-3 reduces aggression.[146]

Fish and omega-3 are associated with better cognition in children. A study of 541 Chinese schoolchildren found that fish consumption predicted sleep quality and that those who ate the most fish had the highest IQ, 4.8 points higher than those who ate none. Improved sleep quality, linked to fish intake, was correlated with IQ. [147]

A study in Northern Ireland found that half of schoolchildren were deficient in vitamin D, with a level below 50nmol/l (I recommend above 75 nmol/l). Another found that low vitamin D levels in childhood were related to behaviour problems in adolescence.[148] Is it any wonder so many children are neurodivergent?

Another nutrient that is rich in marine food is vitamin A. Cod liver oil is a rich source of vitamin A, vitamin D and omega-3 fats. Vitamin A is vital for proper black and white vision and the proper functioning of the retina in the eye, hence its name, retinol, and the idea of eating carrots to see in the dark. Dr Mary Megson, a paediatrician in the USA, identified a particular genetic weakness in several children on the spectrum which would affect their ability to use vitamin A. She associates this with children who won't look you in the eye because they see better on the periphery of their visual field.[149] Giving a source of retinol such as cod liver oil improves eye coordination and vision, helping those with autism who don't make eye contact.

Think zinc and magnesium

My teacher, Dr Carl Pfeiffer, was the first to put zinc on the map for mental health, in the 1970s, thanks to a girl called Lisa.

Lisa was crazy, but her parents had learned how to keep her sane: oysters. If she had a couple of oysters a day, her mind calmed down.

Dr Pfeiffer worked out it was zinc. Zinc is essential for cellular growth and repair, and thus found in all seeds, nuts, beans and lentils, as well as eggs, meat and fish, but nothing beats oysters. Zinc is one of the most essential minerals in pregnancy, along with iron, and babies and children, due to their rapid growth, need more.

Bear in mind that the vegetarian sources of zinc, such as nuts and seeds, also contain phytates, which inhibit zinc's absorption, so those on an exclusively plant-based diet might need more.

The basic calculation for our zinc needs to support growth is 7.5mg a day. (An oyster gives 5.5mg.) But is that really the minimum? What's the optimum? The Nutrient Reference Value is 10mg. Many children fail to achieve this.

Few have explored what zinc intake is needed for optimal mental health. Researchers in North Dakota gave 200 schoolchildren in the 7th grade zinc supplements and found that those taking 20mg of zinc a day, as opposed to those taking 10mg (the RDA) or a placebo, had faster and more accurate memories and better attention spans within three months.[150] The girls, also, behaved better.

Children with ADHD tend to have lower levels of zinc, chromium and magnesium. Some have low levels of copper, according to research in New Zealand.[151]

One study of ADHD children found higher levels of copper.[152] Copper, the main source of which is copper water pipes, and zinc compete, so if zinc is low the body's copper levels tend to rise. It was the copper to zinc ratio that was especially high in neurodivergent versus neurotypical children and predicted the degree of ADHD.[153] The same applies to schizophrenia, with some of those diagnosed having low zinc levels[154] and higher copper levels.[155] Copper is likely to be higher in softer-water areas and in newer houses with copper pipes. Blue staining in baths or sinks is an indication of a high copper level in the water. Both zinc and magnesium levels tend to be lower in those with depression.

Earlier we saw that chromium, a mineral essential for sugar control, helps some people with symptoms of depression. Magnesium, a commonly deficient mineral, is calming. Zinc deficiency is linked to disperceptions both in eating disorders and schizophrenia, as well as depression and anxiety. Both zinc and magnesium are critical co-factor nutrients, activating enzymes that make the all-important brain fats such as DHA and EPA, as well as neurotransmitters, from the food we eat.

Back in the 1970s, when I was studying schizophrenia, there was an agent which turned mauve when added to the urine of schizophrenics. It was called the mauve factor and related to the excretion of an abnormal chemical called a pyrrole. It robs the body of both vitamin B6 and zinc, is reversed by supplementing B6 and zinc, and is an indicator of oxidative stress.[156] Classic symptoms include being pale and socially withdrawn and having white marks under the nails and frequent infections, poor dream recall, lack of sex drive, or periods in girls, and poor tolerance of alcohol.[157]

Checking a child's zinc, chromium and magnesium status, which can be done with a hair or blood sample (*see Resources*), is a standard practice in nutritional therapy, but not routine in mainstream medicine. Red cell magnesium levels and serum zinc are perhaps more reliable, but sampling hair is less invasive in children. A small study found lower hair levels of chromium in those with ADHD.[158] Nuts and seeds are high in all three nutrients, and correcting deficiencies with diet and/or supplementation is a must for neurodivergent children. Greens and other vegetables are rich in magnesium. A placebo-controlled trial giving ADHD children magnesium together with vitamin D for eight weeks showed a major reduction in emotional, conduct and peer problems and improved socialization compared with children given a placebo.[159]

A Polish study from 1997 which examined the magnesium status of 116 children with ADHD found that magnesium deficiency occurred far more frequently in them than in children without ADHD (95 per cent of the children with ADHD were deficient), and also noted a correlation between the levels of magnesium in the body and severity of symptoms. The children were divided into two groups, one supplemented with 200mg of magnesium a day for six months and the other receiving no supplements. The magnesium status of the group receiving supplements improved and their hyperactivity was significantly reduced, while hyperactive behaviour worsened in the control group.[160]

Andrew's story is a classic example of how effective magnesium can be in helping restless, hyperactive children:

> *When he was three years old, Andrew's sleep-deprived parents brought him to our Brain Bio Centre. He was hyperactive and seemed never to sleep. Not surprisingly, he was grumpy most of the time.*
>
> *We recommended that his parents give him 65mg of magnesium daily in a pleasant-tasting powder added to a drink before bed. Two weeks later, his mum phoned to say that he was sleeping right through every night and had been transformed into a delightful child during the day too.*

The four drivers of ADHD

Optimum nutrition has a big role to play in helping neurodivergent children. Multi-nutrient trials have shown improvements in irritability, hyperactivity and self-harm.[161] Raised homocysteine and low B12 or folate in the pregnant mother are associated with greater risk of their child developing ASD and worse symptoms,[162] creating methylation abnormalities that could explain many of the symptoms.[163] Supplementing homocysteine-lowering B vitamins makes symptoms better.[164]

Conditions like ADHD may be the result of either:

- a high-GL diet, with too much sugar
- a lack of essential omega-3 fats
- a lack of critical nutrients such as B vitamins, zinc and magnesium
- unidentified food intolerances.

Adolescents with blood sugar problems and diagnosed with metabolic syndrome, already show the same kind of cognitive deficiencies and hippocampal brain shrinkage found in adults with pre-dementia.[165] That's how important it is to stop children developing a sweet tooth.

Studies by Dr Alex Richardson from the University of Oxford, giving children with ADHD these vital brain fats, have shown an improvement in learning and the behavioural problems that define ADHD.[166] Her book *They Are What You Feed Them*, based on a lifetime of research, explains how diet affects children's behaviour and learning.

Over in New Zealand, Professor Julia Rucklidge tested the effects of giving children aged 7 to 12 who had been diagnosed with ADHD a high-strength comprehensive multivitamin and mineral supplement, including plenty of B vitamins (B6 23mg, folate 267mcg, B12 300mcg, magnesium 200mg, zinc 16mg). A total of 47 children were given the supplement and 46 a placebo. At the end of the 10-week trial, almost four times more children (32 per cent versus 9 per cent) had shown a clinically meaningful improvement in their attention. Also, based on a clinician's assessment and parent and teacher reports, those on micro-nutrients showed greater improvements in emotional regulation, aggression and general functioning compared with those on the placebo.[167]

Autism and the gut

Many children on the spectrum complain of gut problems. Some, though certainly not all, respond well to gluten- and casein-free diets.[168] My strong advice is to test a child for IgG-based food intolerance before embarking on a restrictive diet.

But it's not just milk and wheat that can be a problem, nor do food intolerances only affect those with ASD.

Michael, a five-year-old we saw at the Brain Bio Centre, used to be so hyperactive that he could only go to school on a part-time basis.

He was unable to concentrate on anything, was disruptive in class and also found it difficult to socialize with other children. After taking a YorkTest 113 food intolerance test, Michael discovered he was intolerant to a range of foods, mainly dairy, wheat, oranges, carrots, soya, chicken and pork.

Staff at Michael's school were amazed by the changes in his behaviour just one week after making the dietary changes. He could sit still and calmly draw pictures and went back to school on a full-time basis.

Putting all these pieces together, US researchers ran a 12-month study of a comprehensive nutritional and dietary intervention, enrolling 67 children and adults with autism spectrum disorder (ASD) aged 3 to 58 years and using 50 non-sibling neurotypical controls of similar age and gender. Treatment began with a comprehensive vitamin/mineral supplement, and additional treatments were added sequentially, including essential fatty acids, Epsom salts baths, carnitine, digestive enzymes and a healthy, gluten-free, casein-free, soy-free (HGCSF) diet. There was a major improvement in both autistic symptoms and non-verbal intellectual ability (non-verbal IQ) in the treatment group compared with the non-treatment group, with a gain of 7 IQ points. This is equivalent to what we found in the first vitamin IQ study back in 1987, when adolescents put on a B-vitamin-rich multivitamin had a 7-point increase in IQ compared with those on a placebo over seven months.[169]

Parents in the ASD study reported that the vitamin/mineral supplements, essential fatty acids and HGCSF diet were the most beneficial.[170]

I did a similar thing in a south London school for the BBC. They had challenged me to change the behaviour of disruptive kids in a week.

Of the 30 children, aged six to seven, the teacher said 10, roughly a third, were disruptive or had learning or behaviour problems. The worst was Reece. He couldn't sit still or pay attention and was constantly getting into trouble.

I enrolled Reece's mother and the other parents in a one-week experiment in which they'd give their children no sweets or food with added sugar, additives or colourings, a drink containing vitamins and minerals, and try to eat more fish, fruit, vegetables, nuts and seeds. To measure change, the teacher asked the children to write a story on the day before we started and then again one week later. You can see the change in one week in Reece's stories below.

In the following month, his reading and writing age went up by a year. Now able to sit still and concentrate, he went from close to the bottom of the class to close to the top,. His parents noticed he was worse after eating Monster Munch, which contains monosodium glutamate. Some children are particularly sensitive to this flavour enhancer.

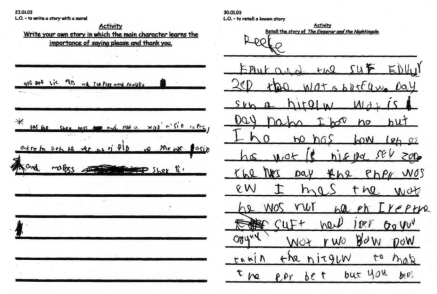

Fig 29. Reece's handwriting before and after 'optimum nutrition'

Eight-year-old Richard is another case in point. Diagnosed with ADHD, he was 'out of control' and his parents were at their wits' end. Richard had also been constipated his entire life. Through biochemical testing at the Brain Bio Centre we found that he was intolerant to dairy products and eggs and was very deficient in magnesium. By looking at his diet, we also saw that he was eating far too much sugar on a daily basis.

He was given a low-sugar, low-GL diet free of dairy and eggs, and also given magnesium and omega-3 supplements. Within three months, his parents reported that he had calmed down considerably and had become much more manageable. His constipation had also cleared completely.

Dr Alessio Fasano, who is also both Professor of Paediatrics at Harvard Medical School and Professor of Nutrition at Harvard's Chan School of Public Health, thinks something is going wrong in the gut, with many ASD children reporting gut problems, including diarrhoea, constipation, belching and excessive flatulence and dysbiosis indicated by an abnormal pattern of gut bacteria.[171]

His findings support a connection between metabolism, gastro-intestinal physiology and complex behavioural traits. This has been confirmed by a small trial 'cleansing' the gut with an antibiotic, then giving 'healthy' faecal transplants to 18 children with ASD.[172] This resulted in significant improvements in constipation, diarrhoea, indigestion and abdominal pain, as well as behavioural ASD symptoms. The improvements persisted eight weeks after treatment.

In some children, wheat and milk may contribute to these symptoms. Professor Fasano's research finds that neurodivergent children show high levels of zonulin, which can lead to leaky gut.[173] The gluten in wheat makes the zonulin levels go up.

ASD children have also been found to have opioid-like wheat and milk proteins in their urine, making these foods especially 'addictive'. This was the discovery of researchers at the Autism Research Unit at the University of Sunderland, headed by Paul Shattock, now known as ESPA Research. They developed successful strategies for helping children with autism known as the Sunderland Protocol.[174]

In summary, to build healthy young brains and minimize the risk of developing symptoms associated with neurodivergence, including ADHD and autism, it is important for mothers-to-be, pregnant women and breastfeeding mothers and their children to:

- Limit or avoid foods with added sugar and follow a low-GL diet.
- Avoid chemical colouring and flavour additives such as MSG.
- Optimize omega-3 intake, also phospholipids, from seafood and eggs, and supplement omega-3 DHA and EPA.
- Optimize vitamins A and D, with sufficient sun exposure to encourage good body stores of vitamin D.
- Ensure healthy methylation with B vitamins, especially vitamin B12 in vegans and those on a largely plant-based diet.
- Check for food intolerances, including gluten, if digestive symptoms are present.

PART 4

Brain Fuel

Discover the optimal diet, lifestyle, exercises and supplements for a super-healthy brain.

23

The Brain-Friendly Diet

How do you work out the best diet to protect your brain and prevent cognitive decline? Generally speaking, there are two ways to approach this question. One is to look at foods that reduce or increase the risk of cognitive decline and the other is to look at diets that reduce the risk, but these usually start with an assumption of what a healthy or not healthy diet is. Either way, and we will do both, what you eat has a massive impact on your brain health. You'll recall the up to 92 per cent reduced risk of Alzheimer's reported in the study in Finland and Sweden that compared those with a 'healthy' versus unhealthy diet in midlife for the risk of developing Alzheimer's disease and dementia 14 years later.[1]

A study in the *British Medical Journal* following over 30,000 people over a decade found that those with a healthy diet were about seven times less likely to have age-related cognitive decline or dementia than those with an 'average' diet and about nine times less likely to develop dementia than those with an unfavourable diet. Their definition of a healthy diet was one high in fish, eggs, fruits, vegetables, legumes, nuts and tea.[2]

Mediterranean diet advantages

These foods are also hallmarks of a Mediterranean-style diet, which, as we've seen, usually means eating more fruit, vegetables, legumes, nuts and seeds, as well as more fish, less meat and sometimes some wine. Early studies on the Mediterranean-style diet reported that high adherence versus low adherence reduced the risk of Alzheimer's by a third.[3]

The most recent study conducted by researchers at Rush University Medical Center in Chicago showed that eating a Mediterranean-style diet called the MIND diet, with lots of vegetables and fruit, keeps your brain 18 years younger.[4] According to the researchers, 'People who scored highest for adhering to the Mediterranean diet had average plaque and tangle amounts in their brains similar to being 18 years younger than the people who scored lowest.'

A similar study in Holland reported that 'better-diet quality related to larger brain volume, grey matter volume, white matter volume, and hippocampal volume. High intake of vegetables, fruit, whole grains, nuts, dairy, and fish and low intake of sugar-containing beverages were associated with larger brain volumes.'[5]

So, following a brain-friendly diet could reduce your risk of cognitive decline by up to 90 per cent, stop your brain shrinking and avoid signs of brain ageing such as amyloid plaques and neurofibrillary p-tau tangles. Let's assume that if they are good for older brains, they're likely to be good for young brains too.

Small changes make big differences

Also, adding in one 'good' food makes a big difference. Rush University's research found that ticking one good food box – such as eating the recommended amounts of vegetables or fruits – reduced amyloid build-up in the brain to a level similar to being about four years younger. In their study, the greatest result was found with those eating greens. Those in the top third of greens consumption had substantially less Alzheimer's-related pathology than those in the lowest third.

'Doing a simple dietary modification, such as adding more greens, berries, wholegrains, olive oil and fish, can actually delay your onset of Alzheimer's disease or reduce your risk of dementia when you're growing old,' said study author Puja Agarwal, Assistant Professor of Internal Medicine at the Rush University Medical Center in Chicago.

Also, reducing bad foods makes a big difference. Replacing just 10 per cent of ultra-processed food by weight in one's diet with an equivalent proportion of unprocessed or minimally processed foods was estimated to lower the risk of dementia by 19 per cent.[6]

Brain-friendly foods

So, what are the foods that are most protective for your brain and cognitive health? In Chapter 13 we looked at the results of one of the first good studies, which was carried out in Norway more than a decade ago by Eha Nurk and Helga Refsum and colleagues.[7] To recap and summarize, they found that:

- *Tea* – the more you drink, the better. The tea benefit has been confirmed more recently in a study in Singapore, with green tea being marginally better than black tea.[8] However, this benefit was not found in a UK Biobank study, which reported tea and coffee drinking to be associated with worsening cognition compared with abstainers.[9] My view is to drink tea, green over black, in preference to coffee, and limit your intake to one of two cups a day.
- *Chocolate* – peaks at 10g, or about 3 pieces – and let's say dark, 70%+, thus with less sugar, is more likely to be better, as sugar is a strong indicator of cognitive decline. More recent studies giving cocoa, a rich source of flavanols, have shown improved cognition, possibly by improving circulation.[10]
- *Grains and potatoes* – reach a plateau at 100 to 150g a day, which is one or two servings max. High-fibre bread was the most beneficial carb food. White bread increased risk. Overall, eating fewer carbs and choosing wholegrains and wholefoods, high in fibre, is a good idea. Sugar and ultra-processed foods are consistently bad news (*see Chapter 11*).
- *Fruit and veg* – the more you eat, the better, though the benefits start to plateau at 500g a day, which is about five to six servings. Of individual fruit and veg, *carrots*, *cruciferous vegetables* and *citrus fruit* were the most positive, as were *mushrooms*. The Rush University study found that those who ate 1.3 portions of *green leafy vegetables* a day, compared to less than one a week, had a dramatically slower decline in

cognitive function, equivalent to being 11 years younger over a 10-year period. *Berries* are particularly protective, especially *blueberries* and *strawberries*.[11]

- *Fish* – is the most protective. The Norwegian study found a peak benefit at about 100g a day, which is one to two servings. A study of all studies by National Institutes of Health researcher M. A. Beydoun and others reported that eating fish once or more each week reduced the risk of Alzheimer's by a third compared with those who ate fish less than once a week.[12] Oily fish, as a source of omega-3 fats, is the best.
- *Olive oil and nuts* – seem to have positive aspects associated with a Mediterranean diet.[13] One study assigned people to a Mediterranean diet supplemented with either a litre a week of olive oil or 30g of nuts a day, which is a small handful, versus a control diet with low fat, and reported reduced cognitive decline with the extra olive oil or nuts.[14] I favour olive oil high in polyphenols (*see Resources*).

Some foods or drinks could go either way. For example, some studies suggest coffee drinking might reduce risk, yet coffee increases homocysteine levels, which is a strong predictor of risk. Alcohol consumption, especially red wine, may reduce risk in moderation, but there's a narrow window of benefit. Wine consumption reduces risk up to 125g a day, which is a small glass. Abstinence increases risk, as does having more than 14 units of alcohol a week, which is equivalent to a medium glass of wine every day, according to a study in the *British Medical Journal*.[15]

What makes a food brain-friendly?

The foods listed above are rich sources of one or more of the following critical nutrients:

- antioxidant vitamins (C and E)
- flavanols and other phytonutrients
- vitamin D
- omega-3 fats
- folate and other B vitamins
- phospholipids and choline

The key components of the diet

Bearing all this in mind, the key components of a diet designed to protect brain health and reduce risk of cognitive decline are:

Eat essential fats and phospholipids
- Eat an egg a day, or six eggs a week – preferably free range and organic. Boil, scramble or poach them, but avoid frying.
- Eat a tablespoon of seeds and nuts every day – the best seeds are chia, flax, hemp and pumpkin (all higher in omega-3). They're delicious sprinkled on cereal, soups and salads. The best nuts are walnuts, pecans and macadamia nuts, but all nuts, including almonds and hazelnuts, are good sources of protein and minerals, as are unsalted peanuts.
- Eat cold-water, oily, carnivorous fish – have a serving of herring, mackerel, salmon or sardines two or three times a week (limit tuna, unless identified as low in mercury, to three times a month). Vegans need to supplement algal omega-3 DHA, as well as choline or lecithin capsules or granules, rich in phosphatidyl choline.
- Use cold-pressed olive oil for salad dressings and other cold uses, such as drizzling on vegetables instead of butter. Substitute frying with steam frying with olive oil, coconut oil or butter, e.g. for onions and garlic, then adding a watery sauce, such as lemon juice, tamari and water, to 'steam' for example, vegetables, perhaps with tofu, fish or chicken.

Eat slow-release carbohydrates
- Eat wholefoods – wholegrains, lentils, beans, nuts, seeds, fresh fruit and vegetables – and avoid all white, refined and over-processed foods, as well as any food with added sugar.
- Snack on fresh fruit, preferably apples, pears and/or berries, especially blueberries.
- Eat less gluten. Try brown rice, rye, oats, quinoa, lentils, beans or chickpeas.
- Avoid fruit juices. Eat fresh fruit instead. Occasionally have unsweetened Montmorency cherry juice or blueberry juice (made from unsweetened concentrate).

Eat antioxidant- and vitamin-rich foods

- Eat half your diet raw or lightly steamed.
- Eat two or more servings a day of fresh fruit, including one of berries.
- Eat four servings a day of dark green, leafy and root vegetables such as broccoli, tenderstem broccoli, kale, spinach, watercress, carrots, sweet potatoes, Brussels sprouts, green beans or peppers, as well as mushrooms. Choose organic where possible.
- Have a serving a day of beans, lentils, nuts or seeds – all high in folate.

Eat enough protein

- Have three servings of protein-rich foods a day if you are a man, and two if you are a woman.
- Choose good vegetable protein sources, including beans, lentils, quinoa, tofu or tempeh (soya) and 'seed' vegetables such as peas, broad beans and corn.
- If eating animal protein, choose lean meat or preferably fish, organic whenever possible.

Eat gut-friendly fermented foods and fibres

- Add sauerkraut, kimchi, live yoghurt, kefir, kombucha, fermented pickles and some unpasteurized soft cheese to your diet.
- Add chia seeds to oat-based cereals.
- Limit or avoid wheat. Have oatcakes instead of bread.
- Eat oats and oatcakes, beans, nuts, seeds, whole fruit and vegetables, having four servings of vegetables a day, raw or lightly steamed.
- Eat prebiotic-rich Jerusalem artichoke, garlic, leeks, onions, asparagus, barley and oats.

Avoid harmful fats

- Minimize your intake of fried or processed food and burnt saturated fat on meat, and cheese.
- Minimize your consumption of deep-fried food. Poach, steam or steam-fry food instead.
- Minimize your intake of refined vegetable oils high in omega-6 (principally soybean oil, corn oil and sunflower oil).

Avoid sugar, reduce caffeine and drink alcohol in moderation

- Avoid adding sugar to dishes, and avoid foods and drinks with added sugar. Keep your sugar intake to a minimum, sweetening cereal or desserts with fruit.
- Avoid or considerably reduce your consumption of caffeinated drinks. Don't have more than one caffeinated drink a day. Tea is preferable to coffee.
- Drink alcoholic drinks infrequently, preferably red wine, to a maximum of one small glass (125g) a day.
- Have up to three pieces of dark chocolate, minimum 70 per cent cacao, or drink unsweetened cacao with milk or plant milk.

It's one thing knowing what to do, of course, and another thing doing it. When you join COGNITION, you'll be given bite-size assignments to make the changes to your diet that will make the biggest difference, with reminders to keep you motivated and on track. It takes approximately three weeks to break a habit and six weeks to make a new, good habit, so whatever you decide to do, you need to stick to it for at least a month.

Whether or not you sign up to COGNITION, by doing the free online Cognitive Function Test at foodforthebrain.org, you'll see which areas you need to focus on. For example, if you score red or amber on 'Up Brain Fats', focus on the 'Eat essential fats and phospholipids' section above. If 'Low Carb and GL' is your weak area, focus on the section 'Eat slow-release carbohydrates'. If it's 'Antioxidants' that come up lacking, focus on the 'Eat antioxidant- and vitamin-rich foods' section. If 'Healthy Gut' is your weakness, focus on 'Eat gut-friendly fermented foods and fibres'.

From the list of recommendations above, highlight three that you aren't currently following and want to focus on for the next month. Write them down in big letters and stick this on your fridge. Make a note, in a month's time, to do the same again, choosing three new areas to focus on.

Going ketogenic

Your brain loves ketones, made from fat and specifically the medium-chain triglyceride C8. A great way to encourage your brain to feed on them is to either do an 18:6 diet for two or three days a week, or have a day or two with no carbs, or go fully ketogenic for five or so days a month, bearing in mind that it takes a couple of days to get fully into ketosis. Let me explain these options.

18:6

This approach means having no carbs for 18 hours or no food at all for 18 hours. An easy way to do this is to have dinner at 6 or 7 p.m., no breakfast, and lunch at 12 or 1 p.m. the following day. The problem is, you'll probably wake up hungry. If you have a hybrid latte (*see page 273*), which includes a tablespoon of C8 oil, this will energize you. (You may want to build up to this by having a teaspoon on the first day, then two, then a tablespoon on Day 3 if you tolerate it fine.) Simply adding a tablespoon to the milk or plant milk such as an oat barista-style milk, especially if you have a frother, makes a delicious creamy drink.

Nigel tried it out:

'I had been feeling less mentally alert, a bit foggy, not my usual self. Patrick gave me a tablespoon of C8 oil in my coffee and I felt noticeably more energized, focused and sharp, particularly as this was after a relatively sleepless night... The effects lasted for around five hours. Not only that, it improved my coffee – a pleasant and creamy taste.'

You can also have a carb-free snack mid-morning, such as kale crackers, crispy nori seaweed and/or olives.

A one or two-day carb fast

An even 'faster' way to switch your liver into making ketones is to simply eat no carbs at all for 24 hours. For example, eat dinner at 6 p.m., have a hybrid latte the next morning, then a no-carb snack such as olives, crispy seaweed or kale crackers at 10 a.m., a no-carb lunch (such as salmon and kale or spinach sautéed in ghee or coconut butter, perhaps with pesto or tahini) at 2 p.m., a spoonful of C8 MCT oil mid-afternoon (*see page 319*), then a no-carb dinner at 6 p.m., if you're going for two days, or a low-carb dinner if not, choosing from one of my recipes. In this example, you effectively eat nothing for 16 hours, and effectively eat no carbs for the full 24 hours.

Five or more days of low-carb, high-fat eating

Learning how to eat low-carb, high-fat does take a bit of instruction, and knowing which foods and which recipes to use. My book *The Hybrid Diet* explains how to do this and gives you recipes to follow.

For those wanting to go one step further, my book *The 5-Day Diet* gives an exact process for not only going ketogenic, but also triggering a cellular self-repair process called autophagy. This helps build new mitochondria in cells and could help brain recovery. It involves eating a low-calorie, low-protein and virtually vegan diet for five days. The reason for this is that both carbs and too much protein, especially meat and milk, switch off autophagy.

Here are some examples to help get you started.

Your morning routine with three breakfast options

Starting off on the right foot sets the tone for the rest of the day. We've learned that it's better to be up for an hour before having a coffee (or tea), although there's nothing wrong with a non-caffeinated option. It's also better to exercise before eating, as in our evolutionary programming to hunt, then eat. So, starting your day with some exercise, either physical or mental, then having your morning coffee or tea, is best.

If you're doing an 18:6 day, break your fast by having a hybrid latte (*see page 273*).

If not, have a low-GL, brain-friendly breakfast, including only foods on the good food list on pages 267 to 269. Three options are given below, namely:

- Get Up & Go with CarboSlow®, low-carb milk and berries
- Oat and chia porridge with blueberries or strawberries
- Scrambled or poached egg with smoked salmon and avocado

Get Up & Go with CarboSlow® is a vitamin- and mineral-rich breakfast shake, also containing the gut-friendly soluble fibre glucomannan. You whizz it up with milk and some berries (*see page 273*). Both eggs and salmon are rich in phospholipids.

Brain-friendly main meals

There are a number of ways you can try out and build up a library of brain-friendly recipes. My *Low-GL Diet Cookbook* is a great place to start, especially if cutting back on carbs is indicated or a challenge for you. There are also a number of recipes in my book *The Hybrid Diet*, which also gives you ketogenic options if you wish to pursue this avenue. If you are vegan but would like to apply as many of these principles as possible without eating fish or eggs, my book *Optimum Nutrition for Vegans* has 100 low-GL recipes. There are also a growing number of brain-friendly recipes in the Upgrade Your Brain Cookapp: foodforthebrain.org/UYBcookapp.

Below, in the recipes section, I've included an example of a salad, a soup and a hot meal, two of which include the use of fish in ways you may not have experienced that consistently get the thumbs-up from people who don't like fish, or rarely eat sardines or mackerel, both of which are high in omega-3 fats:

- Sardine pâté salad
- Smoked mackerel kedgeree
- Primordial soup

These recipes also have very low-carb options for those choosing to have a more ketogenic day.

Snacks

The rule as far as snacks are concerned is to always combine any carb-rich food with a protein-rich food. This slows down the release of the sugars in the carb-rich food. An example of this would be:

- fruit, perhaps some blueberries or a small apple, with some nuts such as walnuts, pecans or almonds
- a vegetable crudité such as a raw carrot, celery, pepper or cucumber, or an oatcake or two, with some hummus (made from chickpeas) or taramasalata (made from fish roe)

- a fully fermented sugar-free yoghurt (or coconut yoghurt for those avoiding dairy) with some berries and nuts

Brain-friendly recipes

Hybrid latte

Serves 1

240ml low-carb, unsweetened almond milk
120ml filtered coffee or run through (less caffeine, more antioxidants)
1 heaped tbsp almond butter or peanut butter (ideally half of each – almond has half the carbs)
1 tbsp C8 oil (*see Resources*)
1 rounded tsp (3g) cacao powder carb
½ tsp cinnamon (good for blood sugar)

- Stir all the ingredients together in a glass or mug.

Note: Leave out the coffee for a caffeine-free option and add more almond milk. Add a cup of ice cubes for an iced latte.

Get Up & Go with CarboSlow®, low-carb milk and berries

Serves 1

1 tbsp (10g) Get Up & Go with CarboSlow®
480ml unsweetened soya or almond milk, or full-fat cow's milk
handful of blueberries, strawberries or raspberries

- Blitz all of the ingredients in a blender.
  [*8 GL/5g carbs*]

Note: Add a teaspoon of chia seeds for extra protein, omega-3s and fibre.
If you're having a ketogenic day, use a zero-carb plant milk.
Make the shake watery, not too thick, and consume immediately after making. The soluble fibre glucomannan in CarboSlow®

absorbs liquid rapidly, and ideally this should happen inside you, as it will keep you feeling full for longer.

Oat and chia porridge with blueberries or strawberries

Serves 1
25g oats
240ml water
120ml carb-free, unsweetened almond or soya milk
2 tsp chia seeds
handful of blueberries or strawberries

- Simmer the oats in the water and milk for 5–10 minutes.
- Add the other ingredients and stir well.

Note: Half a chopped or stewed apple, plus some cinnamon, may be used instead of the berries. Chopped almonds, pecans or walnuts can be used instead of the chia seeds.
Add half a teaspoon of xylitol (0.5 GL) if required.

Scrambled egg with smoked salmon and avocado

Serves 1
2 eggs
olive oil or butter, for frying
1 slice of smoked salmon
½ avocado, peeled and chopped
1 Nairn's rough oatcake

- Crack the eggs into a bowl and scramble well.
- Heat a little olive oil or butter over a medium heat. Add the eggs and cook gently, stirring, until cooked through.
- Serve the scrambled eggs with the smoked salmon, avocado and oatcake.

Note: Easy to put together on a busy morning. This filling breakfast is low on GLs, but full of fats to fuel the brain.

Sardine pâté salad

Serves 1
½ tin sardines
¼ small red onion, roughly chopped
a pinch of finely chopped coriander
a pinch of finely chopped flat leaf parsley
juice of ¼ lemon
4 capers
½ tbsp apple cider vinegar
1 tbsp olive oil
salt and ground black pepper
rocket and mixed baby leaf salad

- Put all the ingredients except the salad in a blender or food processer and blend together. Serve with the salad.

Note: If you're eating low-GL, you could serve with a couple of oatcakes. If you're having a ketogenic day, serve with 100g portion of kimchi and some kale crackers.

Low-carb kedgeree

Serves 4
60g wholegrain bulgur or quinoa or brown basmati rice (makes
    180g cooked; quinoa is the lowest GL and brown rice the highest)
around 275g smoked mackerel fillets
2 free-range or organic eggs
100g frozen petit pois
200g broccoli or tenderstem
2 tbsp mild (not extra virgin) olive oil, virgin rapeseed oil or coconut oil
1 clove garlic, crushed
1 large or 2 small onions, finely chopped
½ to 1 tsp ground smoked paprika or cayenne (depending on how
    hot you like it)
½ to 1 tsp ground cumin
½ to 1 tsp ground turmeric
freshly ground black pepper
1 tbsp tahini
4 tbsp finely chopped flat leaf parsley (to garnish)

- Measure out three times as much water as bulgur, quinoa or brown basmati rice and bring it to the boil. Add your grains and simmer on a low heat, for 8 minutes (bulgur), 13 minutes (quinoa) or 35 minutes (brown rice). Drain any surplus water if necessary.
- Boil the eggs in a pan of boiling water for 6 minutes until the yolks are firm, then cool rapidly under the tap for a minute. Set aside to fully cool before peeling and slicing into quarters.
- Heat the olive oil in a large saucepan over a medium heat and cook the garlic and onion for a minute or so before adding the spices. Let them gently cook for a further few minutes, taking care not to let them burn, until the onions are soft and fragrant.
- Break the smoked mackerel into small pieces and add to the saucepan, stirring them in.
- In the meantime, add the frozen petit pois to boiling water and wait until the water is boiling again, then add the broccoli or tenderstem pieces. Once the peas float to the top, remove from the heat and drain.
- Add the petit pois and tenderstem or broccoli florets to the onions and mackerel. Stir in the cooked grains until evenly coated and then add the hard-boiled eggs.
- Stir in the tahini to make it creamy and season with plenty of pepper – you won't need any salt thanks to the smoked fish and the strength of the spices. Garnish with the parsley.

Note: By using mackerel instead of the traditional haddock, and creamed up at the end with tahini, this spicy kedgeree ends up both high in fat and low-GL.

Primordial soup

Serves 1

1 tsp olive oil
½ red onion, roughly chopped
1 garlic clove, crushed
1 carrot, diced
a small sweet potato (or equivalent portion of butternut squash), peeled and diced
1 tsp fresh root ginger, peeled and grated

a pinch of ground turmeric and cayenne (optional, for those who like things hot)

1 tsp bouillon powder

¼ red pepper, deseeded and roughly chopped

2½ tbsp coconut milk

- Heat the oil in a saucepan over a medium heat and cook the onion and garlic for 3–4 minutes until softened.
- Add the carrot, sweet potato, ginger, turmeric and bouillon powder. Add boiling water to just cover and bring to the boil. Reduce the heat, cover and simmer for 10 minutes or until the vegetables are soft.
- Add the red pepper and coconut milk, reheat if needed, then purée using a blender or food processor until smooth and thick.

The Upgrade Your Brain CookApp

To support your brain-upgrade journey, the charity foodforthebrain. org has a CookApp which not only offers you 300 brain-friendly recipes, but rates all the recipes for:

- GL-friendly to help stabilize your blood sugar and help you lose weight
- brain-fat friendly
- B-vitamin friendly
- antioxidant friendly

You can choose your area of focus, as well as put in any foods you avoid if you're gluten or dairy intolerant, vegetarian or vegan. You then see those breakfasts, main meals, desserts, soups or salads that best meet your brain-upgrade needs.

To find out more, visit foodforthebrain.org/UYBCookApp.

24

Brain Training Exercises

While I've already emphasized the need to use your mind and body in ways to challenge your brain as part of your daily exercise, how do you do this? Also, how do you train yourself to stay focused and centred, not shooting off into states of stress and anxiety?

One of the most practical and effective tools I've discovered for this is HeartMath, which I describe below. If your Cognitive Function Test came up with 'Active Body', 'Active Mind' or 'Sleep and Calm' as needing attention, the HeartMath techniques are particularly good.

Here we'll look at three areas of action – physical, intellectual and emotional – that support your brain upgrade.

Increasing physical activity

Whatever you can do to learn a new physical skill is good for your brain, for example learning *t'ai chi* or yoga, or taking up a new sport. Anything that both builds muscle and involves coordination is great. A simple, practical way is to do the *Burn Fat Fast* exercises (*see page 176*).

Increasing intellectual activity

If you feel you could benefit from some brain training, there are a few options. Generally, I recommend you do 15 minutes of brain training most days, ideally in the morning, at least five days a week.

The ones you are likely to know about are doing a daily cross-word puzzle, Soduko or Wordle. There's a free version of this at: www.nytimes.com/games/wordle/index.html.

Two apps that crank up your brain training to high levels, especially if the above become easy or are not attractive to you, are Brain HQ and Lumosity.

- *Brain HQ* is designed to work through neuroplasticity – the process by which the brain physically changes through learning, experience and training. Making these physical changes to the brain is key to improved brain performance. Every Brain HQ exercise challenges the brain's speed and accuracy of information-processing. Using smart adaptive algorithms, each exercise ensures that the challenge stays at a level just right for driving brain change – not too easy, but not too hard. The result is that Brain HQ exercises rewire the brain, improving brain activation, timing and connectivity between different brain regions. (*See www.brainhq.com.*)
- *Lumosity* is designed to enhance memory, processing speed and problem-solving, all of which are critical to protect against cognitive impairment. It was originally a test in a trial of thousands of participants who either trained on it for five days per week, for 15 minutes each day, or did online crossword puzzles as an active control. After 10 weeks, the Lumosity users had improved more than the control group on assessments of working memory, short-term memory, processing speed, problem-solving, fluid reasoning and overall cognitive function. (*See www.lumosity.com.*)

Increasing emotional stability and building stress resilience

While any form of meditation, including mindfulness, has to be good, it has mainly been researched and shown to help those with cognitive decline. Long-term studies showing that meditation reduces future risk of cognitive decline are lacking, but it is likely.

I would encourage you to pursue a mediation practice if that is your wish, especially if you have a hyperactive mind or get lost in negative thoughts.

One of my favourite books on this subject, which is quite practical, is *Meditation for the Love of It* by Sally Kempton. She helped me write the tenth 'secret' in *The Ten Secrets of 100% Healthy People*, which has a number of exercises and meditations for finding your sense of meaning and purpose.

T'ai chi and yoga are both meditative and involve physical training, so tick both 'Active' boxes. If you can find a form of physical exercise that also helps to get you into the zone, that's excellent for your brain. This could be dancing. Mine is paragliding.

Building stress resilience with HeartMath®

Reducing the negative impact of stress is a vital piece of your brain upgrade. In my experience, no matter how well a person follows a recommended diet or supplement programme, if they remain stressed, their health goals are difficult to achieve. This led Susannah Lawson, my co-author for *The Stress Cure*, and me to explore a range of approaches to find a way to help clients tackle stress, from breathing exercises and guided visualization to referrals to life coaches and Emotional Freedom Technique practitioners.

One of the most effective was a simple technique from the HeartMath system which could reduce the stress hormone cortisol by 23 per cent in just one month and increase the rejuvenating hormone DHEA by 100 per cent.[16] Nothing we'd ever seen before could claim such dramatic success in such a short time – and all from an exercise that took just five minutes a day. So Susannah jumped on a plane and flew to California, the home of HeartMath, to find out more, and later trained as a HeartMath practitioner to enable her to teach the technique to her clients back in the UK. Here's how it works.

The HeartMath system is a scientifically validated way to not only reduce stress, but more importantly to transform the negative emotional and physiological effects experienced when a stressful event occurs. This is crucial, because so many stress-relieving activities – listening to music, having a warm bath, or a massage, or a glass of wine, for example – focus on relaxation *after* the event. Yet by the time you wind down, you've probably already experienced hours of stress and its unpleasant effects. The stress hormone cortisol, for example, stays in your system for hours once released. So the key appears to be learning how to interrupt and transform your reaction to stress, and therefore stop the emotional and hormonal fallout that follows.

Of course, some people will claim they thrive on stress. Some people say, 'Deadlines motivate me.' And as long as you truly perceive stress in a positive way – and are giving yourself adequate time to rest and recuperate – then you may not be having any harmful side-effects. It's when stress leaves you feeling depleted and out of control that it becomes problematic.

You are probably already aware that if left unchecked, ongoing stress isn't good news. Are you experiencing it? Take a look over the list below and see if you experience any of the following on a regular basis:

- finding it hard to think straight
- a negative attitude
- feeling out of control
- anxiety
- tension
- irritation
- anger
- feeling overwhelmed
- heightened worries and concerns
- frustration
- resentment
- hostility

If you answer 'yes' to even one of these, then the chances are that stress is having a depleting impact on your emotional state. This is important, because it's how we are feeling, rather than what we're thinking, that activates and drives the physiological changes that correlate with the stress response. Thus the key to optimal mental health and vitality is directly related to our ability to self-regulate our emotional response.

Simply put, the emotions we tend to label as 'negative' – for example, those listed above – disrupt optimal physiological and

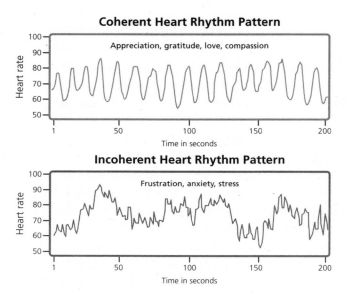

Figs 30 and 31. How a positive or 'renewing' emotion affects the heart rhythm

mental functions and leave us feeling depleted. Conversely, the emotions we label as 'positive' facilitate a wide range of physiological functions, renew our energy and optimize our body's natural regenerative processes. The research that supports these findings calls the latter 'psycho-physiological coherence', or more simply, heart coherence.

How emotions affect heart rhythms

When we think of the heart, we probably visualize a physical organ, but we may also think about the emotional qualities we attribute to it. Interestingly, research by the Institute of HeartMath has discovered that the two are interlinked – that is, our emotional state has an impact on our physical heart rhythm patterns.

The top graph in the figure below shows the heart rhythm pattern that is typical of a positive feeling such as appreciation or gratitude. This smooth shape is what scientists call a 'highly ordered' or 'coherent' pattern and is a sign of good health and emotional balance. The bottom graph shows the irregular, jerky heart rhythm pattern typical of stressful feelings like anger, frustration, worry and anxiety. This is called an 'incoherent' pattern.

Just as our emotions influence our heart rhythm pattern, so our heart communicates with our brain and the rest of our body. This occurs via our nervous and hormonal systems, electromagnetic inter-actions and other pathways. HeartMath research has been able to demonstrate that the signals the heart sends to the brain can profoundly influence perception, emotions, behaviour, performance and health.[17] What's also interesting is that there are actually more connections from the heart *to the brain* than *from the brain* to the heart.

In studying the science of the heart, what the Institute of Heart-Math has discovered is that our heart rhythms have an impact on our thinking. When our heart rhythm is coherent, we are able to access higher-thinking centres in our brain, so can think more clearly and see more options or solutions to problems. But when our heart rhythm pattern becomes incoherent, driven by negative emotions, this access becomes inhibited and we are likely to find our reactions are slower and we aren't able to think so clearly.

Studies have found that people in a coherent state, i.e., when their heart rhythm pattern is coherent, are noticeably able to improve their thinking and performance, whether they be making decisions or playing sport.[18]

Over time, coherence also helps to reduce the stress hormone cortisol, which is produced whenever we experience feelings of frustration, anxiety, anger or despair,[19] and increase the 'vitality' hormone DHEA. Ideally, these hormones should be in balance, but when we experience frequent stress, cortisol can become too high and DHEA depleted. This pattern is found in most major disease states and is associated with accelerated ageing, brain-cell death and impaired memory and learning as well as decreased bone density, impaired immune function, increased blood sugar and increased fat accumulation around the waist and hips.[20]

Getting coherent with HeartMath techniques

The premise of the HeartMath system is different from many other approaches to stress relief, which typically focus on calming down and lowering heart rate after the stressful event has occurred. With HeartMath, you learn a coherence technique that can help you 'reset' your physiological reaction to stress as the event occurs.

Just a couple of HeartMath breaths can help you stop the hormo-nal cascade that triggers the release of cortisol – and you stay coherent, i.e., calm and in balance. Research has found that when practised regularly, the exercise can help you to feel better emotionally and improve your intuition, creativity and cognitive performance.[21] This helps you to become smarter and more resilient under pressure, which is part of the reason why HeartMath has become popular with senior business executives, as well as with the military and healthcare providers.

Quick Coherence® technique

There are three simple steps to practise to get coherent:

1. Heart focus

- Focus your attention on your heart area, in the centre of your chest.

2. Heart breathing

- Now imagine your breath flowing in and out of that area. This helps your respiration and heart rhythm to synchronize. So, focus on this area and aim to breathe evenly, for example inhale for five or six seconds and exhale for five or six seconds (choose a timescale that feels comfortable and flows easily).

Take a few minutes to get the hang of these stages, then introduce step three:

3. Heart feeling

- As you breathe in and out of your heart area, recall a positive emotion and try to re-experience it. This could be remembering a time spent with someone you love, walking in your favourite place, stroking a pet, picturing a tree or scenic location you admire or even just feeling appreciation that you ate today or have shoes on your feet. If your mind wanders, just bring it gently back to the positive experience.

These three steps, when practised daily for around five minutes, can help you feel calmer and more content. It really is that simple. Your heart rhythm pattern will become coherent and your heart–brain communication will optimize to help you think more clearly. Ideally, find time where you can sit down quietly and be undisturbed – for example, first thing in the morning, during your lunch break or when you get home from work – to do this exercise every day. This way, it's more likely to become habit and you can give it your full attention.

Once you've got the hang of this HeartMath technique, you can use it any time you encounter a stressful event – for example, as you start to feel tense in heavy traffic, overloaded at work or sense you are about to face a difficult emotional situation. Just a few heart-focused breaths can help you stay calm and coherent instead of becoming stressed (that's why it's called the Quick Coherence technique). And you can do it with your eyes open, as you walk or talk, so you have a tool to control stress at the direct point you encounter a situation that's likely to trigger a negative or depleting reaction.

How well does it work? Numerous studies have shown that regularly practising HeartMath techniques can have hugely beneficial effects, not only on emotional health and well-being, but also on physical health markers.

HeartMath: Benefits for emotional and physical health

Research into the benefits of using the HeartMath system has focused on a wide range of different audiences, from the very young to the elderly, from medical professionals to the military, students to chief executives, those suffering from mental and physical health problems to athletes. What studies show time and again is that regular use of the HeartMath techniques can produce significant reductions in depression, anxiety, anger, hostility, burnout and fatigue, and corresponding increases in caring, contentment, gratitude, peacefulness and vitality.[22, 23, 24, 25, 26]

A study looking at the daily practice of the HeartMath tools on hormone levels found that after just one month, cortisol, the stress hormone, reduced by 23 per cent and DHEA, the anti-ageing vitality hormone, increased by 100 per cent.[27] The independent lab measuring the hormone samples thought the subjects were on drugs, because they had never seen such improvements in 10 years of operation, processing more than 30,000 samples.

For those suffering with additional health problems, research has shown that practising HeartMath tools and techniques can help to regulate abnormalities. For example, a workplace study of employees with hypertension found that after three months of practising HeartMath techniques, blood pressure dropped an average 10.6 mm Hg for systolic and 6.3 mm Hg for diastolic. Participants also reported improvements in emotional health, including reductions in stress symptoms and depression and an increase in peacefulness and positive outlook.[28]

In a hospital study on 75 patients suffering abnormal heart rhythms (atrial fibrillation) who practised the HeartMath techniques for three months, 71 reported substantial improvements in their physical and emotional health, 56 experienced such improvements in their ability to control their heart rhythms and hypertension that they were able to decrease their medication, and 14 were able to discontinue their medication altogether.[29]

Finally, a small study with diabetics involved teaching a group of 22 participants with both type 1 and type 2 diabetes the HearthMath techniques and monitoring their progress. Six months after the workshop, the participants reported significant reductions in anxiety, negative emotions, fatigue and sleeplessness, along with increased feelings of vitality and improved quality of life. Changes in glycosylated haemoglobin (HbA1c, the marker for sugar damage in the blood) were also observed, with increased HeartMath practice associated with a reduction in HbA1c levels.[30]

Measuring your coherence

As you can see, doing the HeartMath exercise can really help you reduce stress and improve your well-being. It also helps you develop greater resilience and heart coherence. But how will you know?

Further research by the Institute of HeartMath discovered that you could monitor your state of coherence accurately by measuring not just your heart rate (the number of beats), but the pattern of activity between heartbeats. This is called heart rate variability, or HRV. As a result, a simple tool called the Inner Balance™ Coherence Plus sensor has been developed.

The Inner Balance device has a clip that attaches to your ear lobe to pick up your HRV (your ear lobes register a pulse) and then feeds this data through to a hand-held device which tells you how coherent you are (there is also a mobile phone app called Inner Balance which you can download for free). There are three zones – red for incoherent (the state most of us are in), blue for more coherent and green for fully coherent. There is also a breath pacer to help you regulate your breathing, and different levels and modes, so you can adapt your practice as you get the hang of it. (*See Resources for more details of where to buy.*)

> *Pamela was a 55-year-old management consultant who came to see Susannah for help reducing her high blood pressure, heart palpitations and menopausal symptoms. An Adrenal Stress Index test revealed she was in the 'Maladapted Phase II' stage of stress adaptation, suggesting that she'd been stimulating her stress hormones for some time and was beginning to deplete her reserves.*
>
> *Using the HeartMath technique alongside a nutritional protocol, Pamela found that her blood pressure dropped from around 180/139 to 167/101 in four weeks (her GP was also monitoring) and that she was finding it easier to feel less angry and more positive much of the time.*
>
> *After eight weeks, her blood pressure dropped further to 140/90 and she stopped having any heart palpitations. She reported a big improvement in her overall mood and a reduction in menopausal night sweats. Pamela also showed significant progress in her coherence levels and reported enjoying her daily HeartMath practice at home.*
>
> *After 12 weeks, we retested Pamela's stress hormones and found a huge improvement – her results put her in the 'Adapted' category. Her blood pressure stabilized at around 135/90 and her GP was especially impressed.*

Taking HeartMath tools further

As well as teaching you to transform stress, the Institute of HeartMath has developed practices in addition to the Quick Coherence technique for transforming negative attitudes and resolving specific problems. With a qualified practitioner, the HeartMath tools can also be used to help issues such as emotional eating, insomnia, anger/conflict resolution, obsessive compulsive disorder and addictions. And with children, HeartMath tools have successfully been used to help manage ADHD, hyperactivity and anxiety. (*See Resources for how to find a practitioner.*)

You can visit HeartMath's American site, www.heartmath.org, or UK site heartmath.co.uk, for more information and research. There's also a great book written by HeartMath founder Doc Childre called *Transforming Stress*, which gives lots of useful information about using HeartMath tools and developing your practice.

25

Brain Support Tests and Supplements

You will have learned throughout this book that there are four fundamental processes that drive every type of mental illness and ultimately, if out of balance, lead to cognitive decline and Alzheimer's dementia. These are your blood sugar control, your intake of brain fats (omega-3, phospholipids and vitamin D), your homocysteine level, determined by your intake of B vitamins and ability to absorb them, and your antioxidant potential, which is a function of your intake of fresh vegetables, fruit and herbs, and also not smoking or living in a polluted environment.

I call these the four horsemen of the mental health apocalypse. It sounds dramatic, but loss of blood sugar control, with raised HbA1c, and lack of omega-3, vitamin D and B vitamins (and consequent increase in homocysteine), are strongly associated with every major form of mental illness, from ADHD to autism, Alzheimer's, anxiety, bipolar, depression, schizophrenia and Parkinson's. Tackling these four brain-health fundamentals is guaranteed to make you feel a lot better.

Also, many people ask me, 'How do I know if I need to supplement?' The best way to answer this question is to ask your body. Each of these processes can be tested, not to see if you have a disease as such, but to find out how much resilience you have and therefore whether you will benefit from supplements.

Fortunately, it is both relatively inexpensive and easy to test these using a home-test kit supplied by foodforthebrain.org called DRIfT, short for the Dementia Risk Index functional Test. This involves a new technology called dry blood spot analysis. Basically, you prick your finger with an almost painless device you put against your finger and press. Then drip a drop of blood onto the dry blood spot card. Then send it back to the lab. This is available all over the world. Food for the Brain are collecting these test results from thousands of people to redefine what an 'optimum' level means for the best possible cognitive health. From the hundreds of thousands of people who have done the Cognitive Function Test, they can work out what blood levels of these critical biochemical markers correlate with the best cognitive function.

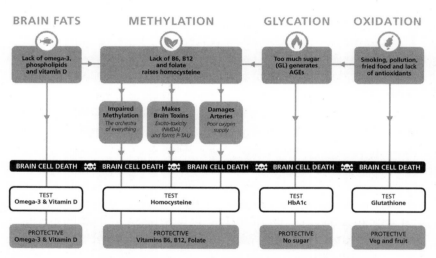

Fig 32. The four drivers of cognitive decline and how to test for them

As you will have learned in Part 2, the critical biomarkers are:

- *HbA1c* for your glucose control (this is what doctors use to diagnose diabetes).
- *Omega-3 index* and *vitamin D* to determine your brain-fat status.
- *Homocysteine* to find out if you're getting enough B vitamins. Many people malabsorb vitamin B12 and consequently have raised homocysteine levels. Anything above 10 needs

supplement treatment, as it is an indicator of accelerated brain shrinkage.

- *Glutathione*, the body's master antioxidant, is the best indicator of your antioxidant potential.

The DRIfT test measures all five from a single pin-prick of blood. (*See foodforthebrain.org/drift.*)

By knowing your levels, you take the guesswork out of what you need, and your test results will then guide you as to what you need to supplement, if necessary. You want to get your homocysteine below 10 and ideally closer to 7mmol/L. The best omega-3 index is above 8 per cent, although many people in Japan, where a lot of seafood is eaten, have an omega-3 index of 10 per cent. You need vitamin D above 75nmol/l for optimal brain health and HbA1c close to 5 per cent – not more than 35nmol/mol, but ideally around or below 30. You want your glutathione index to be in the green.

It is good to retest after three months to find out if you've corrected all your deficiencies. Some of these tests measure substances at 'red blood cell' levels. Red blood cells last for three months. So, if you've taken the right actions, three months later you should have a clean slate of red blood cells, fully loaded with nutrients. That's why it is worth waiting three months to retest.

Once you've got yourself into the 'optimum' or green range, I recommend retesting annually to make sure you're still in the green range.

Food for the Brain combines all these tests into a Dementia Risk Index Functional Test (DRIfT) score. The higher the score, the worse you are. If your DRIfT score is zero, you are in the best brain health. If you score 15, you've got the most work to do to upgrade your brain. (*See Resources for details on these tests.*)

Supplements – are they necessary?

It amazes me that there are still people, including health professionals, who entertain the idea that 'you can get all the vitamins you need from a well-balanced diet'. This conventional view is based on government-supported recommended intakes (RDAs, RNIs, NRVs or DRVs) designed to prevent the classical symptoms of deficiency, such as scurvy in the case of vitamin C. Blood levels of nutrients that prevent classical deficiencies are thus extended to imply that a person has sufficient nutrient status if above these levels. But there is abundant evidence that levels above those used to define 'deficiency' are often associated with adverse signs or symptoms or increased risk of diseases such as dementia, and these levels therefore define a zone of 'nutritional insufficiency'.

There is, furthermore, a growing body of evidence from well-designed studies on specific mental health diseases showing that supplements giving nutrients at levels beyond the basic 'RDAs' delay or reverse the disease or eliminate or ameliorate the symptoms, including cognitive decline. Also, there are many studies showing a steady reduction in symptoms, or diseases, when blood levels of nutrients increase beyond the arbitrary cut-off levels set to prevent classical deficiencies. Thus, neither RDAs nor normal reference ranges given for blood levels of nutrients are 'optimal'.

This illustrates that the definition of 'deficiency' is outdated. Deficiency means a lack of efficiency. If the definition of nutrient deficiency, and its counterpart, sufficiency, were to be defined as the level of a nutrient that relieves the symptoms of disease or promotes its prevention, that definition is not only scientifically supportable but also takes into account the unique biochemical individuality that occurs as a result of genetics, environmental exposure, microbiomics and the ability to absorb nutrients.

While medical and advertising law prohibits the description of a nutritional supplement or food as 'preventing, reversing or treating a disease', this is scientifically not correct. Nutrients *do* prevent, reverse and treat disease.

My overarching principle, and that of the Food for the Brain Foundation, is that of scientific integrity – that is, to be consistent with the prevailing science and share that growing body of knowledge in a way that enables people to restore, maintain and improve mental health. That is the purpose of this book.

Four nutrients are especially relevant in this regard:

- *Vitamin D* – it is now well established that anyone living far from the Equator has to supplement vitamin D for several months over the winter. In 2016, the UK government recommended that everyone supplement during the autumn and winter. Almost a decade earlier, in 2007, I made the same point, but was reported to the Advertising Standards Agency, whose rule states: 'A well-balanced diet should provide the vitamins and minerals needed each day by a normal, healthy individual...' I felt like reporting the government to the ASA!

- *Vitamin B12* – many people, especially over the age of 50, simply do not absorb vitamin B12 well enough for food alone to provide a sufficient supply. The ignorance regarding vitamin B12 is compounded in the UK by the inaccurate reference range for serum B12 of anything above 180pg/ml being sufficient (200pg/ml in the US). This is urgently in need of revision. In Europe and Japan, anything below 500pg/ml is considered deficient. Against this yardstick, two in five people over 60 have too low B12 levels to stop accelerated brain shrinkage. Ignorance regarding B12, and the inability of doctors to prescribe it to those with cognitive concerns, are fuelling the epidemic of dementia.

- *Omega-3 DHA* – in the UK, doctors are not allowed to prescribe omega-3 supplements for any condition, be it depression or dementia, despite all the evidence of its benefits. I first wrote about omega-3 in 1981, and with each decade, recommendations have gradually increased. However, there is still no official Nutrient Reference Value for it. The current guideline is to have 250mg of combined EPA and DHA a day, but this is well below the level of DHA that confers the greatest protection from cognitive decline.

- *Choline* – despite clear evidence of the need for choline, which makes the phospholipid phosphatidyl choline in pregnancy for normal infant brain development, there is no recommended intake. Vegans can be assumed to be deficient unless supplementing.

I prefer to err on the side of caution, that is, to provide the highest optimal level that research suggests improves mood, memory and mental alertness and is consistent with minimizing the risk of cognitive decline. How many have developed dementia waiting for health officials to catch up?

In the chart below you'll see the basic optimal supplemental levels for some of these more vital nutrients that are advisable for everyone to achieve from a good daily supplement programme (assuming you are eating a reasonably good diet) for brain protection.

Then there is the restoration level for correcting imbalances if you are suffering from any of the problems described in this book and feel you need a significant brain upgrade.

Finally, there is the highest level for maximizing recovery if either your cognition is going downhill or you've had a stroke or brain injury. For how to achieve this with combinations of supplements, with optional add-ons depending on your needs, *see page 296.*

Supplement levels

Nutrient	Optimum supplemental	Restoration if cognitively impaired	Maximum brain recovery
Vitamin A	2,500mcg	5,000mcg	5,000mcg
Vitamin C	1,800mg	3,000mg	6,000mg
Vitamin E	300mg	600mg	800mg
Vitamin D	15mcg	25–50mcg	50–75mcg+
Vitamin B12	10mcg	250–500mcg*	500mcg*
Folate	200mcg	400–800mcg*	400–800mcg*
Vitamin B6	20mg	40mg	40mg
Magnesium	200mg	300mg	400mg
Zinc	10mg	15mg	25mg
Chromium	35mcg	200–600mcg	200–600mcg
Selenium	35mcg	100–200mcg	100–200mcg
CoQ10	10mg	90–120mg	90–120mg
Glutathione or NAC	25mg	50–250mg	250–750mg
Lipoic acid	10mg	100–200mg	100–500mg
Omega-3 (DHA, EPA)	1,000mg	2,000mg	Up to 4,000mg

* These high levels are only appropriate if you have raised homocysteine. Ideally supplement the methylfolate form of this vitamin. I do not recommend supplemental folic acid above 200mcg if you have any risk of colorectal or other cancers. Your ideal intake is that which brings homocysteine below 7 mcmol/l.

+ Your ideal intake of vitamin D is that which brings your blood level to above 75nmol/l (25ng/ml), although 100 to 125nmol/l may be optimal. For most people, 50mcg (2,000iu) on a daily basis is too much, but can be good during the winter or for a few months to build up vitamin D stores. Otherwise, don't exceed 25mcg (1,000iu) on a daily basis.

Are these quantities dangerous?

Of all the nutrients listed above, the one that has supposedly been given the most caution is vitamin A – but only for pregnant women; if you are a man, or a woman over 50, this is irrelevant. However, I know of no evidence that even 5,000mcg is a problem in pregnancy. Our ancestors consumed several times this amount.

Vitamin D, at very high levels, can be toxic. If you live in the northern hemisphere, this is unlikely to be an issue even at the highest supplemental doses; however, I advise a maximum of 75mcg (3,000iu) during the autumn and winter, unless this is insufficient to get your blood level above 75 nmol/l. If you live in the northern hemisphere, have dark skin and rarely expose yourself to the sun, you are going to need these higher levels to maintain a healthy vitamin D status. Some people take 125mcg (5,000iu) in winter with no apparent harm.

There is some concern, although not everyone agrees, with high-dose folic acid in people who have pre-cancerous cells, especially in the colon, indicated by polyps. The reason for this caution is that although folic acid prevents healthy cells from becoming cancerous, there is evidence that high doses encourage the growth of pre-cancerous cells into cancer cells. Whether or not this occurs when supplementing a combination of homocysteine-lowering nutrients is not yet known. Given that high homocysteine levels also increase cancer risk, it is hard to say whether the benefit of supplementing such nutrients to lower a raised homocysteine level is of greater benefit than the possible risk of high-dose folic acid increasing the cancer risk in those with pre-cancerous cells in the colon.

These are the only cautions I am aware of. Needless to say, even these cautions pale into insignificance against the risks of either doing nothing or taking the usual plethora of medical drugs.

Building your own brain-upgrade supplement programme

How do you put all this together into your own personal daily supplement programme? There are those supplements recommended for all (*see below*), then various 'add-ons' if you need help with your memory, mood, sleep or levels of stress and anxiety.

Recommended for all

- 2 × high-strength multivitamin–mineral tablets, taken one with breakfast and one at lunchtime. (Note: most high-strength multis are taken in two doses – follow the pack instructions. You want one that gives you at least 150mg of magnesium.)
- 2 × vitamin C 900mg, ideally with extra zinc, taken one with breakfast and one at lunchtime. Since your multi will provide some, the goal here, together with diet, is to achieve 2,000mg a day. If younger, 1,000mg may be sufficient.
- 2 × essential omega-3 and omega-6: dosage 500mg of omega-3 (EPA+DPA+DHA; 50mg GLA), taken one with breakfast and one at lunchtime. Judging by recent research, it may be wise to double or quadruple the omega-3 amount by adding in a high-strength DHA supplement, which is what I do.
- 1 × 'antioxidant formula' (containing resveratrol, lipoic acid, glutathione, CoQ10), taken with lunch or dinner. This is most important for those over age 50 and those undertaking lots of exercise, which increases the need for antioxidants.
- 1 × 'brain-friendly formula' with extra B vitamins and phospholipids, taken with breakfast. You can also increase your phosphatidyl choline intake by taking two 1,200mg lecithin capsules or a dessertspoon of lecithin granules. This is especially important for vegans and those not eating eggs.

The above is what I take daily at the age of 65.

Optional extras

- *Vitamin D* – if you live in the northern hemisphere, or have decreased bone mass, depending on your blood level of vitamin D (which should ideally be between 75nmol/l and 125nmol/l), you would be wise to add 1 × 75mcg (3,000iu) capsule of vitamin D3 during the autumn and winter months. Since it is stored, you can take seven times this amount once a week. It's just as good as daily supplementation.
- *B vitamins and homocysteine-lowering supplements* – if you have any memory concerns or cardiovascular risk, get your

homocysteine level checked. If your homocysteine level is raised (above 7, or above 10, or above 15), take the appropriate levels of homocysteine-lowering nutrients (*see page 106*). Then add the appropriate number of homocysteine-lowering nutrient complexes. You may also wish to double up on a brain-friendly formula containing phospholipids and an antioxidant formula if you want to maximize brain recovery from a stroke or brain injury.

- *Mood support* – if you are struggling with your mood, try increasing omega-3 EPA and chromium to the maximum in the chart above. This will require an additional fish-oil supplement, high in EPA, and a supplement containing chromium. Some supplements provide combinations of vitamin D, zinc, magnesium and chromium, plus the amino acids 5-HTP and tyrosine, which is a great all-rounder. If suffering from atypical depression, then you may wish to try higher-dose chromium, namely 600µg. Most chromium supplements provided 200mcg, so this will require taking three chromium supplements, two in the morning and one with lunch.

- *Anxiety and stress support* – nutrients that help include GABA or its precursors taurine, glutamine plus B6, magnesium and 5-HTP, and either valerian or hops and passion flower. If you feel burnt out, the adaptogenic herbs Reishi, rhodiola, ashwagandha, American and Chinese ginseng and Siberian ginseng may also help, together with the amino acid tyrosine. These are often provided in combination formulas (*see Resources*), although rhodiola (200mg twice a day) and ashwagandha (take 120mg twice a day) have to be supplied individually, as they are classified as medicinal herbs. (*See Chapter 18 for more details.*)

- *Sleep support* – if you are having difficulty sleeping, add 5-HTP (100mg) (or melatonin, 3mg), GABA (1,000mg) and magnesium (200mg) an hour before bed. Some sleep formulas contain combinations of these, or the precursors of GABA – taurine and glutamine. Hops and passion flower also help. Alternatively, try valerian, which is more soporific and, as it is classified as a medicinal herb, is supplied individually. (*See Chapter 19 for more details.*)

Become a Brain-Friendly Citizen Scientist and Activist

Do you ever get the sense that healthcare, as we know it, is broken and you're unlikely to get the help you need when you need it? The old model of running randomized controlled trials to test the effect of usually one factor versus a control group or placebo cannot begin to model what's happening in real life. In any event, these studies select specific people of specific ages and circumstances, so the only way to know if the research finding would work in real life would be to roll it out to the masses.

Anyway, if all the research I've shared with you were endorsed by our so-called health authorities and recommended for use in our healthcare systems, the critical challenge would then be how to motivate people to make these diet and lifestyle changes. That's what we are doing now.

In the 40 years I've been in healthcare, I've seen very few of these critical prevention discoveries put into action, despite the obvious benefits. I've met so many brilliant, committed humanitarian scientists who are bitterly disappointed at how their research findings, which could have saved so many lives, have had close to no effect because health authorities haven't done the right thing.

Apostolos Tsiachristas, Associate Professor in Health Economics at the University of Oxford, costed the saving that would be made if doctors simply tested homocysteine in those over 60 and prescribed inexpensive B vitamins.

'[This] is predicted to be a highly cost-effective policy that could save costs to the UK economy of approximately £60 million per year,' he said.

It was also estimated it would also promote healthy longevity, adding 14 years to life expectancy.[31]

But the discovery that established this simple, inexpensive prevention step was made in 2010, and still nothing has changed. Doctors don't test homocysteine and can't prescribe B vitamins. How many thousands of people would have been saved from the terrible fate of dementia if only our health authorities had listened? We estimate that this prevention approach could easily halve the number of people developing dementia. The latest research by a world-leading team, including two of our Scientific Board members, estimates that 'up to 47–73 per cent of dementia cases could be prevented'.[32] That would mean well over 100,000 fewer people every year in the UK alone getting a dementia diagnosis. If prevention is ignored for another decade, the healthcare system as we know it will be completely bust.

There is another way, which puts the individual at the centre. Many people and organizations are working towards creating a new healthcare system which works directly with the people and is based on what's really driving disease. It has to be based on prevention and, as you saw in Chapter 7, all the major diseases facing us in the 21st century are largely driven by the same factors that lead to cognitive decline. So, the critical issue becomes how to find out what combination of diet and lifestyle changes packs the biggest prevention punch and how to motivate millions of people to make those changes. This book is part of this movement.

How can you get involved? The first step is to become a citizen scientist, which is what happens when you become a Friend of Food for the Brain and complete the Cognitive Function Test. By joining as a FRIEND and becoming a COGNITION user, you are then part of a group of like-minded people committed to educating yourself and taking charge of your own health, with guidance and support.

Behind the scenes, with close to half a million people having completed the Cognitive Function Test already, we are tracking (anonymously) the changes everyone makes and the impact it has on their cognition. Even those who make no changes are important. They are, if you like, part of the control group.

In this way, we can find out what changes make the biggest difference. Then the question is how can we become increasingly effective at encouraging people to make these changes. To that end we've teamed up with a group of leading digital health behaviour change experts, headed by Dr Kristina Curtis, to continually improve our motivational and educational communications with the single goal of driving down risk, in this case for cognitive decline, but the 'side-effects' will no doubt reduce the rate of many other diseases, from cancer to diabetes. Our research is directed by Assistant Professor Tommy Wood from the University of Washington, and we are working with other charities committed to making prevention happen, each collecting critical (anonymized) information and each encouraging positive prevention steps, so that collectively we'll have the real-life data on well over 1 million people doing what they can to take charge of their health.

One such charity is the GrassrootsHealth Nutrient Research Institute (www.grassrootshealth.net). They've tracked data from nearly 20,000 people worldwide through their vitamin D*action project, which started in 2007, measuring aspects of health, vitamin D intake and vitamin D levels. Since then, the project has expanded to include additional data, measurements and tracking for omega-3 levels, inflammation, blood sugar, and more.

They encourage their people to take our Cognitive Function Test and we, at Food for the Brain, also encourage you to test your vitamin D as well as omega-3, HbA1c and homocysteine levels, so we can also track what happens to your body's biology. By combining forces with other charities such as Grassroots, and tracking people's cognitive function changes over time, we can, for example, find out what vitamin D level means the lowest risk, thus rewriting the books on what an 'optimal' vitamin D level actually means.

We are also working with hundreds, hopefully soon thousands of doctors who are encouraging their patients to take the Cognitive Function Test.

What this means is that by completing our Cognitive Function Test, then making the changes you can, you are helping us, along with thousands of others like you, to research, publish, share back to you and learn what really works to prevent cognitive decline and encourage people to take charge of their own health, making the changes they can to improve their well-being, not just for mental but also physical health and future disease prevention.

We are hoping, by the end of 2025, combining forces with other charities, to have in the order of 1 million people involved as citizen scientists, taking the test every six months and following the COGNITION programme, which then tracks the changes made and the impact each has on health.

We, and the organizations we work with, are not-for-profit. We are charities who put all the funds we raise, from people like you who become FRIENDS, back into doing the research, improving the educational impact and reaching more people. We are not beholden to any vested interests. We are funded by you, the people, and working for your benefit.

All you need to do to become a citizen scientist is complete the Cognitive Function Test. Should you wish to support the initiative by becoming a Friend of Food for the Brain and getting involved in the COGNITION brain-upgrade journey, thank you! By following as much health advice as you can, which we track through the online questionnaire, with you repeating the Cognitive Function Test at least annually and ideally every six months, we can find out what happens to health-conscious people like you when they choose to take the steps to upgrade their brain.

I hope you will go one step further and encourage all your friends, family and associates, especially those over the age of 40, to take the test at foodforthebrain.org and support this citizen science initiative.

My mentor, twice Nobel Prize-winner Dr Linus Pauling, whose picture is on the badge below, was described by Albert Einstein as a 'true genius'. He had 48 PhDs! He discovered that vitamin C, in the right dose, was remarkably effective against viral diseases, cancer and heart disease, and, with Dr Abram Hoffer, defined a new paradigm in medicine called orthomolecular medicine, which I call optimum nutrition. Back in the 1980s he said, 'Optimum nutrition is the future of medicine. We have already waited too long for it.' He knew that we were digging our graves with a knife and fork and that the discovery of the vast importance of vitamins such as vitamin C, the B vitamins and also essential omega-3 fats, backed

Fig 33. Citizen scientist

up with good diet and lifestyle, was the only viable way forward in medicine. It still is. This book is dedicated to him, to Dr Abram Hoffer, who first put B vitamins on the map for mental illness, and to Professor David Smith, whose groundbreaking research on homocysteine and B vitamins for preventing Alzheimer's is well worthy of a Nobel Prize but, like Linus Pauling's discoveries, has tragically been largely ignored. But we do not have to ignore it. We can benefit from the committed research of these humanitarian pioneers.

I hope you have learned in reading this book that your brain health is under your control and the only person who can give you a brain upgrade is you!

Wishing you the best of health and happiness,
Patrick Holford

Recommended Reading

Dale Bredesen, *The End of Alzheimer's Program: The practical plan to prevent and reverse cognitive decline at any age* (Vermilion, 2020)

Malcolm Carruthers, *Testosterone Resistance: Fighting for the men's health hormone* (XLIBRIS, 2016)

Doc Childre, *Transforming Stress: The HeartMath solution for relieving worry, fatigue, and tension* (New Harbinger, 2005)

Michael A. Crawford and David E. Marsh, *The Shrinking Brain and the Global Mental Health Crisis: Two problems, one solution* (Authoritize, 2023)

Ivan Crow, *The Quest for Food: Its role in human evolution and migration* (Tempus, 2000)

Georgia Ede, *Change Your Diet, Change Your Mind* (Balance, 2024)

Johann Hari, *Lost Connections: Uncovering the real causes of depression – and the unexpected solutions* (Bloomsbury Circus, 2018)

Abram Hoffer, *The Vitamin Cure for Alcoholism: How to protect against and fight alcoholism using nutrition and supplementation* (Basic Health Publications, 2009)

Martyn Hooper, *Pernicious Anaemia: The forgotten disease* (Hammersmith Health Books, 2012)

Sally Kempton, *Meditation for the Love of It: Enjoying your own deepest experience* (Sounds True, Inc., 2011)

Malcolm Kendrick, *The Cholesterol Con: The truth about what really causes heart disease and how to avoid it* (John Blake Publishing, 2008)

—, *The Clot Thickens: The enduring mystery of heart disease* (Columbus Publishing, 2021)

Geoffrey and Lucille Leader, *Parkinson's Disease: Reducing symptoms with nutrition and drugs* (Denor Press, 2017)

Robert Lustig, *Fat Chance: Beating the odds against sugar, processed food, obesity, and disease* (Hudson Street Press, 2012)

—, *Hacking the American Mind: The science behind the corporate takeover of our bodies and brains* (Avery Publishing Group, 2017)

—, *Metabolical: The lure and the lies of processed food, nutrition and modern medicine* (Yellow Kite, 2021)

Patrick McKeown, *Anxiety Free: Stop worrying and quieten your mind, featuring the Buteyko breathing method and mindfulness* (Buteyko Books, 2010)

Chris Palmer, *Brain Energy* (Benbella, 2022)

David Perlmutter, *Drop Acid* (Yellow Kite, 2022)

Candace Pert, *Molecules of Emotion: Why you feel the way you feel* (Pocket Books, 1999)

Peter Rhys-Evans, *The Waterside Ape: An alternative account of human evolution* (CRC Press, 2019)

Alex Richardson, *They Are What You Feed Them: How food affects your child's behaviour, mood and learning* (Thorsons, 2010)

Resources

Educational and health resources

Health Check (free)

You can have your own personal health and nutrition assessment online using Patrick Holford's free Health Check. This provides you with a personalized assessment of your current health, and what you most need to change, including a metabolic check to gauge your risk of metabolic syndrome, and a BioAge Check.

Visit patrickholford.com and get your FREE Health Check.

Holford Health Club

When you join the Holford Health Club, you'll receive a 40-page health report after completing the 'Health Check' and unlimited access to address and support your needs as your health improves. You can also choose a free Patrick Holford-authored book from a choice of six when joining, Patrick Holford's regular health reports, plus instant access to all past reports online on important health issues; also get your personal health questions answered by Patrick Holford in the Holford Health Club members Facebook group; plus 20 per cent off most seminars, webinars and events; and up to 30 per cent off all books and supplements from HOLFORDirect.com.

Alliance for Natural Health International (ANH)

The Alliance for Natural Health International (ANH) is a non-profit organization founded in 2002 with a mission to safeguard and promote natural and sustainable approaches to regenerating and managing human health worldwide. They support approaches to health and self-care that work with, rather than against, nature, using the tools of 'good science' and 'good law'. Through campaigns, actions, research and education, they have inspired and helped thousands of people, including doctors and other practitioners and companies in the natural health sector, to practise, access or adopt natural, diverse and sustainable approaches to managing human health, with due respect to our planet and its natural resources, on which we depend.

Their website, anhinternational.org, has an extensive repository of helpful information.

They are worth joining and supporting. Email info@anhinter national.org.

Brain Bio Centre

The Brain Bio Centre is a resource to connect you with practitioners using the approach in this book: the Centre represents a collective of nutrition and mental health specialists working with individuals of all ages with a wide range of behavioural and mental health issues. Our registered nutritional therapy practitioners and psychiatrists are experienced in this area of nutrition and provide personalized nutrition and lifestyle recommendations tailored to your specific mental health needs.

Visit foodforthebrain.org/the-brain-bio-centre/.

British Association for Nutrition and Lifestyle Medicine (BANT)

The British Association for Nutrition and Lifestyle Medicine is the official register of qualified nutritional therapists. You can search for a therapist by area and see their specialisms, should you need support with your health issues.

See bant.org.uk.

In Ireland, see the Nutritional Therapists of Ireland at ntoi.ie.

Buteyko breathing

For more information on this breathing practice, visit www.buteyko breathing.org. There are also several books featuring Buteyko, including *Anxiety Free: Stop worrying and quieten your mind, featuring the Buteyko breathing method and mindfulness* by Patrick McKeown.

COGNITION®

COGNITION is Food for the Brain's personalized, interactive brain-upgrade programme to help everyone dementia-proof their diet and lifestyle, based on the recommendations of our expert Scientific Advisory Board. It guides you, step by step, with interactive support, giving you the means to lower your Dementia Risk Index closer to zero, our goal being to get you under 10 per cent (in the green) within six months. How? You'll start receiving doable instructions, simple exercises and encouragements, and reminders to make gradual changes to your diet and lifestyle, with supportive 'engagements', including access to free apps and an online forum where you can interact with and learn from others and share what works for you. You'll have your own library of health-enhancing resources, and can choose to receive reminders by e-mail or WhatsApp, as well as being able to join our Facebook group and attend Zoom sessions to help you achieve your goals.

You'll have your own COGNITION Dashboard tracking exactly how you're doing as you move towards your goal of dementia-proofing your diet and lifestyle.

Visit foodforthebrain.org and take the Cognitive Function Test first to access COGNITION.

COGNITION for Smart Kids and Smart Teens

This is Food for the Brain's personalized, interactive brain-upgrade programme for parents to assess and guide their children's habits for optimal mental health, happiness and emotional balance. From the age of 12, the 'teen' completes their own assessment and receives their own guidance.

See foodforthebrain.org/smartkids.

Cognitive Function Test

The Cognitive Function Test is the first-ever free, validated, digital version of what gets measured in memory clinics, tried and tested by almost half a million people. It takes about 15 minutes to complete, and must be done without interruptions and on a screen no smaller than a tablet or computer – not a phone. It is followed by a questionnaire about your nutrition, lifestyle and medical history, which then assesses your Dementia Risk Index and lets you know exactly what's driving your future risk.

Visit foodforthebrain.org.

Emotional Freedom Technique (EFT)

EFT is a therapeutic psychological tool that involves tapping on the body's energy meridians while using positive affirmations to clear emotional blocks and embed new positive behaviours. Sounds bonkers, but it can be surprisingly effective!

Visit www.emofree.com for more information.

There is no central body of EFT practitioners, but some are listed at eftregister.com and at aamet.org, or do an internet search of your local area.

Eye Movement Desensitization and Reprocessing (EMDR)

EMDR was developed by an American clinical psychologist called Dr Francine Shapiro in the 1980s. It's a well-researched therapy for treating psychological trauma.

Visit emdrassociation.org.uk for more information and a listing of accredited therapists in the UK and Ireland.

Food for the Brain Foundation

The Food for the Brain Foundation is a non-profit educational charity, founded by Patrick Holford, which aims to promote awareness of the link between learning, behaviour, mental health and nutrition; and to educate and provide educational material to children, parents, teachers, schools, the public, the catering industry, health professionals and the government. The website has a free Cognitive Function Test. It takes 15 minutes to complete. Depending on your score, it tells you what to do to improve your memory. The charity, and its work helping people prevent dementia, is funded by people becoming Friends of the charity (£50 a year or £5 a month). As a Friend, you have access to all educational information and receive regular updates.

For more information visit foodforthebrain.org.

GrassrootsHealth

GrassrootsHealth is a non-profit public health research organization founded in 2007, dedicated to promoting optimal health worldwide through research, education and advocacy, with a primary focus on the role of vitamin D. Through evidence-based nutrient education, resources and their citizen-science approach to research, they empower individuals to make informed decisions about their health, including mental health, and healthcare providers to move research into practice.

With a panel of 48 senior vitamin D researchers from around the world contributing to its operations, GrassrootsHealth has been running the world's largest public health intervention study – the D*action field trial – to solve the vitamin D deficiency epidemic worldwide. Participation involves measuring vitamin D (and other nutrient) levels from home, completing health surveys that include supplementation data, calculating how much supplementation might be needed to reach a target nutrient level, and retesting to determine if the target level has been achieved.

Learn more at grassrootshealth.net or daction.org.

Institute of Functional Medicine (IFM)

As the leading voice for functional medicine for more than 30 years, IFM is advancing the transformation of healthcare for patients and practitioners worldwide. It supports the confident and competent practice of functional medicine through high-quality education and certification programmes; partnerships across medical disciplines; and advocating on behalf of functional medicine clinicians and patients around the globe. IFM is a 501(c)(3) non-profit organization, and the only organization providing functional medicine certification along with educational programmes directly accredited by the Accreditation Council for Continuing Medical Education (ACCME), in line with the principles in this book.

For more information, or to find a functional medicine practitioner, please visit ifm.org.

Institute for Optimum Nutrition (ION)

The Institute for Optimum Nutrition, founded by Patrick Holford, offers both full- and part-time degrees in nutritional therapy for those starting their nutrition journey. For medics, allied healthcare and CAM practitioners, ION offers a Graduate Diploma Integrative Functional Nutrition. Courses are university validated. Additionally, ION offers a range of CPD and validated short courses.

Visit ion.ac.uk or visit them at Ambassador House, Paradise Rd, Richmond, TW9 1SQ, UK, tel: +44 (0)20 8614 7800.

International Society for Orthomolecular Medicine (ISOM)

The purpose of the International Society for Orthomolecular Medicine (ISOM) is to raise awareness and further the advancement of orthomolecular medicine throughout the world by creating educational programmes and events for professionals and the general public; curating and providing information and resources related to orthomolecular medicine; and uniting existing and future orthomolecular groups and organizations. It is a registered charitable organization based in Canada.

For more information, visit isom.ca.

Psychiatric drug withdrawal

If you'd like help withdrawing from psychiatric medication, visit leap4pdd.org/resources-for-individuals/. This provides resources and information for individuals about prescribed drug dependence and withdrawal. This list is not exhaustive, but has been put together by people with lived and/or professional experience of prescribed drug dependence.

You may also find this website useful, iipdw.org/, and my podcast, 'Are you hooked on anti-depressants?', encouraging, at patrickholford. podbean.com/e/are-you-hooked-on-anti-depressants/.

Psychiatry redefined

Led by renowned integrative psychiatrist Dr James Greenblatt, Psychiatry Redefined provides the most comprehensive scientific, practical, convenient and cost-effective training available in integrative and functional psychiatry. Their clinician-led online courses, fellowship programme, intensive programmes, and seminars and conferences will help you target and treat the root causes of mental illness, providing your patients with a greater chance of lasting recovery and wellness.

Learn more at psychiatryredefined.org.

Qigong Institute

The Qigong Institute has a list of teachers around the world, plus much more information and details of research.

Visit qigonginstitute.org.

T'ai Chi Foundation
This has information on what's available across North America, as well as the UK and Europe.

Visit taichifoundation.org.

T'ai Chi Union
The T'ai Chi Union lists many UK-based instructors on its website at taichiunion.com.

Foods and other products and services

Brain-friendly recipes

Upgrade Your Brain Cookapp
Hundreds of recipes, completely in line with the principles of this book, are available in the Upgrade Your Brain Cookapp that supports this book. The GL, antioxidant, brain-fat and B-vitamin status is given for each recipe, so you can build menus that support your brain health.

Available from foodforthebrain.org/uybcookapp.

Full-spectrum lights

Block Blue Light
Full-spectrum light bulbs, usable in any light fitting, such as a table lamp, angle-poise lamp or downlight, are available from blockbluelight.co.uk/collections/sleep-enhancing-lighting/products/full-spectrum-light-bulb.

Measuring ketones and glucose

Keto-Mojo GKI meter (GK+ in United States)
Widely recommended by healthcare professionals this essential biofeedback tool measures blood glucose and ketones with a single prick of your finger and allows users to download readings using the free MyMojoHealth app. Users can graph/track progress, view trends and calculate GKI (Glucose Ketone Index), as well as send data directly to their coach or practitioner. Measuring glucose and ketones results

in better adherence and therefore better outcomes. You'll receive a 10 per cent discount on starter kits when you use the code FFB10 at checkout. In return, Keto-Mojo donate a portion of the proceeds to Food for the Brain to help with their research. Committed to empowering, Keto-Mojo enhances lives by providing powerful tools and resources that support lifestyle changes. Visit keto-mojo.com.

Ketoscan Lite

This device measures breath ketones. You can use it as often as you like, and others can too. After 300 tests you'll need to buy a new cartridge. It costs £99.99 but if you use the code PH20, you get £20 off. It's the easiest to use and gives you readings on the device, so you don't need to link it to an app on your phone or computer, although that's possible for keeping a record of your scores.

Other products and services

Bioidentical progesterone

This is available as an over-the-counter cream in some countries, but in the UK it is only available on prescription as a licensed capsule, Utrogestan, in one fixed strength. There are, however, some advantages to transdermal application, such as a possible reduction in some of the unwanted side-effects, and transdermal creams can be prescribed by a practitioner and made by a compounding pharmacy (see Specialist Pharmacy below).

Centre for Men's Health

The Centre for Men's Health provides expert advice, diagnosis and treatment for men with Testosterone Deficiency Syndrome (Low T), erectile dysfunction (ED)/impotence, or prostate health concerns and health problems. Their team of doctors specializes in andrology, urology and men's sexual and general health. With 30 years' experience, the Centre's men's health clinics in London have helped thousands of men regain their well-being and vitality and return to a fulfilling sex life.

Visit centreformenshealth.co.uk.

CherryActive

CherryActive is a deliciously healthy, low-GL cherry juice. It is sold in a highly concentrated format, so mix a 30ml (1fl oz) serving with 250ml

(9fl oz) water. Each 946ml bottle contains the juice from over 3,000 cherries – that's half a tree's worth – and contains a month's supply.

CherryActive is also available as a dried cherry snack and in capsules. It's available in health-food shops and online at both holfordirect.com and active-edge.co.uk.

Drop of Life olive oil

This is a healthy extra virgin olive oil from a naturally evolved olive variety with an exceptionally high polyphenol level and with a low acidity.

Available from holfordirect.com.

Get Up & Go with CarboSlow®

This is a delicious breakfast shake combining wholefoods with vitamins, minerals, essential fats, protein and super-soluble glucomannan fibre. (*See page 271 for more about this.*)

There is no need to take a multivitamin and mineral if you have Get Up & Go, since it provides optimal levels of all vitamins and minerals.

Available from holfordirect.com and health-food shops.

The Marion Gluck Clinic

One of the UK's leading hormone clinics, whose doctors prescribe bioidentical hormones, and their academy also trains doctors in how to prescribe them.

Visit mariongluckclinic.com.

HeartMath and the Inner Balance™ Coherence Plus

This sensor and app are an innovative approach to improving wellness and performance through monitoring your heart rhythms and self-regulating your thoughts, feelings and physiology. The sensor clips onto your ear to monitor your heart rate variability (HRV), and enables you to practise HeartMath coherence techniques and bring yourself into a state of high stress resilience.

Use the code FFB10 to receive a 10 per cent discount when buying from either the HeartMath UK store (www.heartmath.co.uk) or US store (www.heartmath.org). HeartMath kindly make a donation to Food for the Brain to help their research.

Visit the above websites for resources, details of events, training, HeartMath Coaches and products.

Susannah Lawson

Susannah Lawson is a certified HeartMath trainer and practitioner, offering group training and one-to-one coaching. She is also a qualified nutritional therapist, kinesiologist and teacher/practitioner of subtle energy healing.

Visit susannah-lawson.co.uk for more details, or contact Susannah via mail@susannah-lawson.co.uk.

John Levine's Alpha Music – Silence of Peace

Based on the centuries-old therapeutic use of specific musical scales and arrangements, the music of John Levine helps you enter a more relaxed and peaceful state of mind. *Silence of Peace* is excellent for promoting a good night's sleep.

To download, visit silenceofmusic.com/ and use the code FFB. They will match your discount with a donation to the Food for the Brain Foundation.

Specialist Pharmacy

Specialist Pharmacy compounds bioidentical progesterone and other hormones in various dosage forms, including transdermal creams, via a private prescription from a practitioner.

Visit specialist-pharmacy.com

Tests

Adrenal stress test

This test measures levels of the stress hormones cortisol and DHEA in saliva at periods throughout the day.

An adrenal stress test is available from Genova Diagnostics. Genova is a referral laboratory, so testing can be arranged only via a doctor, nutritional therapist or other registered healthcare professional.

Visit gdx.net.

Coeliac test

Coeliac Screen

A reliable home-test kit that gives immediate results is Coeliac Screen, which is available from most leading pharmacies, including

Lloyds, Boots and Superdrug. You can buy online from personal diagnostics.co.uk/coeliacscreenorder.

Dementia Risk Index functional (DRIfT) test

This is a home-test pin-prick blood test for five tests: homocysteine for B-vitamin status; omega-3 and vitamin D for brain-fat status; HbA1c as a measure of blood sugar control; and glutathione index for antioxidant status.

It is available from foodforthebrain.org/drift/.

Food intolerance tests

Food intolerance can be tested from a blood sample with a home-test kit.

YorkTest

If you live in the UK, go to yorktest.com and enter the discount code FFB10 in the basket for a 10 per cent discount. If you live in the USA, go to yorktest.com/us and enter FFB10US in the basket for your $10 discount.

YorkTest will match your discount with a donation to Food for the Brain to help support their research.

Genetic testing

Genetic polymorphisms in the ApoE4 and MTHFR gene can be tested through a buccal (mouth) swab.

Genova Diagnostics

Genova Diagnostics offers these tests on referral from a healthcare practitioner, such as a nutritional therapist.

Visit gdx.net. Available in the USA and UK.

Glutathione Index (antioxidant status)

Glutathione is the body's master antioxidant. When it is fully loaded, it's called 'reduced', and once it is spent disarming oxidants, it is called 'oxidized'. The glutathione index calculates the ratio between reduced and oxidized glutathione to give you an accurate measure of your antioxidant potential. It is the best way to check if you're eating enough antioxidants and polyphenols or need to increase your intake or supplement.

Order from foodforthebrain.org/tests.

HbA1c (long-term glucose measure)

Haemoglobin A1c is a measure of how healthy average blood sugar levels have been in the recent few months, and is a better representation of blood sugar health than a single glucose measurement, since glucose levels vary throughout the day. HbA1c is the compound formed in the blood when a haemoglobin molecule in a red blood cell binds with a glucose molecule in the blood; the resulting molecule is also known as glycated haemoglobin (sugar-coated or damaged red blood cells).

It can be a good indicator of glucose intolerance even in the absence of abnormal fasting glucose levels indicating the need to reduce your intake of sugar, carbohydrates and alcohol.

A level above 6.5 per cent (48 mmol/mol) is considered diabetic. You certainly want to get your score below 5.4 per cent (36 mmol/mol).

Order from foodforthebrain.org/tests.

Homocysteine test

Homocysteine can be measured through your GP but few GPs do this. Above 11 mcmol/l is associated with accelerated brain shrinkage; 7 mcmol/l or less is probably optimal.

Health practitioners can order tests from private laboratories such as Genova (www.gdx.net). Foodforthebrain.org offers a home-test kit, using a pin-prick of blood. See foodforthebrain.org/tests.

Leaky gut test

This test involves measuring a marker of intestinal permeability, zonulin, either in stools or serum.

It is offered by a number of laboratories, including Genova (gdx. net) and Viva Health Laboratories (vivahealthlabs.com) via a health-care practitioner.

Mineral analysis

Your mineral levels can be measured by a hair tissue mineral analysis.

Mineral Check
This test is available from Mineral Check, or via a nutritional thera-pist, if you also want comprehensive interpretation.
Visit www.mineralcheck.com or call 01622 850 850.

Omega-3 test

An omega-3 test measures EPA and DHA, the two very important omega-3 fatty acids that are found in fatty fish and other marine sources and are essential to our health.

The Omega-3 Index is a measure of the amount of EPA and DHA in red blood cell (RBC) membranes. The result is expressed as a percentage of total RBC fatty acids, and is a long-term and stable marker of omega-3 status. Experts recommend an Omega-3 Index of at least 8 per cent.

Food for the Brain Home-test kit
This is available from foodforthebrain.org/tests. Once you have your Omega-3 Index result, we will advise you what you need to eat and/or supplement to bring your score above 8 per cent.
Order from foodforthebrain.org/tests.

Platelet serotonin and other neurotransmitters

Platelet, as well as blood and urine, levels of serotonin, acetylcho-line, dopamine, adrenalin, noradrenalin and GABA are available, on referral from a healthcare practitioner, such as a nutritional ther-apist, from Genova Diagnostics and the World Health Laboratory.

Genova Diagnostics
Genova Diagnostics test neurotransmitter metabolites in urine, on referral from a healthcare practitioner. Visit gdx.net.

World Health Laboratory
Regulierenring 9, 3981 LA Bunnik, The Netherlands; worldhealth laboratories.com; phone: +31 30 2871492

Vitamin D test

A vitamin D test measures 25(OH)D3, the major circulating form of vitamin D in the blood and the commonly accepted measure of vitamin D status. Circulating 25(OH)D3 levels reflect endogenous production as well as vitamin supplementation. Optimal levels of 25(OH)D3 are certainly above 32ng/mL (80 nmol/l) and ideally over 40ng/ml (100nmol/l).

Order from foodforthebrain.org/tests.

Supplements

Patrick Holford has formulated a range of supplements to support optimal health, with a focus on brain health. The backbone of a supplement programme is an optimum multivitamin and mineral, with extra vitamin C and essential fats, both omega-3 and 6. These are provided in the Optimum Nutrition Pack.

If over 50, the enhanced version, the 100% Health Pack, provides extra antioxidants such as 'AGE Antioxidant' (*see below*) and 'Brain Food', a source of phospholipids.

Antioxidant formulas

A good all-round antioxidant complex should provide vitamin A (beta-carotene and/or retinol), vitamins C and E, zinc, selenium, glutathione or cysteine, anthocyanidins of berry extracts, lipoic acid and co-enzyme Q10 (CoQ10).

Examples are Holford's 'AGE Antioxidant', Viridian's 'Antioxidant Formula' and Solgar's 'Advanced Antioxidant Nutrients'.

Awake Food

Supports alertness and energy. Contains key B vitamins, which contribute to energy metabolism, tyrosine and three forms of ginseng.

Available from holfordirect.com.

Brahmi

Containing 300mg of Brahmi leaf, this is available from viridian-nutrition.com.

Brain Food® Upgrade Pack

This provides a daily strip of the three key building materials for brain-cell membranes. Includes 'Connect' – high-potency B12 plus other homocysteine-lowering B vitamins; 'High Strength Omega-3', which contains essential fats at potent levels (770mg EPA and 510mg DHA); and 'Lecithin', which contains one of the best natural sources of the phospholipid phosphatidyl choline, which is needed for brain health.

Available from holfordirect.com.

C8 oil – Keto fast®

Ketofast is a pure form of C8 oil, the most effective MCT oil. Each tablespoon provides 15ml of pure C8 derived from coconut oil, without any additives. Take 1 to 3 tablespoons (max 45ml). Each 450ml bottle provides 30 × 15ml servings, a month's supply.

Chill Food

'Chill Food' is a blend to calm and help sleep. It contains magnesium with amino acids, theanine, 5-HTP and GABA precursors (glutamine and taurine), and hops. Take before bedtime. For a 'reset', it works well to have two in the evening and then two 'Awake Food' the next morning.

Available from holfordirect.com.

Digestive support

Includes probiotics, glutamine and digestive enzymes. Any decent digestive enzyme needs to contain enzymes to digest protein (protease), carbohydrate (amylase) and fat (lipase). Some also contain amyloglucosidase, which digests glucosides, found in certain beans and vegetables noted for their flatulent effects.

Try Solgar's 'Vegan Digestive Enzymes' or Holford's 'DigestPro', which contains both these enzymes, probiotics and glutamine.

Some people have low levels of betaine hydrochloride (stomach acid). You can supplement this on its own, and if it helps digestion, this might be your problem. Try Biocare's 'Betaine plus HCl'.

Get Up & Go with CarboSlow®

A delicious breakfast shake combining wholefoods with vitamins, minerals, essential fats, protein and super-soluble glucomannan fibre. (*See page 271 for more about this.*)

There is no need to take a multivitamin and mineral if you have Get Up & Go, since it provides optimal levels of all vitamins and minerals.

Available from holfordirect.com and health-food shops.

Homocysteine support supplements

These should include TMG, vitamin B6, riboflavin (vitamin B2), zinc, folic acid (ideally as MTHF) and vitamin B12, ideally as methylcobalamine. Options include Holford's 'Connect', Solgar's 'Gold Specifics Homocysteine Modulators' and Higher Nature's 'H Factors', Cytoplan's 'Methyl Factors' and Viridian's 'Homocysteine Support Complex'.

Lion's Mane and Reishi

Pure organic concentrates are sold as Mico-Leo and MicoRei.

Available from hifasdaterra.com.

Mood Food

Supports the 'feel-good factor'. Contains B vitamins, L-tyrosine and 5-HTP, TMG, zinc and chromium. It is slow-release.

Available from holfordirect.com.

Omega-3

The most important omega-3 fats are DHA and EPA, the richest source being cod liver oil. The most important omega-6 fat is GLA, the richest source being borage (also known as starflower) oil.

Try Holford's 'Essential Omegas', which provides a highly concentrated mix of EPA, DHA and GLA, Biocare's 'Mega-EPA', a high-potency omega-3 fish-oil supplement, also Seven Seas 'Extra High Strength Cod Liver Oil'. All these products have consistently proven to be the purest when tested for PCB residues, which are in almost all fish. Cod liver oil also contains vitamin A. Nordic Natural's DHA Extra provides 480mg of DHA per capsule. Minami provide a high-dose EPA (500mg), a vegan DHA providing 2,540mg of DHA per capsule and good supplements for children. Holford's 'Brain Food Upgrade' provides 510mg of DHA in two capsules.

Phospholipids and phosphatidyl choline

Holford's 'Brain Food' provides eight nutrients, including key B vitamins such as B12, B3 and B5 (pantothenic acid), as well as folic acid and phospholipids, both phosphatidyl choline and phosphatidyl serine, to support the healthy functioning of the brain, with specific nutrients contributing to psychological function and normal mental performance (*see holfordirect.com*). Lecithin and lecithin capsules also provide phosphatidyl choline.

Vitamin D

Comes in two forms: D2 from plants and D3, mainly extracted from lanolin in the wool of sheep. D3 is more effective.

Many companies sell vitamin D products. Holford's 'Vegan D3', derived from lichen, provides 3,000iu. Cytoplan have a vegan D3 product, derived from lichen, providing 2,500iu. Viridian has a 2,000iu capsule and drops. This is the amount you need for a winter top-up. Available from www.biocare.co.uk and also holfordirect.com. Healthaid have a range of products going up to 20,000iu for a short-term top-up of vitamin D stores to correct deficiency, available from www.healthaid.co.uk.

Supplement suppliers

Reputable supplement suppliers in the UK include:

Biocare – biocare.co.uk
Cytoplan – cytoplan.co.uk
Higher Nature – highernature.co.uk
Holford – holfordirect.com
Solgar – solgar-vitamins.co.uk
Viridian – viridian-nutrition.com

Index

Italic page references indicate a diagram or table